FIRE IN THE BONES

FIRE IN THE BONES

BILL MASON
AND THE CANADIAN
CANOEING TRADITION

JAMES RAFFAN

A Phyllis Bruce Book
HarperCollins*Publishers*Ltd

The author thanks the Mason family for the use of the photographs on the cover and within this book. Endpapers taken from Bill Mason's working map of the Oiseau Bay area, Lake Superior.

Canadian Cataloguing in Publication Data

Raffan, James
Fire in the bones : Bill Mason and the Canadian canoeing tradition

"A Phyllis Bruce Book".
ISBN 0-00-255395-3

1. Mason, Bill, 1929-1988.   2. Canoes and canoeing - Canada.
3. Canoeists - Canada - Biography.   4. Painters - Canada - Biography.
5. Motion picture producers and directors - Canada -Biography.   I. Title.

GV782.42.M37R3 1996   797.1'22'092   C95-932439-9

96 97 98 99 ❖ HC 10 9 8 7 6 5 4 3 2 1

Text printed on 50% recycled paper

Printed and bound in the United States

to keepers of the fire

His word was in mine heart as a burning fire shut up in my bones, and I was weary with forbearing, and I could not *stay*.

Jeremiah 20:9

CONTENTS

ACKNOWLEDGEMENTS

WALKING BILL MASON'S PATH has taken me to the camps and kitchen tables of a host of remarkable people who, without exception, have welcomed me and given freely of their time and wisdom. Without Bill's generosity of spirit, as reflected in the hospitality and stories of the people who knew him, this would have been a very different (and much thinner) book.

Joyce Mason never said no. Paul and Becky Mason and their spouses talked and listened with patience and courtesy. Bill's sister Elizabeth McKenzie and her family in Selkirk, Manitoba, took me in as one of their own, introducing me to Sadie Mason.

Many of Bill's friends, colleagues and co-workers willingly put aside projects of the day to talk, especially: Ken and Susan Buck in Old Chelsea; Don and Willy Campbell in Winnipeg; Christopher and Glenn Chapman in Uxbridge; Wilber Sutherland in Toronto; Wally Schaber in Ottawa; Albert Labun at Manitoba Pioneer Camp; Kathleen Shannon in Nelson; Mike and Carolyn O'Connor in Goulais River; Ralph Ellis in Toronto; Blake James and Alan Whatmough in Ottawa; Bernard Lutz at the NFB in Montreal; and Tony Tascona in St. Boniface.

Paddlers from across Canada and around the world went out of their way to give something back for the things Bill had taught them, including:

Bill Morgan and Deb Baglow in Anola, Manitoba; Patsy Barker, Perry McGregor, Don Starkell, Bruce Talbot, Jack Blair, Donna Kurt, Julianne Schaible, Doug Ingram, and Julie P. Howgate in Winnipeg; Terry Fuchs in Kingston; Morton Asfeldt in Camrose; Alan Short in Aberdeen.

Thanks also go to many other people who contributed to this project in significant ways including (with apologies for the indignity of a list): David Alexander, Kingston; Tina and Albert Angenent, Seeley's Bay; David Archibald, Newburgh; Gary Babcock, Lake Superior Provincial Park; Katherine and Alan Balmer, Seeley's Bay; Alan Barwin, Kingston; Mike Beedell, Martindale; Jane and Peter Billings, Seeley's Bay; Jacqueline Boileau, Atikokan; Ken Bowman, Winnipeg; Isabel Bourdon, NFB, Montreal; Jim Brown, Winnipeg School District #1; Alex M. Bryans, Kingston; Philip Chester, Deep River; Bruce Cockburn, Milton; Dr. Ted Cuddy, Winnipeg; Jack and Cathy de Graaf, Seeley's Bay; Gerald D'Eutremont, NFB, Montreal; Gordon Deval and Linda Kepron, Winnipeg; George Drought, Hamilton; Phyllis Ducharme, Winnipeg School District #1; Bob Edwards, Ottawa; Gerald Finley, Kingston; Jim Foster, Canning; Harry Gutkin, Winnipeg; Alex M. Hall, Fort Smith; Brenda Hans, Yellowknife; Trudy and Kevin Hartley, Seeley's Bay; Andrew Human, Walkerton; Dale Lapham, Wawa; Jane, Steve, Erin & Kevin Jonah, Riverview, N.B.; Ernie Kuyt, Edmonton; John LaForgia, Rochester, Minnesota; Roger MacGregor, Ivy Lea; Mrs. Ken McCaskill, Winnipeg; Ian and Sue McKenzie, Banff; Jeff Miller, Orillia; Tom Meadows, Winnipeg; Jacqueline Moen, Rochester, Minnesota; Duane Murray, Manitoba Pioneer Camp; Barrie Nelson, Malibu, California; Alan Oates, Somerset, England; Verne and Anne Parrett, Cold Spring Head; Nick Pipoli, Bachawana Bay; Christine Robertson, Kingston; Ian Reid, Selkirk; Marta Scythes, Newburgh; Tom Shoebridge, Ottawa; Marney J. Simmons and sons Ryan and Andrew Wilcox, Black Rapids; Ranjit Singh, Guelph; Doreen Sisto, Selkirk; Jack Smyth, Winnipeg School District #1; Ron Tozer, Algonquin Park; Leon and Dory Trenholm, Chapman Settlement; Pierre Trudeau, Montreal; Jim Dale Vickery, Ely, Minnesota; Kirk Wipper, Toronto; Ron Williamson, Dunrobbin; Moiya Wright, Old Chelsea.

Finally, special appreciation to my colleagues at Queen's University Faculty of Education—Bert Horwood, Louise Cowin, Heidi Mack, and especially Jan Carrick—who taught courses, read drafts and filled the gaps while I was away on sabbatical, and when I wasn't; to my insightful and even-handed publisher and editor Phyllis Bruce; to Bill, wherever you are; to my wife Gail, who ate the toast even though it *was* burned; to daughters Molly and Laurel who paddled in rain and still managed to smile; to my mother-in-law, who gives without asking; and to my parents whose unconditional support buoys me always. Many thanks.

INTRODUCTION

ON A PROMISING SEPTEMBER DAY, I'm searching for Bill Mason on the blue-water edge of the Canadian Shield, north of Sault Ste. Marie. Lake Superior has been calm as I have made my way west from Michipicoten Mission. The fall sun has reached its zenith and is noticeably lower in the sky than just weeks ago; my left side is hot, but there's a chill creeping in from the shadows on my right. Swells begin to rise from the direction of Devil Island or Michigan or wherever it is that the character of this lake originates. They lift and settle this canoe as if I'm paddling on the back of a benevolent monster. Fortunately, the boat has been here before—Bill's boat. It knows the beast. There is safety in that.

Bill's widow, Joyce, has lent me this loved, old 16-foot Chestnut Prospector. The red canvas is cracked and faded. The ribs and planks are brittle. But the slat seats still squeak, and that nostalgic smell of cedar and old varnish wafts up from the sun-warmed floor as I make my way along the coast. The plan is to visit some of Bill's favourite haunts. Today I'm headed for Denison Falls and will sleep there in one of his old Baker tents. The boat spins as a rogue wave rolls under its keel, turning me broadside in the troughs. It's a great old canoe, but too small for a lake this size to notice. Time to head upriver. I fight to maintain balance as the waves break and tumble back in the shallow water along the sand spit that protects the river from the lake. I catch a curler and surf into the calm water on the other side.

The sign on the first inside says "Dog River. Since 1632." Somebody's trying to make a point. Bill always called this river "The University." He always talked about a cherished spot a couple of miles upstream from the lake: Denison Falls. He filmed it, painted it, described it in his books. I've come along the coast to pay my respects.

Two or three bends upstream from the sign, I'm debating with myself whether I'm actually gaining or losing ground against the current. Should I pull a little harder and get to that eddy there, and then across to that big rock over there? Travelling alone like this, talking to myself, reminds me of Friar Tuck and the way he muddled through Sherwood Forest supplying both sides of a running argument. Bill prayed a lot when he was out here. Maybe now is the time. Or should I forgo the upstream paddling, save breaking my paddle on the bottom as I flail to make headway, and start tracking up the shore?

I tie lines to the bow and stern painter rings, let the boat angle freely into the current, coil up the loose ends and begin making my way unsteadily along the boulder bank of the river. It's not a very big river and the water appears to be low, but it's surprising how much pull the canoe exerts on the ropes. Looking back at the empty red canoe, I am caught by a momentary twinge of deep sadness. Bill *is* gone.

The valley is deep here, and the trees are mostly birches and conifers with a few mountain ash sprinkled with vermilion berries. The forest hues are bronze, not red. Lofty hemlocks diffuse sunlight into cascades of laughing riparian light that follows me up the valley, highlighting the banks. Behind, the gulls, the noisy birds, have stayed to argue on the spit. But for the most part, the forest here is quiet. Ahead, the river chuckles away on rocks and riffles centre stream. I turn and look again at the red canoe silhouetted against the shining river, somehow expecting him to be sitting there, feet up, enjoying the free ride.

I'm doing my best not to get wet feet, but before long the boat catches on a gravel bar and I must wade in, in my wellies, to move it. Three steps later I've got one long, tall soaker; then the other. The river is not all that deep, and it's not all that fast-flowing, but there is a current and the canoe feels heavy on the lines. One almighty tug, one slip, and I'm wet to the waist.

Two hours later, I'm thoroughly soaked, tired but pleased to be reaching a sharp left swing in the river where the map says the falls are supposed to be. I pull up the canoe by an eddy and slosh my way up the shore to catch a glimpse of this place that so caught Bill's fancy. There it is, Denison Falls, running across the river, maybe 20 feet high. I'm surprised. Like the man, perhaps, it looks bigger in the films.

I strip—even in an out-of-the-way place like this, it's a trick to convince yourself that you are in fact alone—and carefully lay out my wet shirt, pants and red woollen socks on the smooth grey rocks to dry in the sun. Barefoot, I make my way back up the rock-strewn riverbed to the base of the falls. There's another rushing stream coming in on the right—Jimmy Cash Creek. It's almost more appealing than the big falls. Nice spot, but it is difficult to imagine why Bill got so excited about this place. Denison Falls seems pretty ordinary.

There appears to be a steep trail that starts at the point where a worn hawser dangles from an overhanging cedar tree down a vertical rock face beside the falls. I haul myself up the rock, scramble up the trail and make my way through the bushes, apparently cutting high across another sharp bend in the river. Then, suddenly, I'm aware of a physical murmuring in the air and the ground around me. Under a deadfall, a few more excited steps along the path, and I've found what Bill discovered more than thirty years ago.

The path opens to an outlook commanding a stirring view of Denison Falls. It begins above me in the coloured hills on the far side of the river, a line of black water steps out over a mist-shrouded brink; it splits with abandon on a pillar of black rock, wheels with a flick to the crowd, then bubbles itself into a filigreed fan that flutters and falls to the river below. The view suspends time, for an instant, for an hour. Bill always said he felt closer to God in places like this. Just breathing the mist-dampened air makes the transcendency of that notion close enough to touch.

Sometime later, shadows lengthen and I start to get cold. Surely those clothes are dry by now. I return on the path, climb under the broken tree and down the steep, slippery path, onto the rope gingerly—it's different trusting your life to a line when you've seen the extent of its tenuous anchor close up—and back down to the river below. I pick up and pull on my jeans and shirt. Bending to get my socks, I find only one, lying flat and crispy on the rock. The other is gone. Gone. Gulls might steal a sock, but not now, not in the fall, and besides they're probably still bickering at the lake. The only bird I've seen all day is a circling lone osprey. The sock, apparently, has just vanished.

It's classic Mason. I start to laugh. The silliness of the missing sock is too much. For a minute I'm certain that a puckish Bill is hiding in the trees somewhere nearby, with his battered hat and his favourite canoeing shirt, killing himself laughing and waving one red sock on a stick for all the otherly world to see. It was his kind of joke. "Mason, you little weasel, what have you done with my sock?" I call exasperatedly in a voice that is swallowed without echo by the autumnal woods.

And so it has been for nearly two years now looking for Bill Mason, checking out his favourite spots, talking to his friends and family, following his trail from one side of the country to the other. Writing the story of his life has been a little like the Denison Falls trip, hoping chance and serendipity might leaven safe, scholarly instincts. Bill's geographic lifeline links Winnipeg, where he was born, to Old Chelsea, Quebec, where he died. I've found it helpful to think of his life as a gradual eastward movement, over time, away from Winnipeg, east past Lake of the Woods, Quetico, the north shore of Superior, and Algonquin Park, to Ottawa. His career rises gradually along that line through the making of *Paddle to the Sea, Rise and Fall of the Great Lakes* and his other early films, climaxing with the release of *Cry of the Wild*, his feature film about wolves that outsold every film except *The Exorcist* in its first week of release in New York City. The wolf film days were the high times that led to a turning-point in his life in the mid-1970s. Mason was dining with the Queen, playing broomball with Prime Minister Pierre Trudeau, and being asked to speak around the world. At this point in his career, on the occasion of his investiture as a film maker into the Royal Canadian Academy, he startled his University of Manitoba School of Art colleague and previous RCA inductee, Tony Tascona, with the news that he was going to quit filming and turn back to painting, his first love. It was a transition he struggled with for the rest of his life.

Being a keen paddler myself, following Bill the canoeist was easy. It was the best excuse yet for getting out to the wild. Getting at Bill the artist, however, was a very different story. I began these explorations by attempting to whittle a likeness of Paddle to the Sea using Holling C. Holling's famous children's book as a guide, just as Bill had done. It was a chance to think with my hands, as Bill frequently did. But the task was *much* more difficult than I had ever imagined. Artistically, the result was disappointing. Carving the canoe, with its many symmetries, was facile, but bringing form—and proportion—to the little Indian figure was another story. In the end, when the Band-Aids were all used up, and the work as finished as I could make it, I was frustrated and a little embarrassed at the tawdry effort. I simply dumped Paddle on the basement bench to collect dust, until the summer.

I threw in Paddle and a few old jars of Testor's model paint, almost as an afterthought, packing for our annual summer pilgrimage to Nova Scotia. Paddle would "go to the sea," and maybe that would release a little of his Masonian wisdom. On a day when it was too hot to swim or even walk the flats, I got out Paddle and, hesitantly at first, began to apply the paint. Almost magically the wood came to life. Our two young daughters began inviting their beach friends to hold Paddle while perusing the dog-eared book. On sleep-overs there were fights about who would hold Paddle while the book was being read. And in that transformation I glimpsed the world for an instant through Bill Mason's eyes. To everyone else who bought the book at Eaton's in Winnipeg back in the 1940s, and since, *Paddle to the Sea* was a charming story about a carved wooden toy. To Bill, who purchased the book in his teens, Paddle was a magical being he could bring to life and share with children and adults around the world through the medium of film. From the moment Bill saw the illustrations in the book, Paddle was alive in his imagination. It would take him nearly fifteen years to transfer the vision in his head to moving images on the cinematic screen, but that is exactly what he did.

And so began the career of one Canada's most prolific and success-ful film makers—eighteen films; sixty-odd honours, including two

American Academy Award nominations and two British Academy Awards; and a gilded international reputation as a sensitive creator, canoeist and voice of wilderness preservation. The strange thing is that, while everyone, it seems, loved Bill Mason's work in film, Bill could never rest on his accomplishments. Perhaps the greatest burden he carried with him—and one substantiated by his faith and sense of artistic mission—was the need to seek out the next challenge, never to rest on his accolades. The story of his life that you are about to read is one of enviable success, creative freedom, supportive family, tantalizing projects and a life's work that most artists in the world of film can only dream about. But in walking Bill's path, in seeking out his favourite locations, his friends, co-workers and family—in efforts to explore his life comprehensively, I have uncovered a story that has its moments of great sadness and disappointment. Bill Mason died at 59 with every kudos, every success, every award a film maker could hope to achieve, but, ironically, he may have died a resolutely frustrated artist, his passing coincident with the tumultuous end of one career and the trepidatious beginning of another.

I knew Bill, but primarily for only one period of his life, when we collaborated on several projects in the 1980s. Even with those sporadic encounters I had learned to admire his qualities as a canoeist, a dreamer and a lover of adventure who would much sooner go out the door than in. There was something about Bill that drew people to him. What kind of person would win almost every award possible for film making and then quit making films because, he said, he was really a painter? What kind of person would impel strangers to name their children in his honour? What kind of person would move other strangers to tears on hearing the news of his death?

I started this book with a clear destination in mind, like the North Pole from Guelph, Ontario, to celebrate Bill's life and work, and to answer a few of these questions. But a life, it turns out, is more complicated than I had ever imagined. Bill Mason was a son, a brother, a father, a husband and a film maker who loved to create with his hands and who lived to canoe; but like other Canadian heroes, Mason was also a mythical character, larger than life, wilderness man—white beard, floppy hat, plaid shirt, red bandana, cutoffs and a long summer tan—keeper of the wild, painter in the red canoe. It helps to begin to think about Bill first as a person, a person from whom an enduring myth emerged. Bill the man had a life that could be portrayed as points on a line—significant events, achievements and contradictions ordered in time. Bill the myth was a much more elusive character; the wilderness icon was created by Bill himself, first in the process of editing *Cry of the Wild* and later the Path of the Paddle series, but it very quickly developed a life energized elsewhere. These two Bill Masons lead to at least two intertwining obligations for his biographer: the first demands that life be written as linear, birth at one end, death at the other; the writer's obligation is to demarcate significant points on the line and to highlight patterns that emerge, to highlight the facts. But, as writer and paddler Robert Perkins remarked, "Life is what happens between the facts." Put another way, poet Bronwyn Wallace characterized this other human essence as powered by "the stubborn particulars of grace."

At one level, this story of Bill Mason's life is an assemblage of facts. But I hope there is also, within these words, a prospect for readers to see between the facts, to ponder the stubborn particulars, even to imagine that a life isn't linear at all; some lives are spherical and have at their centre a focus, or essence, around which everything else is ordered and from which a vital talent is derived. This is a story about one man, but—depending on one's point of view and the extent to which Bill's life is seen as facts or particulars, as a line or a circle—this is also a more universal story in which a reader might find him- or herself or something elemental about red canoes, white water and the lure of the wilderness.

The curious thing about Bill Mason's huge popularity and influence was his simplicity. My favourite images of him—and the ones, I suspect, that have made the most difference in changing the way we think about who we are and where we live—are those of a solitary, far from the adulation, alone in his red canoe in a wilderness like Algoma or Algonquin Park. There he is oblivious to man or machine, paddling, watching, listening, suspended in a reverie piqued by regard for nature and fixed by faith that there is a lesson to be learned from immersion in the Canadian wild. Sometimes, when I'm alone on the water, I hear the chatter of waves on the shore and the scolding of a red squirrel in the pines; at other times, I'm sure it's Bill's hearty laugh I hear on the wind. But in a blink he is gone, leaving only the rhythmic dip of cherry paddle in bright water, and the echoes of a uniquely Canadian story.

J.R.
Seeley's Bay, Ontario
November 1995

1

THE MAN AND THE RED CANOE

A SINGLE RED CANOE PIVOTS playfully next to the Mississippi River in Carleton Place, southwest of Ottawa. Evening light warms its chipped wooden gunwales and shadows its gentle curve from stem to stern. Star bursts of tiny cracks and scratches in the patina of painted canvas give a sheen to the boat as it turns in rhythm with the music. Underneath, balancing the canoe on his shoulders, blasé about poise or whom he might hit in the process, is a diminutive man in grey flannels, white shirt and burgundy tie. It is only when the twirling canoe narrowly misses the bride, clapping in a joyous circle of family and friends, that someone grabs the dangling painter as it sweeps across the polished dance floor, stops the pirouette and leads the man outside and back to the river. A spontaneous cheer rises above the music. People applaud and hoot for the spirit of the man, Canada's own Mr. Canoehead—Bill Mason—dancing as only he would, at his son's wedding.

It is June 18, 1988. Mason's 5-foot 4-inch, 130-pound frame is tanned and lean. He will be sixty on his next birthday, and there is much to celebrate. Son Paul, with whom he paddled so many Canadian rivers in the making of his best-selling instructional films and canoeing books in the Path of the Paddle series, has found a new paddling partner; he is growing up, moving on, marrying the love of his life. At the wedding Mason is surrounded by family—wife, Joyce; daughter, Becky; sister, Elizabeth; nephews, nieces and relatives of every stripe—from Winnipeg and the greater Ottawa area. He has just given Paul and his new bride, Judy, a hand-drawn card on which a cartoon character asks them to select one red Chestnut Prospector canoe "from the pile" at the Mason homestead at Meech Lake for their wedding present. Paul and Judy paddled to the Carleton Place Canoe Club, after a simple marriage ceremony in a nearby church, and now Bill is celebrating their new life together, remembering old times, in the only way he knows how—with a canoe and a laugh and a show for the audience.

Anyone who looked closely that night as Bill Mason danced with his beloved Prospector canoe in the Carleton Place Canoe Club would have seen a hospital identification bracelet tucked under the starched cuff of his dress shirt. Two days before the wedding, he had been admitted to Ottawa Civic Hospital for tests to get to the root of a serious intestinal problem. He had signed himself out for the wedding. On the day following the wedding, the Sunday, before returning to the hospital, he canoed whitewater on the Petite Nation River, north of Ottawa, with his nephews from Winnipeg and other wedding guests. On Monday he underwent a CAT scan and on Tuesday he was diagnosed with terminal cancer. In four months he would be dead, at fifty-nine.

During his life Bill Mason captivated the hearts of people across Canada and around the world. He became an icon for wilderness, with his floppy hat, white beard, plaid shirt and red canoe. His last six films—four in the Path of the Paddle series, and two features, *Song of the Paddle* and *Waterwalker*—made Bill a canoe legend. Two books about canoeing, which grew out of the film work, cemented his place in canoeing history. And while people, young and old, turned to Mason's books and films for advice on canoeing—the technique, the stroke details, the "how-to goods" on every aspect of the sport—they also got tips on how to relate to nature. Over the years there have been dozens of instructional books and films produced by and for canoeists but what drew fans and admirers and set Bill in a class of his own was the man himself—the man who could not hide his love for life, for canoes and for the wilderness, even if he had wanted to; the man who would dance with his canoe.

Had Mason plopped his red canoe in the water that night, instead of returning to the wedding, he would have paddled downstream, as he had done countless times previously, past Appleton, Almonte, Pakenham, and out to Arnprior, at the confluence of the Mississippi and Ottawa rivers. Since leaving Winnipeg in 1959, he had made the Ottawa valley his home, a voyageur highway swelled at every turn by Quebec waters to the north and Ontario streams to the south. With his friend Wally Schaber, he had crashed down the steep Laurentian hills on the Quebec side every spring on rivers like the Dumoine, Black, Fildegrande, Coulonge, Picanoc and Petite Nation; and on lazy summer days and the misty mornings of late August he had made his way down the big rivers of Algonquin Park, including the Petawawa, Barron, Madawaska and Opeongo. He travelled with friends and family, any-body he could cajole into joining him for 5:00 A.M. departures, and stopped to paint or to listen to the way the echoes of a loon change as the air gets crisp and cold. And just for fun, on an afternoon whim, he had sometimes filled his boat with truck inner tubes and gone for a whitewater frolic on the main channel of the Ottawa, at Beachburg, or for a flatwater toot on the Bonnechere, the Jock or the Mississippi, stop-ping in at Carleton Place for ice cream or a glass of cold water.

Had he carried on down the Ottawa, even solo and in the dark, past Masson, Thurso, Papineauville, Hawkesbury and Montreal, he would have relived other adventures—his nights at the National Film Board in Montreal, his days with Blake James in the Gaspé, looking for locations to shoot the ocean scenes for *Paddle to the Sea*. And should he have stopped for the night to sleep in his cherished Baker tent, he would have set it up with a view of the stars and the crescent moon and, long after the candle had been extinguished, would have dreamed of places and possibilities for a man and his canoe.

Anybody who ever talked to Bill Mason would learn that his favourite canoe trip was the one he had just finished. After canoeing the Nahanni, he raved about that; after the Hood River trip with singer Bruce Cockburn, he raved about that, though he wouldn't tell people how disappointed he felt on encountering silence after running to the top of an esker and howling his head off expecting a chorus of wolves to reply. After the Dumoine, he might speak rapturously about the nuance

3

of change in rapids as water levels rise and fall, or he might complain about the garbage he'd found on the big campsite on Lac Benoit. And after a day's outing on the Mississippi, he would say *it* was his favourite because it is *so* beautiful and so close to home, or because he happened to see there a flight of geese heading south against the sun. Or he might duck the questions altogether and just say, "C'mon, let's go. It's too nice a day to sit around gabbing!"

Unconventional though it may be to begin a person's life story at its end, the image of Bill at his son's wedding is highly symbolic of a man who loved his canoe, who cherished life and who defined himself and spoke to the world as much through his actions as through his words. Bill rarely danced in the conventional way—or at least, not very often, according to his wife, Joyce—but in so far as dancing is action charged with the rhythm of its surroundings and with the zest of its actor, Bill Mason was a dancer for his whole life—Mr. Bojangles with a camera and a canoe, full of life, full of passion.

In his actions and in the rich experiences of his life, Bill crystallized for a generation the Canadian wilderness tradition and wisdom of his elders, among them Ernest Thompson Seton, Grey Owl, Tom Thomson, Calvin Rutstrum, Sigurd Olson and Eric Morse. Look closely at Bill's life, though, and it's full of paradox: he was not a great reader, and yet he carried the words of the masters in his heart and conveyed them in his work; he thrived on the company of others and loved the comradeship of team sports—especially hockey in the starched blue winter air of Winnipeg and Meech Lake—and yet he craved solitude for his painting. Collaboration with others was in many ways the bane of his professional film making; he was inarticulate, not handy with words, and yet he was a masterful storyteller, writing award-winning film scripts and best-selling canoe books; he was physically small and was sick much of his life with asthma and various other life-threatening conditions, and yet he became the epitome of the robust wilderness man, the modern-day voyageur, travelling the woods alone, heaving his canoe through haystacks and souse-holes in the wildest of rapids, and carrying huge packs over craggy trails all through the Canadian Shield; he could sit for hours—days even—at an editing table in his film studio at Meech Lake, and yet, when it came to painting, he always said the biggest problem was sitting still long enough to finish an image. Catchy contradictions worth exploring.

When Bill died in his log home on the shores of Meech Lake on October 29, 1988, his passing was marked by almost every national newspaper, radio and television outlet in the country, noting his legacy of films and books and his presence as part of the environmental movement. In time, when the popularity of his films was documented, Bill Mason would emerge as the most successful film maker in the history of the National Film Board of Canada. Records would show that, as a body of work, his films were borrowed, purchased and seen by more people than those of any other NFB film maker since the inception of the Film Board in 1939. And from his work at the NFB comes another central informing image from this fascinating life.

In *Paddle to the Sea*, Mason's first film with the NFB, there are many memorable images that include the carved toy canoe and its Indian occupant: a snake swimming up and over Paddle as he sits in a marshy backwater; Paddle getting away from a little boy who finds him on the shore of a lake, and the boy's dog refusing to fetch the little canoe; Paddle going over Niagara Falls; Paddle being caught in a raging forest fire. The adversity this little figure overcame in many ways parallels the early years of a young boy born on the banks of the Red River. Close up, that life was fraught with scrapes, moments of unspeakable strife, ups and downs to shake the most resilient of characters, meanders and backwaters to test even the most patient of souls. But, from a distance, especially with the broad vision of time, there was pattern, flow and purpose—destiny even—in Bill's life, moving ever forward on the river that was his faith and his belief in himself.

2

CANOES AT GRAND BEACH

IT WAS A WONDER THAT THE BOY survived at all. Born William Clifford Mason in Winnipeg's Victoria Hospital on April 29, 1929, the first child of Sadie and Bill Mason was a very tiny baby. Anyone who came to visit the proud mother in hospital would have seen her struggle not to panic when the baby rasped and coughed. From the beginning, he was beset with respiratory problems, leading later to asthma, which would pester him into adolescence. On those first nights in the hospital, someone would have to sit him up and massage his back to help him breathe. Thinking about those at once joyous and worrisome days, Sadie remembers fearing at times that her son would expire from lack of breath. After the doctor decided to allow the baby to be taken home, Sadie Mason— by instinct, pure determination or a combination of both—would sleep, as only a mother would, in Bill's room in a little bed beside his crib, listening for the slightest wheeze. Night after night she would take him in her arms, feed him, rub his back and sing him to sleep. When Sadie got too tired to continue, she would go into the next room and wake her husband, who would take his turn walking with Bill to ease his breathing. People remarked at the time that, even with all the love and care his parents provided, it was astonishing that the child prevailed.

The Winnipeg into which Bill was born was a crumbling commercial and industrial empire, soon to be devastated, like the rest of the country, by the Great Depression. The Canadian Pacific Railway, which had come to Winnipeg fifty years earlier, had brought with it manufacturing and service industries that made the city the wholesale, administrative and financial hub of the West. But, in 1919, the Winnipeg General Strike signalled the start of serious economic decline and social ferment in the proud city. By April 1929, in what was called "The Bull's Eye of the Dominion," factories were closing and unemployment was rising at unprecedented rates. But though he was born at the beginning of the Depression, Bill Mason was spared the indignity and hardship felt by many Winnipeggers of the time: his father and both grandfathers had work, and the family home was warm and filled with the helping hands of grandmothers, and other relatives from both sides of the family who did what they could to help him get started in the world.

It was a stable, conservative home environment. Mason's father and namesake, William Thomas Mason, had moved to Winnipeg with his parents as a boy, from Birmingham, England, in the early part of the century. He grew up during the city's boom years, graduating from Grade 11 at age sixteen and finding employment immediately as a clerk with the Great West Life Insurance Company, where he remained—reluctantly, as time progressed—until retirement. Bill Sr. was twenty-five when son Bill was born. By then he had been at Great West Life for nearly a decade, and with Sadie's careful budgeting they had been able to purchase a small white two-storey frame house in South Winnipeg.

Like her husband, Sadie Fair was also the child of a family that had emigrated from the Old Country, in this case, Dublin, Ireland. She met Bill Sr. at a United Church Sunday school in St. Vital, another suburb of Winnipeg, where her friend May lived. Even after Sadie completed high school and went to work at the T. Eaton Company in Winnipeg, she continued to visit May. It was on one of those weekend visits that she met the man she would marry. After that first meeting, the dashing young Mason kept sidling up to May, enquiring hopefully, "Why don't you ask Sadie to come up and stay for the weekend? And why don't you bring her to Sunday school again?" Sadie knew that her mother was set on another fellow for her, but fell in love with the handsome lad with a career position at Great West Life, and married him instead.

For the seven years prior to the birth of his sister, Elizabeth Catherine, Bill Jr. lived the life of an only child. He was frail and small, and his mother fussed over him constantly. The Masons lived at 162 Morley Avenue in the suburb of Riverview, an orderly grid of lots and modest houses tucked inside a sweeping oxbow in the Red River, just south of the place where La Vérendrye had built Fort Rouge in 1738, at the confluence of the Assiniboine and Red rivers. Bill's father would leave in the morning and walk west, past neatly planted boulevard hardwoods that in later years would arch over the streets, shading the wonderful old neighbourhood. On Sundays, Bill and his parents would take that same sidewalk, west to Osborne Street, where they would catch the Park Line street car and head north to church in the centre of town. Almost as soon as he could walk, and certainly as soon as he could draw, little Billy would accompany his parents to church, where he would often position himself on his knees on the floor, facing the pew between his parents. Here he would draw while the preacher delivered the message of the day. In those preschool years, Bill created elaborate drawings in church—of trucks and buildings, fires and fire engines—and on the way back south on the street car he would regale his parents with elaborate narratives of what was going on in his work, who was doing what to whom and why. By the time they trundled him back up Morley Avenue for lunch in the sunny family kitchen at the back of the house, or on the porch outside at the front or the back, Bill's attention would be onto something else, fighting crooks or wild Indians on the great plains of his imagination.

Feeding that hungry imagination and shaping the world of the preschool Bill Mason were two sets of very different grandparents who lived nearby. Perhaps because Bill was the first grandchild, perhaps because his parents individually never really broke the habit of deferring to their own parents in family matters, perhaps because these people influenced the young boy's life at a time when he was most impressionable, the legacy of his grandparents was substantial and long lasting, and in the fullness of time would turn out to be more significant than that of either parent.

His father's parents, Thomas and Elizabeth Mason, both born in Stratford-on-Avon, England, had emigrated to Canada in 1907. Thomas became a printer for the T. Eaton Company when he arrived in Winnipeg, and despite his having very bad asthma that was exacerbated by the volatile inks and solvents in his workplace, stayed in this job until his retirement. He was a quiet and benevolent soul who loved his children and grandchildren; however, like the rest of the family, he was very much under the thumb of his wife, Elizabeth, who judged everyone, everything, every action and inaction, against a rigid set of Christian principles derived from her Plymouth Brethren upbringing.

Granny Mason was an imposing character, physically generous and psychically severe, a woman who dressed in black and spent most of her time sitting in a rocking chair with a bible in her lap, while the rest of the family waited on her and suffered the imposition of her judgments on their every move. That Bill's paternal grandmother had these characteristics would have had only minimal effect on the family—presumably they could have chosen to visit, or not, as the spirit moved—except for the fact that Bill's mother, Sadie, felt compelled to attend Granny Mason in the way of an indentured servant.

Almost daily, Sadie would parcel up Bill, and later, Bill's sister, Elizabeth, walk out to Osborne Street and take the street car through various transfer zones to visit Granny Mason. Arriving at her mother-in-law's house, Sadie would do the laundry, clean the house as required, and do the baking, while Granny Mason sat in her chair and rocked with her bible. It was a strange situation that Sadie remembered with more than a tinge of regret in her later years. The extent of this servitude to Granny Mason on Sadie's part was a mystery—in the end, even to Sadie. Speaking about this long after Granny Mason had died, she said that Mrs. Mason had had more control over her and her family than her own parents or anyone else. Although Granny Mason's two daughters lived in the area with their husbands and families, and apparently were as dutiful as daughters should be, they felt nothing like the compulsion borne by their sister-in-law Sadie to do their mother's bidding. On occasion Sadie would be invited to visit with her neighbours or be asked to bake for church or neighbourhood functions, but would have to concoct excuses for delaying those tasks until she had tended to Granny Mason's needs.

Granny Mason's world was a grim amalgam of guilt and servitude to her God, a world of fear and retribution. It was a world of black and white; no grey. You were either going to heaven or going to hell. With the exception of reading the Bible and worshipping the Lord, almost everything else—books, films, games, secular music, cards—was the work of the devil. Once, when Elizabeth was small, she inadvertently slipped and asked Granny Mason for playing cards. Sadie, who always had an ear cocked to make sure the children were toeing the line with their grandmother, quickly interrupted: "She means old Christmas cards to play with. Don't you, Elizabeth!" For all the orthodoxy in following the ways of the Lord in the Plymouth Brethren traditions, Granny Mason was very fussy about her medicinal tonic, which had to be near to hand and had to be Five Star Brandy; lesser brands would not do. The liquor store was a common diversion for Sadie on her way to Granny's house.

As apparently joyless and severe as this grandmotherly world was, there can be little doubt that Granny Mason's faith in God became an integral and unavoidable part of the intellectual and spiritual nurturing of her grandchildren. Where Bill might draw a picture and launch into a boy's story of adventure and intrigue on the Manitoba plains, Granny Mason would counter with biblical stories of Cain and Abel, of Esau and Jacob, or of the Tabernacle and Moses leading the exodus out of Egypt. Bill would listen quietly. For a boy like Bill Mason, who loved to draw and who had a talent for storytelling, there was understandable pressure to internalize the possibly unholy passions of the day, and to retreat as required to a rich and adventuresome imaginary world inside his head. Everyone in Granny Mason's orbit learned that certain things were simply better left unsaid. Silence, after all, was more difficult to judge.

The world of Bill's maternal grandparents was very different. Tomas and Catherine (Kate) Fair were churchgoing folk but, unlike Granny Mason, seemed almost instinctively to know how to reach out and nurture a growing extended family.

Tomas Fair was born in England in the late nineteenth century and was sent to Dublin to work in the laboratory of the Royal College of Surgeons, where he met his future wife. For a while things were grand for Tomas and Kate, but shortly after the arrival of their second child, the Fairs decided to emigrate to Canada to find more opportunities. Tomas went ahead to look for work and landed a job in Winnipeg with the Canadian Northern Railway. Kate was to follow soon after, but what was supposed to be an August 1914 departure for her and the children was delayed until November of that year as transatlantic shipping was choked with the movement of troops and supplies to support the growing war effort. Perhaps because of these early insecurities, the Fairs established priorities for themselves and for their children. When Sadie took an interest in and finally married a handsome lad she'd met at the young people's group of a friend's church, the Fairs took it upon themselves to provide as much support as possible to the clan as it grew.

For young Bill Mason—or "Billy," as he was called—one of the most significant aspects of this assistance was the Fairs' renting of a cottage each summer at Grand Beach on Lake Winnipeg. Developed by the CNR just prior to the First World War, Grand Beach was one of only three beach-style resorts around the southern cusp of Lake Winnipeg. Victoria Beach, to the north, was where the more well-to-do folk summered. Winnipeg Beach, across the lake, was predominantly Jewish. By contrast, Grand Beach was populated by Jews and Gentiles alike and was very much a blue-collar haven designed by and for employees of the railway. On the site was a large hotel, a dance pavilion, a boardwalk and 312 identical cottages laid out in 26 rows, one for each letter of the alphabet, 12 cottages deep, stretching into the poplars and cottonwoods on the shore of the lake. As a CNR employee, Grandpa Fair joined the throng in an annual, twelve-dollars-per-week, summer pilgrimage to Grand Beach, and was eventually able to purchase a cottage on the Grand Beach site.

These were halcyon days for young Bill and they contrasted sharply with his Winnipeg world, cloistered and constricted by the whims and edicts of Granny Mason. The air was different at Grand Beach. The people were free and happy there. There was so much to do: places to explore, fish to catch, boats to row. On cool August evenings, Bill could climb up onto Grandpa or Grandma Fair's lap beside the big, black McCleery stove, drink cocoa, eat cinnamon toast, play cards and enter the wonderful worlds of *Treasure Island*, *Robinson Crusoe* or *Gulliver's Travels*, read as only a grandparent can.

In June, Sadie and the children would take the train to Grand Beach to spend the summer with the Fairs. Bill's father would carry on with his job and would take the "Daddy Train" up to Grand Beach on weekends. And for his annual couple of weeks of holiday, Bill Sr. would bring his bathing suit and a change of clothes to join the rest of the family at play. At summer peak, as many as 13,000 people a day travelled the 54 miles from Winnipeg to Grand Beach on as many as a dozen trains. Families would rent cottages, and in the evenings dating couples from Winnipeg would arrive at the Grand Beach dance pavilion on the "Moonlight Special"; for one dollar, you could leave Winnipeg after work and be back by midnight, having danced the night away. On warm summer evenings such tunes as "Brother, Can You Spare a Dime?," "My Gal Sal," "Swanee River" and "Red Sails in the Sunset" would float through the Grand Beach dunes. Families would walk the famous Grand Beach boardwalk along the sand beside the dance pavilion, intermingling with amorous dancers catching a breath of fresh air, eating hot dogs or five-cent greasy French fries from Mr. Reynold's chip concession, washing them down with Kik cola, Stone's ginger beer or Coca-Cola. Despite the Depression, Grand Beach thrived in the thirties. Word had it that every baby in the greater Winnipeg area nicknamed "Sandy" had been conceived in the soft, warm sand under the Grand Beach boardwalk, to the tromp, tromp, tromp of a thousand feet resounding overhead.[1]

Each cottage at the beach came with an icebox and a book of tickets for ice collected from Lake Winnipeg by Natives from the nearby Grand Marais Reserve. Grandpa Fair always made a point of feigning befuddlement on ice day, letting on to young Bill that he couldn't for the life of him remember where the ice house was. That was Bill's cue to take his grandpa in one hand and the little wheeled ice cart's handle in the other and go down towards the station, to the ice house, for a 25-pound block of ice. Occasionally, when he was a little older, a little bigger and a little stronger, Bill would take the same wagon down to meet the trains and earn a little chip money by helping people move their luggage from the train to their cottages.

The same Native people who cut ice for the Grand Beach cottagers caught pickerel and sold it each morning, two fillets for a quarter.

Young Mason no doubt had his turn heading out to mingle with the fishmongers, each trip teaching him something more about the world of his growing up. Writer Barry Broadfoot describes those mornings this way:

> At 7:00 A.M. the call "fresh fish, fresh fish" was heard in the land and my mother would take two quarters from the teacup on the shelf above the stove and I'd run out to join the small crowd around Manuel, the half-breed—now they try and add dignity to their wretched state by calling them Métis. Manuel was a huge man, always dressed in black pants and orange sweater, and his hands were forever bleeding slightly from nicks caused by his flashing filleting knife. . . . The fillets were the biggest, thickest, juiciest, and bone-free I have ever tasted. . . . Those pickerel fried in butter and served with heated stewed tomatoes and bread smeared thick with raspberry jam and a tall glass of milk were enough to send any ten-year-old, red-blooded Canadian boy rushing out onto the trail to do battle with the toughest kid on the block.[2]

No doubt one of those other, though smaller, red-blooded Canadian boys fuelled and informed by Manuel's wares and repartee was little Billy Mason. And as friendly and outgoing as Bill was, on the occasions when he took his fishing pole to the trestle where the spur line to Victoria Beach headed north of the creek that fed the Grand Beach lagoon from the south, he too would have encountered the gracious old gentleman who fished there regularly on a hot summer afternoon, counselling youngsters who happened by about the world from his point of view. Barry Broadfoot remembers the man saying to him, "You'll find that fishermen are the nicest people in the world. Jesus must have thought so too because he chose five as his Apostles." Had young Mason been given such advice, it would perhaps have been the only tale of Grand Beach that met with Granny Mason's approval.

Looking at the world in which Bill Mason spent his formative years, one can see elements that impinged, subconsciously perhaps, on his imagination. On the trains to and from Grand Beach, for example, would have been posters and other material produced by the railway and the federal government, who, in the early 1930s, were actively promoting canoe vacations in the vast wilderness places made accessible by train. Picture a boy on his way to Grand Beach, sizzling with anticipation of swimming, fishing and canoeing, sitting before a poster of red canoe, blue lake and rocky shore, day-dreaming to the trundle of the moving train, or a tired adventurer on the way back to Winnipeg, being lulled to sleep, full of canoe nostalgia.

For many Canadians, especially those in the art community, the images of empty red canoes in railway promotional material had a very real and tangible attachment to the memory of Tom Thomson. J.E.H. Macdonald, fellow artist and founding member of the Group of Seven, had recently painted a canvas[3] in which the empty red canoe expressly symbolized the memory of Thomson. The railway had played a very significant role in the lives of these, and other, Canadian painters, as it enabled them to reach the wilderness areas they loved. It is likely that young Bill was exposed to echoes of these painters as he rode the rails from Winnipeg to Grand Beach and back.

Another Canadian who would have sat before those same posters as he passed through Winnipeg, about the time Mason turned one, was none other than Wa-sha-quon-asin, Archie Belaney, a.k.a. "Grey Owl," changing trains in Winnipeg on his way northwest to Riding Mountain National Park to establish a beaver colony in protected space. Belaney had taken part in a well-publicized government film-making effort to raise awareness of the plight of the beaver. News of the day records him moving through Winnipeg with pet beavers Rawhide and Jelly Roll, who travelled in fine style in an elaborate government-constructed beaver box complete with a 4- by 6-foot tank with bath, drying platform and upper-tier living quarters. Later that year, Grey Owl[4] would make the news a second time with the much-heralded publication of his first book, *Men of the Last Frontier,* in which he described early days on Bear Island in Temagami and Biscotasing in Northern Ontario just prior to the outbreak of the First World War, and provided an important context for Bill's later work in highlighting the symbolic importance of wilderness travel in the Canadian imagination:

The trail, then, is not merely a connecting link between widely distant points, it becomes an idea, a symbol of self-sacrifice, and deathless determination, an ideal to be lived up to, a creed from which none may falter. . . . Stars paling in the East, breath that whistles through the nostrils like steam. Tug of the tump line, swing of the snowshoes; tracks in the snow, every one a story; hissing, slanting sheets of snow; swift rattle of snowshoes over an unseen trail in the dark. A strip of canvas, a long fire, and a roof of smoke. Silence.

Canoes gliding between palisades of rock. Teepees, smoke-dyed, on a smooth point amongst the red pines; inscrutable faces peering out. Two wooden crosses at a rapids. Dim trails. Tug of the tump line again: always. Old tea pails, worn snowshoes, hanging on limbs, their work is well done; throw them not down on the ground. Little fires by darkling streams. Slow wind of evening hovering in the tree tops, passing on to nowhere. Gay, caparisoned clouds moving in review, under the setting sun. Fading day. Pictures forming and fading in glowing embers. Voices in the running waters, calling, calling. The lone cry of a loon from an unseen lake. Peace, contentment. This is the trail.[5]

These are the literary images that Bill would paint with his brush and camera, and with which he would become synonymous in the public imagination.

A year before Grey Owl passed through Winnipeg, a pair of teenage adventurers from Minnesota, looking for the adventure and romance of Grey Owl's mythical "trail," paddled north on the Red River almost by the Masons' front door on Morley Avenue. Eric Sevareid, then seventeen, and later to become a well-known American television commentator, canoed with a friend from their home in Minneapolis to York Factory, near the mouth of the Hayes River on Hudson Bay, before they paddled up the nearby Nelson River, where they caught a southbound train on the newly opened Hudson Bay Railway, a distance of 2,250 miles. This remarkable achievement in recreational wilderness canoeing was in many ways ahead of its time, for in those days the railway was the way to access the wilderness. Canoes were used for day trips, in the manner of the customers of Nelson's Boat Livery at Grand Beach lagoon. Recreational canoeing, especially extended wilderness tripping, was very much in its infancy.

Grand Beach was a venue of consequence for Bill that buoyed his interests and growing independence. He was supported by his parents and the Fairs in his need to explore, to make mistakes and to learn by doing. Whether by virtue of his being small for his age, or simply by disposition, these early years set the pattern for the rest of his life: Bill was either with family or alone; there is little talk of summer friends or pals on the beach. He learned to swim on his own and to accept responsibility for forays away from the cottage on his own. On one of these occasions, he went fishing in the reeds along the edge of the Grand Beach lagoon, set apart from Lake Winnipeg itself by the mile-long spit of white sand for which the place became known. No one was more surprised than Grandpa Fair when Bill arrived home, helped by a neighbour, with a 38-inch jackfish (pike). Not knowing what to do with such a monster, Bill's mother insisted that he keep it outside until someone could fillet it and cook it. There he proudly guarded that fish in a metal garbage can until the cutting was done.

The lagoon was a place of great fascination for young Bill, only partly because it contained monster fish. The lagoon's other draw was Nelson's Boat Livery, the place with a collection of rental row-boats and canoes. For a few cents an hour and a small deposit, people could head out and paddle on water protected by the Grand Beach dunes. The lagoon was always calmer and more forgiving than capricious Lake Winnipeg. When the big lake was calm, however, holidayers would paddle or row themselves around to where swimmers were gathered, and, in the heat of a summer day, would be inclined to forgo their deposits, leaving their rented boats pulled up on the beach. It was here that Bill's lifetime love affair with canoes began. Later on, his dad would rent a canoe for an hour and the two of them would go fishing in the lagoon, but in the early days, especially later on in the afternoon, while his family cavorted in the water, young Bill would wander over to one of those canoes abandoned on the beach, park himself in it and dream of far-away places.

When, at Bill's urging, his father finally rented a canoe for a week, there was no turning back. In *Path of the Paddle*, Mason describes this rental as "the happiest time of my whole childhood."[6] Even at an early age, Bill found the canoe to be a very visceral experience—whether he paddled it or not—and it linked almost organically with the stuff of his imaginings, having a natural resonance. For the first time in his life he had a tangible connection with a device that could take him—just him—to the ends of the earth. Canoes at Grand Beach magically transported him from what *was* to the limitless possibilities of what *could be*. Bill was never happier or prouder than on the day he found an old paddle in the reeds that the Fairs and his parents allowed him to keep, a paddle still marked with the weathered logo of Nelson's Boat Livery. This first paddle—purloined though it was—would be with him for the rest of his life.

The beach, station, dance pavilion and lagoon, roughly north of his family's cottage, were known territory for Bill. As he grew older, he explored south and west as well, past the communal wash house and the little store, and out to the south bluffs that were exposed to the full expanse of Lake Winnipeg. Here, down a walkway, sat a giant wooden wharf, where the commercial fishing boats docked, and at which the Lake Winnipeg ferries from Selkirk and points south on the Red River would disembark and load passengers. Subject to the full reach of the often turbulent lake, on windy days the wharf shuddered as waves pounded boats against wooden pilings, trapping spray that shot like geysers up and over planks and people alike. But on days when the waters were calm, Bill would, without the knowledge of his grandparents or his mother, clamber down into one of the canoes or row-boats tied up at the wharf and paddle it back and forth as far in any direction as the tether would allow. Here, often alone, the young boy would sit for hours at a stretch. When it was too rough, or too busy, he would fish off the end of the pier, or just watch, happy in solitude and equally happy to chat with anyone who chanced by. In these early years, a pattern emerged that would only get stronger and more pronounced as time went on: Bill was resourceful, self-sufficient and comfortable with his own company.

In later years Bill returned to the beach from time to time, long after the dance pavilion and hotel had gone, and revisited the site of the old wharf on the main lake, now reduced to a tired platoon of wooden pilings doing their best to defy the power of water and ice at the edge of Canada's sixth-largest lake. It remained a vital place for him. After his death, Bill's sister, Elizabeth, would make the pilgrimage up to Grand Beach and always take a moment to wander through the alders to the site of the old wharf where her brother had spent so many happy times.

Grand Beach—the lake, the beach, the wharf, the train—became for Bill a haven of freedom and possibility, of escape from the religious and intellectual confinement of home. The route from Winnipeg to Grand Beach, following the meandering course of the Red River, joined home and his first journey away from home and as such defined the first arm of a triangle that, when completed, would encompass his life itself. In time he would move east, along the base of this triangle, to a point just over the Ontario border, where he would go to summer camp; then, when he finally got away on his first long canoe trip, it would be on the Winnipeg River, which connected camp and cottage. Until he actually built and paddled a boat of his own, however, the Grand Beach cottage was by far the most significant point in Bill's summer triangle.

3
—

RED RIVER DAYS

LIKE MOST WESTERN MUNICIPALITIES in the 1930s, Winnipeg was covered with black soil that billowed in with trains eastbound from the parched plain. The dirt served to widen the apparent differences between the luxurious homes of the rich along the rivers at the centre of town and the tenements and shanties of the poor in Winnipeg's North End. These years of drought and economic hardship sent scores of vacant-eyed hopefuls to the trains in search of work. Prime Minister R.B. Bennett, and later Mackenzie King, refused to take responsibility for these jobless Canadians, insisting that their care was a provincial mandate; the upshot was fiscal collapse for the four western provinces and appalling standards of living for the unemployed. Winnipeg, though better off economically than other prairie municipalities, had massive unemployment and shared the look, the feel and the pall of hopelessness that pervaded the West in the 1930s. At night, along the rivers and in hollows by the tracks, fires in encampments of the dispossessed sent smudges of woodsmoke into the air, adding to the city's dingy appearance.

But nestled in a horseshoe of land just south of the town centre, bordered by Osborne Street to the west and a sweeping oxbow of the Red River to the east, was the borough of Riverview, which, for families like the Masons, whose breadwinner remained employed through the Depression, was a greener and more hopeful place than the enclaves of the less fortunate. For a child like Bill, the Depression had little meaning until he read about it in future years. For those who had food to eat, a nice home and a wonderful summer retreat at Grand Beach, life was good.

For the first seven years of his life, Bill reaped all of the family attention and benefits accorded an only child. That he was a diminutive and frail boy, constantly bothered by his asthma, made his parents, aunts, uncles and grandparents even more attuned to him than they might otherwise have been. When Bill was two, Santa brought a packet of crayons, a joyous occasion the youngster celebrated by making a mural on his bedroom wall. Recalling this event years later, Sadie speaks almost with pride of the artistic accomplishments of her son at such an early age. Children with siblings or less understanding parents might have been summarily scolded for such a crime and fired off to bed with no supper. Not Bill: this first indication of artistic prowess was rewarded with drawing paper and a lot of encouragement to continue.

In September 1934, Sadie took her five-year-old son by the hand and, together, rounding the corner onto Carey Avenue in Riverview, they walked the one block to Riverview Elementary School. So began Bill's checkered school career. Riverview is an imposing three-storey, fortress-like red-brick building. Row upon row of large sash windows line up on either side of a dominant stone entryway with dark brown double doors and an arched window overhead that lights the main stairwell. Walking up the four broad stone steps that first day of school must have been a daunting experience for a boy who was barely tall enough to grasp the handle on the heavy front door and certainly not strong enough to open the door on his own.

In later years Bill would tell people he failed Grade 1 because he was always thinking about canoes. By all accounts he didn't actually fail, but from the moment his school career began, his teachers and his parents worried about his spotty aptitude for book learning. In school Bill turned to what he did best, artwork, and making things with his hands; his imagination was never captured by words or numbers. In that Grade 1 classroom in Riverview School, when the afternoon light streamed in

through the ceiling-high windows, the teacher would invariably find little Billy Mason engrossed with a large rectangular sandbox that sat on a
table in the corner of the room, making landscapes, and little people,
and rivers with cups of water to float the canoes he would fashion out of
construction paper, Plasticine, or anything buoyant. A photographer
from the *Winnipeg Free Press* was in the school one day in early fall that
year and caught a photo of a tiny boy standing beside the sand table in
his short-legged breeks, pleased to show the world what he'd done.
Billy's Grade 1 teacher, who went to the same church as the Mason
family, more than once expressed her concerns to them about his trouble applying himself to anything but artwork and the sandbox.

Bill came by these predispositions honestly. Sadie had drawn a bit
in school, and might have had a flair for art if she'd taken the time to
exercise that talent. Bill's dad, too, might have been an artist, had he
not done the right and respectable thing and taken a job the moment
he stepped out of Grade 11. A handsome man, tall and lean, with a
shock of black hair and a natty trimmed moustache, Bill Sr. might have
been a hockey player too, for it seems he was more than competent at
just about anything. Sports and artistry, unfortunately, if not seen by
Granny Mason as vocations linked to the devil, were certainly not
proper ways for a grown man to support his family.

The circumstances under which Bill Sr. came to have the job at
Great West Life are not clear. What is certain, however, is that this large
insurance firm was a safe and secure place of employment, offering
benefits and a lifetime of steady income for its family of employees; it
was also increasingly obvious, as time progressed, that the job at Great
West Life was one Bill Sr. loathed. If his dad did take an interest in
Bill's schooling, and especially in his artwork, it was from afar. Looking
back after Bill Sr. died, some people thought the father might have
been jealous of the artistic success of the son.

The one thing Bill Sr. did do with enthusiasm was share with his
son his love for the game of hockey. Several fathers in the neighbourhood procured from the city a piece of tax-distressed land at the river
end of Oakwood Avenue and formed what they called the Riverview
Community Club. The CNR donated a boxcar, and with materials
scrounged from basements and new housing sites in the area, club

members were able to fashion hockey boards, hang a rudimentary lighting system, and refit the boxcar as a warming hut, with benches, a framed-in door and two 45-gallon drums for a stove. A small levy on members allowed miscellaneous supplies to be purchased and, eventually, as the club got rolling, they were able to hire "Whitey," an unemployed man from Arnold Avenue, as caretaker, for ten dollars a month. Whitey cleared the rink when it snowed, flooded it when required, and operated a small canteen inside the boxcar warming hut.

As soon as young Bill could stand on his own two feet, his dad had him outfitted with skates, and the two of them whiled away Saturdays and evenings with other Riverview fathers and kids learning the not-so-gentle art of hockey. When he was old enough, Bill tripped down to the rink on his own and, despite his small size, shinnied in with the best of the big kids. They played their hearts out every day of the week, except Saturdays after supper when Foster Hewitt, as sports columnist Trent Frayne recalled on Hewitt's death in 1985, would crackle across the radio and "tell us, the millions of us spread right across the country, brought together in living rooms and kitchens and bathtubs and cars and on lonely dark farms and in small snow-packed towns and in brightly lit cities from one ocean to the other, all of us in our mind's eye watching the matchless giants on the ice below." Emulating the spins and passes of their wireless heroes from the Leafs and the Canadiens—players like Charlie Conacher and Rocket Richard—amid shouts, catcalls, the ring of skates and the muffled thumps of pucks and players on the makeshift wooden boards at the Riverview Community Club, the young skaters were playing an endless game that began as soon as the ice was laid in, in the fall, and continued until blades were awash in the spring, panting under the stars by night, and by day puffing white breath into the crisp air of a Winnipeg winter afternoon.

Young Bill was physically much smaller than his Riverview contemporaries and spent much time alone, on the rink and off. Whether he did so because he liked it or because he was excluded by the neighbourhood children his age because of his size, no one seems to know. What is clear is that by disposition (or resignation), Bill was never discontent with his solitude. When left to his own resources—with his paints and crayons in his room, or outside with a hammer, or with the freedom to wander down to the river's edge, winter or summer—he could entertain himself for hours. At the Riverview Community Club rink, in his inimitable way, Bill struck up a friendship with Whitey the caretaker and soon won the man's confidence, enough, at least, that Whitey felt comfortable going home at the prescribed time and leaving Bill to lock up the boxcar. Often, after all the other children had departed to do homework on an evening, Bill would be there alone, in an oasis of light, skating one way and then the other, practising his hockey skills, or sitting inside by the fire, by himself, stuffing in poplar cordwood, counting his goals, and dreaming of hockey stardom, before locking up as promised and making his way home for Sadie's cinnamon toast and cocoa.

Bill was promoted to Grade 2 at Riverview with a wink and a nod from his first grade teacher. Besides art, drawing, Plasticine work and anything that involved creativity and manual dexterity, little about school caught Bill's fancy. But there was one topic that sustained his interest throughout his school days; he was captivated by the voyageurs. With remembered summer smells of varnished cedar canoes in the hot sun at Grand Beach to bolster the imagining, he spent his school days dreaming of river life and the portage trail. Whether it was Frances Hopkins's evocative renderings of birchbark canoes and brigades of trail-toughened wilderness paddlers that he saw in prints on the walls of Riverview Elementary, or etched reconstructions of Canadian history, especially the fur trade, in schoolbooks of the day, the images Bill saw in school combined with his passion for canoes to create many a reverie at Riverview.

Throughout these early years, Bill suffered constantly from shortness of breath. Sadie estimates that, by this time in his life, he had seen just about every medical specialist in the greater Winnipeg area about his respiratory troubles, to no long-lasting effect. Grade 2 was going much the same as Grade 1 had, with Bill missing school or, when he was there, finding every excuse imaginable to attend to his studies through art and various hand construction projects. But it was a year made much the richer on the home front with the arrival in spring of his sister, Elizabeth. Elizabeth's birth meant there was more going on when he had to stay home, but still Sadie packed up now two children and transported them across town to Granny Mason's to do her chores there.

With seven years of having his parents and grandparents all to himself, Bill could have found Elizabeth's arrival quite a shock, but it seems not to have had any repercussions. Studied tolerance might best describe the way in which a grade-school brother tolerated a toddler sister. Bill never complained, at least not publicly, about his size, but he was teased about it, and the fact that his sister surpassed him in height and weight by the time she was five must have had an effect.

In the years after Elizabeth was born, Bill took to sleeping on the screened-in porch upstairs at the back of 162 Morley Avenue. From there he looked out on the laneway between his street and Bartlet Avenue and on most nights he could look towards the river and see the lights of Riverview School forming a city constellation as they passed through the rusted metal screens. He could lie there on the daybed and watch shifting wisps of cloud in the prairie skyscape of a long summer evening and listen to the last vibrant musings of cicadas settling in for the night or the escalating sputter of snipes spiralling up over open fields towards the river. Or, when all had quieted, he could watch the neighbourhood bats dart past the screens and wonder about them until he drifted off.

The upstairs porch was a haven for Bill, in spite of a demand by Elizabeth, when she was old enough to care, for equal time in the alternative sleeping quarters. Bill was not fussy about such a move, but capitulated. As Elizabeth readied herself for the sleep-out, Bill set to work with a spool of black button thread, rolling yards of it into a tight little ball and tying that off on a long lanyard of thread. He carefully placed the ball under the sheets of the daybed, then waited until Elizabeth was all tucked in and the light was out. From his room, he pulled the end of the thread, causing the ball in the bed to move like a spider or a mouse—Elizabeth especially hated mice. That was it for Elizabeth and the porch.

Although the seven-year age gap hindered Bill and Elizabeth from becoming playmates, there was a gender gap too that had to be bridged. This was not the case, however, when their cousin Bob Tipping was born in 1937, the year after Elizabeth, providing Bill with a friend for the rest of his life. Bob was an only child, and a bit of a loner by all accounts, like Bill, and came to consider his cousin first as an "older brother," and in only a few years as an "older, shorter brother." Bob's mother, Agnes (Sadie's sister), began spending summers at the Fairs' Grand Beach cottage, where Bill taught Bob, as he grew, about the secret places—fishing in the lagoon, getting ice from the ice house with Grandpa Fair—and about the magic of boats and big waves at the Grand Beach wharf.

Bob Tipping's generation came along at just the right time for Bill to relive his early teens and to continue playing the games he loved so much with a brand-new crowd who, for a time, were about his size. After about age ten or eleven, Bill's contemporaries all began the inexorable growth spurts of puberty. Instead of being just bigger than Bill, they became *much* bigger, and of course their interest in forts and hockey waned, as did their prepubescent disdain for girls. Bill would not go through puberty until he was nearly eighteen, and even if he had mustered the courage and the interest to carry on in the orbits of his Riverview contemporaries, there was his love for hockey that needed to be exercised. With cousin Bob Tipping and his contemporaries, such as Jim Foster and Ian MacMorran, Bill could continue his hockey dreams and play his heart out, at least for a few more years, without too much danger of getting flattened on the ice.

What other lasting psychological effects smallness had on Bill during his youth one can only guess, but what he lacked in size in the eyes of his peers he made up for with artistic talent. Whether it was science drawings, maps or geography projects or illustrations—anything artistic—Bill was legendary among his school chums. He won all the school prizes for art. To this day, his former neighbour and Grade 6 classmate Ken Bowman remembers struggling in science to draw a likeness of a woodpecker in his notebook. Sitting in his in-laws' backyard on Oakwood Avenue in Riverview, Ken Bowman thinks back fifty years and recalls trying to get the lines right. The head just wouldn't cooperate. At some point in the process, Ken's classmate Billy Mason, who'd finished his woodpecker and much background detail besides, happened by and, with a couple of flicks of the pencil, repaired Bowman's rendering, leaving him frustrated by his own insufficiencies but amazed at the talent of his friend.

A 1942 school photograph conveys how small Mason was compared with others his age, like Ken Bowman. Fifteen girls and seventeen boys are standing with their teacher on the front steps of Riverview Elementary, girls in the front, in skirts and tunics, some with jackets or cardigans, boys in the back, in collared shirts and V-necked sweaters; only four of them, including Ken and Bill, are wearing neckties. They're smiling proudly; as is typical in school pictures, the girl third from the left in the front row has her tongue stuck out. But Bill doesn't even come up to Ken's shoulder. Even if he weren't teased unmercifully about his size, there can be little wonder about why he found so much companionship with cousin Bob and his younger, shorter friends.

Bob and Bill kept in touch throughout their lives but, with Bob in Vancouver and Bill in Ottawa, they never had the closeness in adulthood that they had as boys. Bob described this wonderful kinship in a letter written after Bill's death in 1988:

> Bill's preferred team sports were football and hockey, both of which involved physical contact, and at times lost tempers and physical challenges. Despite his size, Bill never backed down when faced with such challenges. He developed a strategy for dealing with larger adversaries which, in wrestling terms, could be called the "full Mason." He would grab an opponent by the arm, twist it behind his [the opponent's] back, then shift his grip from the arm to the fingers, which he could twist even more. More than once I found myself face down on a playing field with Bill's knee in my back, forced to utter "Okay, Bill."
>
> During my mid-teens I had a bit of a hockey career, and Bill would always be in attendance at our important games, shouting encouragement while standing in a snowdrift at one of the outdoor rinks or along the boards at the only indoor rinks Winnipeg then had—the Amphitheatre and the Olympic Rink. Bill was also uncompromising when it came to the standard of play he expected of me, and therefore his loyalty didn't come without a price tag. He would always be waiting for me as I left the ice at the conclusion of a game and would let me know how well he thought I had played. If his assessment was unfavourable, he let me know in no uncertain terms, but he was always generous with his praise when it was warranted.

Jim Foster, one of Bob's friends, remembers big debates among the younger boys about whether or not Bob's cousin Bill could play with them. And then, when they decided he could (as was always the case because he invariably had been the initiator of the game), there would be some earnest conversation about which side would get the benefit of this ringer player who, by dint of higher skill level and better coordination, would always score goals and make touchdown plays.

In many ways Riverview in the 1930s was a kids' paradise. There was hockey at the Community Club. Forts were built, raided and built again. Occasionally someone would set fire to the grass in the vacant lots near the river and everyone would muster in to see the fire crews extinguishing the blaze. There were picnics at City Park and rides on the roller-coaster at River Park, where south Osborne Street met the muddy Red River. Older children would pack a lunch, skate 40 miles down the river to Selkirk and return by bus. And there were the movies at Mr. Besler's Park Theatre.

Attending the Park Theatre on Osborne Street was one activity that appealed to every Riverview resident, young and old alike. It was here, on a Saturday afternoon, that Bill Mason first encountered the magic of film. Much to Granny Mason's chagrin, Bill would follow the neighbourhood tide and, for five cents, would enter the Wild West world of cowboys and Indians. The stories that unfolded at the Park Theatre were quite different from those spun in church by his Sunday-school teachers, and the audience, by and large, was rowdier as well. Had it not been for Mr. Besler, who was willing to put up with a theatre full of rambunctious children, those American frontier images of cacti, horses, mesas and heroes on horseback would never have come into Bill's consciousness.

Saturday afternoons were wild with water pistols, cap guns and homemade gizmos, like a contraption involving a coat hanger, an elastic band and a couple of metal washers that made delightful fart-like utterances on the leather seats of the theatre when the movie action got slow. Western movies the likes of *Lightning Bill*, *The Lone Ranger*, *King of the Cowboys*, *Aces Wild* and *Adventures of Red Ryder* were the worst for poor Mr. Besler. Gangs of kids from Riverview and Fort Rouge, the borough of Winnipeg on the west side of Osborne Street, would arrive with water pistols, in season, or, alternatively, toy six-guns and pockets full of rolled caps. When the wagons circled and the fighting on the screen intensified, the kids would join the fray, as Barry Broadfoot recalls:

> When the fighting [on the screen] got intense and the war whoops splintered the air, every kid was standing on his seat and firing at the screen, picking off Geronimo or Crazy Horse or Sitting Bull with an ease that astonished us. The sound of a hundred cap guns blasting away almost drowned out the screams of the girls. The acrid, blue, sulphurous smoke almost obscured the screen.
>
> Mr. Besler would signal for the movie to be stopped, a spotlight would throw his shadow on the screen, and he would say, "Children, if you do not stop this I will close down the show."
>
> We didn't think he meant it until a tough guy from the Arnold Street Gang dropped Mr. Besler in his tracks with nine fast shots from his six-shooter. End of show. No more killing movie-house owners.[1]

It was among the chaos and the excitement, as actors like Buffalo Bill Jr., Chief Thundercloud, Lee Powell, Roy Rogers, Smiley Burnette, Don "Red" Barry, Bob Nolan and The Sons of the Pioneers galloped through Riverview, that Bill developed a fascination with film.

4

FIRST NIGHT OUT

BY APRIL 21, 1942, when Bill turned thirteen, Winnipeg had changed. The Second World War had kick-started the national economy and put people back to work, and since 1940 there had been a dramatic turnaround in prairie fortunes. Oil, potash and uranium extraction industries had diversified a region that had once been solely dependent on wheat. Trains were full of commodities and raw materials, cars in the streets sparkled, store windows were full of new merchandise, and people were picnicking along the Red and Assiniboine rivers, where the hobo camps had been.

Beyond appreciating the more obvious aspects of the economic recovery in Winnipeg, the Mason family was affected little by the war. Art continued to be the principal focus of Bill's life at home and school, and by now he had won a substantial number of awards. Bill Sr. continued to trudge down to Great West Life each day. Liz had started school. Sadie persisted in tending to a newly widowed Granny Mason. The Fairs were still managing to hang onto the Grand Beach cottage, although, financially, they had not weathered the 1930s altogether too well and there was preliminary talk of selling the place. Always busy, Bill was hunched over his drawing table, oblivious to family affairs, this time working on plans for a big construction project.

He had a yen to build a boat. What sparked it no one seems to remember. It may have been something he'd found in an issue of *Popular Mechanics* or *Mechanics Illustrated* or one of the handyman's journals, or it may have simply been a design copied from one of the boats he had seen pulled up on the riverbank at the end of Morley Avenue or at the boat livery downstream, towards the Norwood Bridge. Whatever its origin, Bill had a plan. With the money he had saved from using his wagon to help people with their luggage at Grand Beach, along with birthday change, in his pocket, he got permission from Sadie one Saturday to take the street car to a lumber store near the centre of town. It took two or three trips on the trolley to lug home the 8-foot strips of one-by-two and the other purchased supplies, but eventually he had everything he needed lined up and ready to go.

Bill made it abundantly clear to his parents and grandparents—to anyone who would listen, in fact—that he was *not* making a canoe. (It may be that Bill was well aware of fears harboured by most folk about the dangers associated with canoes.) *He* was building a *kayak*. On the long hot July days that summer, as Canadians fought in the skies over Europe, Bill used hand tools, glue and the make-do spirit of compromise that everyone who'd grown up during the Depression had learned to fashion matched pairs of roughly oval wooden cross-frames, notching each one carefully for the longitudinal members. He then glued, screwed and nailed the whole skeleton together, and using canvas duck Sadie had helped him find, he stretched and tacked the covering over the whole frame, in the manner of the aircraft manufacturers of the day, leaving a hole for the paddler on the top side. The finishing touch was a coat of blue enamel that sealed the seams and shrank the material, fitting it even more tightly onto the frame.

Anyone within range was drawn into the backyard on Morley Street to behold what Bill had made. The boat wasn't particularly pretty to look at, but it was reasonably symmetrical, and it actually did float, for a time anyway, with a person in it. No one was more impressed with the effort than five-year-old Bob Tipping and his chums. And for Bill, the boat was a landmark effort in at least two respects:

having had eight largely unremarkable years at school, except for his successes with art, and having never really excelled at anything physical because of his size, he had finally transcended all of that, designing with his head and crafting with his hands something which everyone, even sister Liz, praised. It was with this boat that he left home for the first time to spend a night alone in the woods.

Bill gathered together a blanket and a few supplies, and the paddle he had found in the reeds at Grand Beach. In two or three trips he lugged all this down past Riverview School, past the boards and the boxcar at the Riverview Community Club, and down to the poplar and cottonwood thicket at the edge of the Red River. It was something his parents thought they should support, having watched him struggle so hard to complete the boat. But Sadie was almost beside herself when Bill announced on his last trip down the back-porch stairs that he would be out all night. Recalling that day later, in her ninetieth year, she recounted:

> I went down in tears with him to the woods by the river on the other side of King George and King Edward hospitals. He put the kayak in there, and he had a net to put over the top of it. And he took a pillow and a blanket because there was no such thing as sleeping bags in those days. We never thought of sleeping bags.
>
> And he said, "Now, Mum, don't worry because it's going to be a wonderful night. At dawn, I want to watch all the little hedgehogs and muskrats and see how they get up in the morning, and how they treat their young." He was thirteen, and just so small.
>
> I said, "Now, Billy, come home. Get home by about ten o'clock, son." Because in August it was still fairly light at ten o'clock. However, he didn't come home. I worried all night that he would get up, put the boat in the water and get drowned or something.
>
> And next morning I'm in the kitchen, ironing, and he walks in and says, "Oh, Mum! I can't wait for Dad to get home! Oh, it was wonderful. I saw hedgehogs and I saw muskrats,"

and he named about four different little animals. He watched
them take their young, take the young out onto the river.
And he said, "I wished I'd had a camera." That started his
love. And after that, I can't say we worried about him.

It was a milestone outing for Bill. Not only had he built himself a
craft in which he could be totally independent, but he could finally con-
summate his part in the great historic drama that had been playing in his
mind's eye for nearly a decade: he could be a voyageur. For years in his
imagination he had worn buckskin, and smelled the sweet birch, cedar
and pitch-pine of bark canoes; in the manner of the sturdiest of
voyageurs, he had shown the overbearing *bourgeois* and the rest of his
fellow *engagés*, time and time again, that he could carry twice what they
could; he could paddle longer, sing louder, and guide a canoe in swift
river current with the best of them. That night, by the Red River at the
foot of Osborne Street, as he had drawn his net over the upturned belly
of his "canoe," rocked down the outer ends and crawled in for the
night, he was a real voyageur, living independently in the natural world.

The Masons soon moved from 162 Morley Avenue to 209
Oakwood, two blocks south and a little closer to Bill's first solo campsite, which made it easier for him to spend more nights alone by the
river. The new house was brick, a step up from the clapboard on
Morley Street, but perhaps most exciting of all for Bill was the fact that
he was the sole resident of the two small rooms on the upper half-
storey of the place. To the left, up a straight, narrow staircase off the
main hall in the middle of the house, was his tiny bedroom, looking
east across open lots to the old rink and the river. To the right, at the
top of the stairs, was another little room in the apex of the house that
became his first real studio. The rooms on the main level were small as
well: a bedroom for Elizabeth; one for his parents; a kitchen with back
porch and a front living room, spanning the modest width of the
house, with a fireplace at the east end. And in the basement was space
for utilities below the stairs, a small storage room, and a large finished
rec room with electric fireplace on the south wall.

By now the Riverview Community Club was doing so well that it
had expanded and moved to a new property bordered by Ashland

Avenue and Eccles Street. Whitey's boxcar and the rudimentary rink at the end of Oakwood were replaced by a much more substantial frame club house with washrooms, proper changing benches with clothes hooks, and a much more organized concession. Outside there were two rinks with real boards, lines on the ice, lights and bigger leagues for the growing kids of Riverview.

It was while living at 209 Oakwood that Bill graduated from Riverview Elementary and struck out for Kelvin High School. The kayak had expanded his horizons and given him access to the river; Kelvin High School, closer to the centre of town, would take him into a more cosmopolitan atmosphere. Known for its academics and its musical stage productions, Kelvin drew from a variety of Winnipeg boroughs besides Riverview. Here Bill encountered classmates who were French-speaking, Jewish, Ukrainian, Polish, and who, on the whole, were more well-to-do and worldly than the children of Riverview. The Second World War was coming to a close as Bill completed his first year at Kelvin. That year, in the yearbook, there was a seven-page "Honour Roll" of Kelvin alumni killed or taken prisoner during the conflict.

In Grade 10, in Room 18, with Mr. Borland, Bill was elected class secretary and won an award for another still-life oil painting of three vases and a string of beads arranged before a cloth backdrop. The photo of that painting in the yearbook may well be the first publication of his work. The class photo for that year shows a handsome group of students, girls in their ties and tunics, boys in their shirts, ties and jackets. Dwarfed by 6-foot classmates, Bill was tucked in at the end of the second row, among the girls, looking more like a mascot than a member of the class.

It was in the Inter-School Christian Fellowship that Bill found his extracurricular home at Kelvin. Through the club he met kindred Christian spirits, in particular, a wise and giving Christian friend and mentor, Wilber Sutherland, who would shadow Bill like a guardian angel for the rest of his life. These were people with whom he could engage his active imagination, who didn't laugh at his size, and who were prepared to listen to his ideas and share his irrepressible optimism and zest for life. By Grade 11, Bill was on the ISCF Executive as publicity convener.

After Wilber Sutherland, Chuck Tipp would be the second ISCF

mentor in Bill's life, and as with Wilber, there was a practical and prag-
matic aspect to the relationship—in Tipp's case focused on canoeing—but
there was always the Christian foundation that grounded the friendship.

Bill's art continued to flourish in Grade 11. Miss Carey, the Kelvin
art teacher, took a shine to Bill and gave him extra lessons to develop his
talent. That year he had two winning paintings from the annual art competition reproduced in the yearbook: another still-life oil, this one featuring miscellaneous ceramic pots and vases from the dusty shelves at the
back of Miss Carey's art room, and a second, much more adventureous
piece depicting a high-prowed oak fishing boat, complete with net buoys
and two fishermen, tying up at one of his favourite places in the whole
world—the Grand Beach wharf. And that year he used his emerging
artistic confidence and his self-deprecating humour to modify the class
photo. He cut out the heads of his classmates, who were all boys by this
time, from the standard class-photo and assembled them all into a crazy
cartoonscape, photo heads pasted onto drawn bodies. Hughie
McComb's head was pasted on the body of a bull caught on the cow-
catcher of an errant train, and big Eddy Mazur was reduced to the role
of a pencil holder for a likeness of Bill himself, who sits in the corner of
the drawing at an inclined drawing board. A voice bubble beside the otherwise tied-up Mazur says, "Duh, look out or I'll pound yah." Among
barnyard animals, monkeys, Tarzans (two) and various other depictions
of Neanderthal human nature—hockey players—sits a cut-out photograph of Mason's own head atop a tiny cartoon character who needs
three books on the stool under him to reach his drawing board. Another
bubble, attached to Bill's mouth says, "Any resemblance in this cartoon
to persons living or dead is purely intentional."

By the end of Grade 11, when most of his classmates were moving
on to Grade 12 in preparation for university, trade school or the search
for work, Bill accepted an invitation from Miss Carey to spend the year
with her in the art room, painting and doing art full-time. Even though
he was assigned to a class with Mr. Young in Room 16, he spent every
day with Miss Carey, practising his craft, and learning about the French
Impressionists and how one needed to extend these techniques to
achieve the look of Jackson, Lismer, Macdonald or other members of the
Group of Seven. In the yearbook that year, Bill is characterized simply as

"Kelvin's gift to ART." The only surviving piece of art from that period of his school life is a detailed and symmetrical, almost architectural, pencil rendering of a classical building façade with a majestic stone stairway leading to a grand arched entryway, with mezzanine, rotunda, Corinthian pillars and plinths, and bronze lions.[1]

Another painting from this period of Bill's life that has survived is one that he did in secret in his studio at home, an oil called *After the Game*. Over a period of weeks, unbeknownst to any of the other teenagers in Riverview, Bill invited his cousin Bob and friend Jim Foster up to his studio, where they dressed in their hockey gear and posed for a painting Bill was doing. In spite of anything he may have learned from Miss Carey about Group of Seven technique, *After the Game* appears more informed by the illustrative work of Norman Rockwell than by that of any other artist.

Like most children of the 1930s, Bill had grown up with the images of Norman Rockwell. The cover of the *Saturday Evening Post* the month before his birth was the famous "Doctor and Doll" image, depicting an aged physician with his stethoscope firmly planted on the doll of an anxious little girl. Throughout his childhood, Bill must have encountered some, if not all, of Rockwell's covers, in boxes at the Grand Beach cottage, in magazine racks at his grandparents' homes, or on the newsstand at the Winnipeg train station. His knowledge of Rockwell is evident in the secret hockey painting.

After the Game shows a scene inside the club house at the Riverview Community Club, and tells the complete story of a boy's hockey world in the Winnipeg of the day. Detailed examination of the painting, as it hangs this very day inside a glass case at the much-renovated club house and Community Centre, reveals the intensity, the joy, the aches and pains, and the pure, unadulterated love of outdoor hockey. Outside, through the windows at the far end of the club house, there is snow banked up on two oval rinks, one with boards, one without. Telephone poles girding the boarded rink support wires on which are spaced sombrero shades and bare bulbs. Inside stands a player's father in fedora and trench coat, holding the hand of a younger brother or sister, waiting for the boys to change. To the right of the windows, a boy in full hockey gear has just come in the door; he has a scarf around

35

his head and looks almost paralysed by the cold. The main element in the painting, reaching from the windows to the foreground is a two-sided bench, with head-high hooks, on which sit four players, also newly off the ice: one is struggling to pull off his long hockey hose; another grimaces as he holds toes, trying to coax the blood back into his frozen feet; the player on the fore end of the bench tries simultaneously to drink and fend off the boy beside him, while a little black and white terrier, sensing this momentary lapse in concentration, tries to bite the hot dog in the boy's other hand. On the left side of the frame is the canteen, where a shortish boy stands on tippy toes on his skates, purchasing something from the woman behind the counter. Another child, who has changed already, digs into the pockets of his pants, with a nonplussed look on his face, trying to find enough money to get his treat. Best of all, and most like Mason himself, although he could be any one of the other figures in the painting, there are two boys in the foreground obviously in the thick of a heated argument, both still in full hockey regalia. The boy on the left, in Montreal colours, holds up four fingers, while the boy on the right, dressed in a Toronto goalie outfit, defiantly holds up two fingers. There's a PeeWee hockey schedule taped to the curve of the canteen counter and all around the room are the skates and trappings of a very busy bunch of ten-year-old boys.

All of the figures in *After the Game* have either light brown or dark brown hair, and have a certain sameness about them in size and build. As cousin Bob Tipping noted: "Most of the players should look the same because Bill made me model for almost the entire team."

By fall of 1944, when Bill was fifteen, the Fairs reluctantly sold the Grand Beach cottage, an event that marked the end of an era for Bill. His access to nature was gone. Although Grand Beach was far from the wilderness he would come to know, its water, dunes and forests had become attached in Bill's mind to a trove of memories and formative experiences. Outings on the river, and with young people from the church, had shown him that those same feelings could be kindled closer to home, and so when the Grand Beach cottage was sold, he naturally turned to these experiences in the church community to keep his connection with the natural world vibrant. He had learned through

ISCF at Kelvin, from speakers like Wilber Sutherland and Chuck Tipp, about a new summer camp that was getting started on Shoal Lake, 93 miles east of Winnipeg and the source of the city's water. Manitoba Pioneer Camp, as it was called, was first established at a former Presbyterian Indian School on Shoal Lake; later, a permanent camp setting was established on one, and then two, islands farther out in Shoal Lake, through the philanthropy of hot-drink magnate Hugh Lorne MacKinnon, a board member with Inter-Varsity Christian Fellowship. Local Native people at Shoal Lake were hired to maintain the site and to operate a water-taxi service to the island, and the railway that had been built for the construction and the maintenance of the aqueduct from Shoal Lake to Winnipeg ensured easy transport for staff and campers to and from the site.

With the Grand Beach cottage gone, Bill pleaded with his parents to send him to this new camp. They managed to find the money and signed him up. Writing about this significant moment in his life much later in *Venture*, the IVCF newsletter, Bill recalled:

> My first year at camp was the most memorable. The awards I received for canoeing, swimming, campcraft and archery were only colourful patches of felt but I'll always remember the sense of accomplishment I experienced.
>
> Even before going to camp, I was obsessed with a love for the canoe—a love which has never diminished. Under the leadership of Chuck Tipp, I came to see canoeing as an art form as well as a vehicle to take me into the wilderness—a world unchanged and unspoiled as God had created it.
>
> My first impression of Pioneer was that it was a beautiful and special place but I came to realize that it was more than that. Pioneer was people—people like Chuck Tipp, Bill Steeper, Stan Steinmann and many others whose lives reflected the life of Christ.[2]

The canoes at Manitoba Pioneer Camp in those early years were classical cedar-strip olympic-style racing boats made by the Lakefield Canoe Company, with sharp entry lines, V-bottoms and almost no rocker, or longitudinal curve along the keel. The kind of canoeing Bill and the other campers learned from instructor Chuck Tipp, in the sheltered bay off the southeast shore of MacKinnon Island, was flat-water racing posture and technique. Photos of the day show Bill "kneeling up," as it was called, with one knee on the bottom behind the centre thwart and the other foot planted firmly ahead. This position gave racers the height from the water and reach required to allow the energy from a wide-bladed, square-tipped and very tall paddle to be efficiently transferred and applied to the motion of the boat. In those days, canoeing was something that was done in the vicinity of the dock. If a group wished to go farther for a cook-out or an overnight, they were ushered to nearby locations around the lake by motor-boat. Canoes were considered much too unsafe for transportation, and the techniques the campers were learning were too energy-expensive for anything other than short sprints. In the years to come at Manitoba Pioneer, however, Bill Mason would almost single-handedly change this style of canoeing.

This move to Manitoba Pioneer Camp was a tremendous relief for Bill, to know that what he had loved most and felt about his summer haven at Grand Beach could be re-created in another place, and, as important, Manitoba Pioneer allowed him spiritual and emotional release from the tyranny of Granny Mason and his father's increasing unhappiness at Great West Life. By now the Second World War was over, and returning veterans were being integrated into the workplace, often being reinstated through the demotion and displacement of those who had been promoted in their absence. At Great West Life, those who had not fought became increasingly bitter as they watched this process unfold.[3] Bill Sr., though never cheerful about his job, became even quieter and more withdrawn, often into drink, and never more so than the day one of his colleagues in the mail room committed suicide as an apparent result of his postwar displacement.

Getting away from home for Bill meant escaping the shadow of his father's unhappiness for a time. Entering the relaxed Christian environment of Manitoba Pioneer Camp also meant that he was exposed for the first time to much less restrictive Christian beliefs than the stiff Plymouth Brethren principles with which Granny Mason judged and girded the clan. Camp gave Bill his first real instruction in canoeing, but it was to have another equally profound effect on his spiritual life. In *Venture* he recalled:

> Pioneer Camp influenced me in other ways as well. It led me to an active church life at Elim Chapel. The concern for God's created world and our environment [I learned there] became the basis of nearly all my films and books. My knowledge of God and my relationship with His Son, Jesus Christ, began at Pioneer Camp. I should say it began on a summer day in 1945 when Mr. MacKinnon took me to the train destined for Manitoba Pioneer Camp.[4]

5

GROWING TIME

IN THE YEARS LEADING UP to the sale of the Grand Beach cottage and the start of Bill's time at Manitoba Pioneer Camp, all was not well on the spiritual side at home. What had been Riverview Presbyterian Church was now part of the United Church of Canada, a 1924–25 blending of the Presbyterian, Methodist and Congregational churches that resulted in the largest Protestant affiliation in the country. Called "the most self-consciously Canadian of all churches" because of its desire to include all ethnic groups, the United Church was hailed by many as ideally suited to Winnipeg's multicultural railway population. Despite vehement de-nunciations of liquor, gambling and pornography, by Dr. James R. Mutchmor, the new church's secretary for evangelism and social service, Grandma Mason was not amused. As far as she was concerned, the United Church had taken over the Presbyterian Church, and she could chunter on about this for hours, always invoking the intransigent princi-ples of her Plymouth Brethren youth. One Sunday in the mid-1940s, the Masons' affiliation with Riverview United Church came to an abrupt end, and they went looking for a new place to worship.

At Sunday dinner, Grandma Mason, in her black dress and ruffled white collar, was quizzing Bill and Liz about what they'd learned that morning in Sunday school. Over the years she had been in the habit of rocking back and forth in her chair, lecturing them on Christian morality while Sadie cleaned and cooked. "So what did the teacher tell you about today in Sunday school, Billy?" she asked. With the restraint that Bill had learned to use when questioned by his grandmother, he reported that the teacher had told them all about the Northwest Mounted Police. "The Northwest Mounted Police! In Sunday school!" Grandma Mason never darkened the door of Riverview United Church again, and dutifully following her lead, because it was easier to capitulate than to rebel, were Sadie, Bill Sr. and the Mason children.

The Masons tried a nearby Unitarian church but that didn't suit much either. However, through the Christian teachings and fellowship of his friends at Kelvin ISCF and the people he was meeting through Manitoba Pioneer Camp, Bill convinced his family to try the Elim Chapel, slightly more evangelical than what they had come to expect at Riverview Presbyterian, but nevertheless a congregation of kindred Christian spirits, especially for him. Elim Chapel had an active young people's group that met on Thursday nights for Bible study and to plan weekend outings and activities. From the moment Bill joined the congregation he became an active participant in the Elim Young People's Group. Granny Mason approved wholeheartedly of the disciplined Bible study, though she was very suspicious of the other things the young people might be up to. When she heard that Bill had been bowling on a Saturday evening she glowered.

Bowling or not, Bill thrived at Elim. Before long, he was publicity convener for the Young People's. He'd fashioned a logo for the group and had printed an announcement card for their various activities. As his influence grew in the group, Saturday activities moved outside and got a little more adventuresome. Teens who bowled one week would find themselves hiking in Assiniboine Park or paddling on the Red River the next, or snowshoeing, or skiing, or being swept up in any number of crazy outdoor ploys hatched by the infectiously enthusiastic Mason. More often than not, the Thursday-night get-togethers and gatherings for hot drinks after skating on a Saturday afternoon would be in the Masons' basement rec room at 209 Oakwood. They were never long there before a rousing Ping-Pong tournament would get under way, with Bill at the centre of the action.

Of all the benefits afforded Bill by his association with Elim Chapel, and especially the Elim Young People's, none was more influential than the friendship with Elim pastor and Young People's adviser Dr. Fred Mitchell. Dr. Mitchell's only son had died in infancy; bright, vivacious and diminutive Billy Mason may well have filled that gap in Dr. Mitchell's life. In any case, Dr. Mitchell was more of a father to Bill, in many respects, than was Bill Sr. It is about this time in Bill's life that his father faded almost completely from the scene, surfacing only occasionally in family lore as a sour and unhappy man who hated his work and leaned on the bottle, especially at holiday time. With his father more or less out of the picture during these important years of his life, Bill was hungry for someone to fill that role. As such, the surrogate father–and–son bond between young Bill and Dr. Mitchell was a place to begin a wonderful kinship centred on evangelical faith and Christian fellowship. Thinking back on this relationship, Bill's mother recalled, "Dr. Mitchell *made* Bill."

In spite of the intellectual and spiritual nurturing offered by Dr. Mitchell, by the winter of 1946 Bill was seventeen and still tiny. His family were anxious to the point of embarrassment about his slow physical development. He was active and coordinated, but he just didn't seem to grow. They took him to every available specialist for his asthma over the years, without result, and now began canvassing the Winnipeg medical community to find out why Bill was half the size and weight of other boys his age. They were also concerned that, at seventeen, Bill's voice had not broken, and he had no facial hair, no characteristic growth spurt, no secondary sexual characteristics at all. People teased Elizabeth about her brother's diminutive size.

Sadie and Bill Sr. got no satisfactory answers from doctors in Winnipeg. In desperation, they went to Dr. Stewart, their family physician, who recommended that they take him to the Mayo Clinic in Rochester, Minnesota, *the* place in North America when all else had failed in medical diagnosis. The following summer, Sadie and Bill left Elizabeth with the Fairs and took a day's train journey south to the Mayo brothers' innovative, multispecialty group practice in Rochester, the first and only one of its kind in the world at that time.

Records indicate that patient No. 1-495-107, seventeen-year-old

William C. Mason of Winnipeg, Canada, was admitted on August 16, 1946; the chief complaint was "lack of growth." Bill's initial physical exam lists his height as 4 feet 7 inches, and his weight at 65 pounds. A hand-written note below this says: "Patient is a 17 year old male who appears about 12 years old according to physical build and voice characteristics. Family history mentions Elizabeth, "9 years old, 4' 7½" tall, weighs 73 lb," quantifying the differences evident in a photograph taken that summer at Coney Island, near Kenora, in which nine-year-old Elizabeth is noticeably bigger than her seventeen-year-old brother. Bill Sr. and Sadie's heights are listed as 5 feet 8 inches and 5 feet 4 inches, respectively.

The recorded clinical history indicates that, with the exception of a few allergies and his bronchial asthma, by now controlled with regular shots, Bill reported being entirely well all his life. Further revealed is the fact that, on both sides of the family, there were members who were small until a growth spurt to normal size in their late teens. For example, Grandpa Fair made it to 5 feet 11 inches but he didn't get there, the report indicates, until "later in life when he grew some more." One gets the sense that Bill's parents were much more concerned about his size than Bill was at the time. That sense is confirmed by a Mayo endocrinologist who, after a variety of tests over a period of six days at the clinic, made the following note on Bill's chart: "Under development. With his family history there is a good chance he would develop normally later. However his parents are anxious for RX [prescription medication]. Had injections once a week for 20 weeks [in the year prior to the Mayo visit]. Would give 3X a week in large doses and see effect."

Bill rarely spoke in later life about any of this. He was self-reliant and independent from the day he was born, and never seems to have doubted himself. The image of Bill that emerges from all accounts of the Mayo Clinic visit is of a person who was as interested in the trappings and machinery of an ultra-modern hospital as he was worried that there might be something wrong with him. But physical size, growth and change are so important in children, especially in the adolescent years through puberty, that his smallness and slowness in development, his high voice and lack of whiskers must have been cause for some ridicule. The fact that he was different may have had something to do with the choices he made to spend much of his time alone in his room or studio, with his art and his dreams.

Later in life, he needed to be alone to create. At some level this connection between creativity and solitude can be linked directly back to his size and the troubles he went through as a teen.

Bill was prescribed large doses of human pituitary extract and/or refined growth hormone therapy, which made him grow, eventually, to his adult height and weight of 5 feet 4 inches, 135 pounds. The doctor at the clinic, a diminutive character in wing collar and white coat, with strong hands and kindly eyes, according to Sadie, sought to reassure Bill and his mother. Reaching out and taking Bill by the shoulders, he said: "Your body is small but it is one hundred percent perfectly proportioned. You will grow. You keep on with your art, and you keep on with what ever you want to do. You keep canoeing. You can be whoever you want to be."

Back in Winnipeg, Bill's dad started to mark his height on his bedroom wall. Finally, he began to develop. His voice changed, and fuzz on his lip began to darken. He continued with his art through Grade 11 and spent his intensive year in the art room with Miss Carey. A photo of Bill at the inclined drawing board in his Oakwood Avenue studio—perhaps taken as he worked on *After the Game* or fiddled with the class cartoon for the yearbook, or lettered certificates for his dad—shows an intent and handsome young man in V-necked sweater, collar and tie, hair slicked back, with dirty fingernails, distinctly in need of a shave.

There seems never to have been any doubt about what Bill would do when he completed high school. Going to church at the Elim Chapel, the family had passed the Winnipeg School of Art in the old law courts building on Portage Avenue. It was a fact in those days that, if one wanted to pursue a career in art, one enrolled at the Winnipeg School of Art. Bill had built enough of a portfolio of work, and had enough of a reputation with Miss Carey and others, to solicit a sheaf of favourable letters of recommendation. Although he appears to have passed Grade 11, there was fortunately no academic entry requirement for the course in commercial art. Admission at the time was based on "evidence of aptitude in the field of art as determined by the faculty."

Bill took to his art courses with the same enthusiasm that seemed to touch everything he did. Tony Tascona had been at the Winnipeg School of Art for two years when Mason arrived and remembers a feisty little guy who was cocksure and interested not so much in art history, studying the masters and developing his own painting technique, as he was in refining his lettering technique and perfecting his skills as a commercial artist:

> He always went his own way. . . . It was like he was in a world all his own, doing his own thing. He hustled jobs working part-time for these commercial art firms in Winnipeg. We knew he was doing really well financially. He was winning design awards, and getting commissions. But as far as I was concerned, anybody who concentrated on commercial art was selling out. I was strictly into fine art. Anybody who did commercial art was held in low esteem by those of us who wanted to be fine artists.

Bill did grow, not a foot, but 9 inches, and nearly doubled his weight, during his time at art school. But this physiological disruption took its toll. As had happened at Riverview and Kelvin, he missed a fair amount of school. However, his asthma improved as his body matured, which made it much easier for him to exert himself, especially in the winter. Some days, he just couldn't manage school, but on the days he did go, in his inimitable style it was full speed ahead. Pictures in the *Winnipeg Tribune* two years running show Mason and friends competing in the annual winter carnival snow-sculpture contest, with Bill, bigger but still small, apparently leading the charge.

In 1950, as Bill was completing second year, the Winnipeg School of Art was taken over by the University of Manitoba. This automatically put him in line for a university diploma instead of paper recognition from a private art school. The amalgamation increased the range of possibilities available for elective courses for Bill and his classmates—they could now take courses in the schools of Architecture, Interior Design and Home Economics. Bill used all media and did his lessons and assignments with relish. What he didn't complete during the time he was at school, he took home to work on in his little studio on Oakwood Avenue. The three principal instructors at the time—William McCloy, Richard Bowman and John Kacere—were all fine artists, printmakers and painters with experience in commercial art and a variety of other media. Gissur Eliasson and Robert Gadbois taught lettering and design. While there were opportunities to develop skills as a painter and to interact with well-known painters of the day, Mason appears not to have taken advantage of these, concentrating instead on his skills as an illustrator and commercial artist.

Some members of the class were entering their work in juried and non-juried shows, putting their work out for public comment and display. Classmate Tony Tascona tells the story of painting a watercolour of a downtown streetscape, with fences, garbage cans, back lanes, laundry blowing one way, smoke blowing another, and, by mistake, a chimney on a roof right above a window. His classmates encouraged him to put it in the Non-Jury class at an art show at the Winnipeg Art Gallery across the street from the School of Art. Four of them were walking up the stairs of the gallery when they met A.Y. Jackson and Frederick Varley walking down the stairs with Mr. Eastman, the gallery director. "What do you have there, boys?" they inquired. Varley said, "Hmm, looks pretty interesting." Tascona had decided to price the painting at $10 but, having had this endorsement from the Group of Seven, by the time they got to the space on the third floor, where the Non-Jury show was to be displayed, his price had risen to $35.

Bill, in his way, followed his own agenda. In April of his third year, he submitted *After the Game* by mail to the O'Keefe Art Awards in Toronto. Other paintings he did at that time were mostly oils and highly realistic in nature, adhering quite rigidly to the conventions of composition. Given the choice, he would have forgone working from the skeletal structure out, to the musculature, the skin, to the layers of colour and shadow—the kind of exploration that his classmates underwent to understand artists such as Rembrandt. While classmates in pursuit of careers as fine artists studied the making of illusion with paint, turning a two-dimensional canvas into a three- or even four-dimensional plane, Bill was off on his own, honing the skills of an illustrator and commercial artist.

Even though he may not have sought opportunities to mingle with the likes of A.Y. Jackson and Frederick Varley, Bill had heard about Tom Thomson and the Group of Seven throughout his school life.

And whether by accident or by design, there is striking resonance and similarity between some of his early paintings and those of these other artists, especially Thomson. An oil painting of the Osborne Street underpass at the CNR yard in Fort Rouge, a location he passed on the way to church and to Kelvin High School, for example, shows lines and colours that are eerily reminiscent of Thomson's *View from the Window of Grip*. Subject-matter alone links him with Thomson and his Group of Seven friends when he paints scenes around Manitoba Pioneer Camp, on Shoal Lake, and other wilderness locales. And when one compares Bill's early paintings with Thomson's, there is remarkable similarity in the space and attention given to skies, and the point of view is low, like that of the canoeist, emphasizing shorelines and landscape in the vastness of space. Bill's early work was measured and controlled and could never be described as having the Thomsonian "smash and stab of passion flying before thought,"[1] but there can be no doubt about Bill's fascination with Tom Thomson. They connected intuitively in an unspeakable love for art, canoes and the wilderness. Bill's wilderness dreams may well have been informed and energized by the colourful joy, power and artistic emotion in Thomson's rocks, trees and skies that surrounded him in his formative years.

It was no secret to Tony Tascona and other members of his class that Bill vicariously thrived on the life and work of Tom Thomson. What classmates perhaps did not understand, however, was that Bill's affection was primarily for Thomson's solitary wilderness lifestyle—the self-reliant man in the red canoe—rather than for Thomson's Algonquin Park subject-matter or style of painting. Tascona occasionally teased Bill about this, telling him that he was going to die in his canoe, referring to Thomson's untimely and mysterious death by drowning in the black waters of Canoe Lake in Algonquin Park. "Not a chance," returned the ever-defiant Mason, time and again, as the good-natured taunts came his way.

In truth, Bill lacked the patience to sit and paint, or to spend the time studying the masters. Life was hockey, football, canoeing, snowshoeing, weekend camping, discussing the Bible with Dr. Mitchell and the Elim Young People's Group, or painting alone in his room. Granny Mason's suspicions about anything not biblically sanctioned—movies, bowling, cards, mounted police and painting—may also have haunted and hampered Bill Mason's art to some extent. So, as his skills as a paddler and outdoorsman grew for all to see in public, his skills as a painter remained largely private and hidden. In his mind, he very much thought like an artist. Bill studied the great Canadian painters like Tom Thomson by paddling his homemade kayak—now with "The River Speeder" stencilled in paint on either side of the cockpit—down the centre of Oakwood Avenue during the great Red River flood of 1950. Like Thomson's, Bill's artistic viewpoint was from a canoe on the water, and these formative experiences at home and at Grand Beach taught him much about the movement of water, the shading of prairie skies; about reflections and the shifting nuance of sun on the green leaves of summer.

The flood caused massive damage, and a great number of people were displaced for months, including the Masons. When the dike near Churchill Avenue broke, the water rose quickly in Riverview. Sadie rushed to the basement and took the trunk in which she had been saving all of Bill's early artwork and other family treasures and put it onto the Ping-Pong table, thinking the water would never rise that high. By the time the water had crested, it had not only filled the basement at 209 Oakwood but it had mucked the floors and carpets of the first floor of the house as well. The house was damaged, though not irreparably; however, Bill's early paintings, cartoons and other work were destroyed completely in the flood. Granny Mason was the first to remind them all that the Lord works in mysterious ways. She might even have felt that the loss of such frivolous material was God's judgment on her grandson, who was growing away from her. Faith and family were all there was to hang on to in times of trouble. Of course, by this time, with strong reference points at Grand Beach and Shoal Lake, Bill was looking anywhere but the soaked basement of the family home. He was hungry for work and for new adventures in the world beyond.

6

WEEKENDS IN WHITESHELL

IN THE SPRING OF 1950, Bill received his Diploma in Commercial Art from the University of Manitoba School of Art and, picking up on some of the part-time, freelance connections he had made at art school, went to work immediately as a commercial artist at Phillips, Gutkin and Associates, a fast-growing Winnipeg advertising firm. Bill had a practised hand as a young commercial artist and an impressive portfolio, including by now published logos for the ISCF, Inter-Varsity, Elim Chapel Young People's; dozens of cartoons with his own unique characters; and, of course, his oil paintings of boats at Grand Beach, scenes from Shoal Lake and Osborne Street, and a curious portfolio of Indian paintings and Western scenes inspired by the westerns he had seen at the Park Theatre and in a book called *Indians of North America* by Diamond Jenness, and painted mostly for his dad, a western-film buff. The young man John Phillips and Harry Gutkin hired the day he arrived through the frosted-glass door of their third-floor studio/office above Royal Drugs and CKY Radio at Portage and Main was not so much a trained commercial artist with a freshly minted diploma as an enigmatic, creative and enthusiastic character whose life appeared to revolve around his art. Harry Gutkin remembers Bill as "an ambitious young man who showed a lot of talent."

Phillips, Gutkin and Associates had been in operation since 1948, feeding the voracious advertising appetite of Winnipeg companies such as Eaton's, The Hudson's Bay, Trans-Canada Airlines, Birks, Great West Life and the big Western co-operatives. Bill began as what Harry Gutkin called "an in-betweener," meaning he was the person who would take a creative idea from someone else, develop it in graphic form and then pass it on to more experienced artists, retouchers and photo engravers, who would complete the finished text, artwork and layout for an ad. From the very beginning, however, Bill worked at home on both the developmental and the final aspects of the campaigns from the office and was never shy in showing his superiors at Phillips/Gutkin that he could turn his hand to all aspects of the commercial artist's craft.

Like his hero Tom Thomson, who got his start as a commercial artist at Grip Limited in Toronto, Bill had ambitions to move beyond being an in-betweener and used this first job as a place to learn every aspect of his craft. Thomson, when he was getting started in commercial art, began with the tedious, anonymous and in-between job of socking in the dots and tints on Ben Day plates. He went on to become the "best letter man in the country," but rumour had it that whatever vocational interest and aptitude Thomson had for commercial art, he kept a drum full of water in the studio at Grip so he could practise his paddling strokes through the winter. Bill never got that far in modifying his work environment, but there is little doubt that many of his Phillips/Gutkin hours were spent elsewhere in his imagination, until something new came along that piqued his interest.

The principal focus at Phillips/Gutkin shifted very soon after Bill joined the firm from the creation of print ads and catalogue work—although that remained important—to animation. Harry Gutkin and John Phillips had sensed the importance of television in its developmental stages, but they also saw a large potential market in industrial 35mm film and animation. They brought in animators from various places in Europe and the United States—Jan Kameinski from Poland, for one, was hired and later became the political cartoonist for the *Winnipeg Tribune*, Barry Helmer from Vancouver was another—and they began developing their own animators, people like local artists Blake James, from Beauséjour; Barrie Nelson, whose family owned the canoe livery at Grand Beach; and eventually a cocky kid from Riverview who seemed too talented and too motivated to leave buried in the art department. As he had done in his first days at Phillips/Gutkin, Bill began in animation as an "in-betweener"; Barrie or Jan would design and draw the main characters, leaving the time-consuming and tedious jobs of filling in backgrounds and movement to apprentice artists like Bill.

Bill had had absolutely no training in film. He had mastered the basics of photographic engraving at art school, and that entailed learning about emulsions, exposures, dark-room techniques and printing, but until he encountered these film makers and animators, who worked in the same space for a subcompany called PGA Films, the closest he had come to knowing how film production and animation worked was watching Mr. Besler emerge from the projection booth at the Park Theatre to chew out a Saturday-afternoon audience about cap guns, squirt guns or rude noises on the seats. He took to this on-the-job training in the manner of the most zealous apprentice, asking questions, watching over people's shoulders and pitching in whenever a hand was needed. He was a natural.

One "Girl Friday" in the PGA office at the time was Doreen Jefferson, a woman who was supposed to be answering the phone, filing and taking dictation. But, like everyone else in the firm, even stenographers and clerks were expected to do what was required to get the jobs done. In the rush of deadlines, Doreen was enlisted in all kinds of unusual roles for these wacky film makers. On one occasion she found herself spending the whole morning riding a corn broom and jumping off a chair in the studio while the animators photographed her in every possible pose in the air. These photos were then used as base material to animate a scene of a witch flying through some magical land of retail make-believe.

Doreen even found herself upstairs on the roof one day doing an ad for Trans-Canada Airlines. Bill was among the crew who set up and photographed this sequence, which involved her dashing around, being photographed against the Winnipeg skyline with a suitcase in her hand. From this set of stills, the animators were able to create a series of images that came together as a polished ciné spot for the airline.

Don Campbell, one of the original photographers at Phillips/Gutkin, fondly remembers those early days in the studio at Portage and Main:

> We were a close-knit group down there because we were working eight hours a day, seven days a week, and anything that happened, we were all sort of together in this thing. Every once in a while you had to let off steam, and I recall on a number of occasions we had some good parties up in the PGA studio. And in the corner there'd be a big argument going on, and everybody would be feeling pretty good. And Billy would be right in the middle of it—the loudest one in the whole works—with his Coca-Cola in his hand! Everybody was sloshed, and there was Billy with his soft drink. He wouldn't smoke or drink or anything.

Contrary to the popular mythology about how Bill spent his first paycheque from Phillips/Gutkin, he did not buy a canoe, although that would happen soon; with the inspiration and instruction of Don Campbell, Bill purchased a Rolleiflex still camera to photograph some of the places he had found on explorations with the Elim Chapel Young People's Group. Love of photography and adventuring made Mason and Campbell fast friends, Campbell taking the lead, at least at first, with the technical aspects of photography, and Mason returning the favour by teaching Don about canoeing, tenting and campcraft, and the woodsmanship skills he had honed at camp. They would rent a canoe in Winnipeg and head out by car or by train on weekends, and before long, with his artistic eye and Campbell's instruction, Bill's $2\frac{1}{2}$- by $2\frac{1}{4}$-inch slides rivalled those of his professional colleague.

As Bill found his place in the commercial-art world, he took on staff roles at Manitoba Pioneer and became a force in the evolution of the camp canoeing program. Overnights no longer involved motorboats for getting campers out to campsites around the lake; gradually, the sleek, polished cedar-strip racing craft at the camp were being replaced, at Bill's instruction, with new ultra-durable (by contrast), lighter and more seaworthy canvas-covered wooden canoes, with names like Chestnut, Peterborough, and Old Town, that allowed staff and campers to move into the early stages of a canoe-tripping program at the camp. It made sense, then, that one of the first places Bill would take Don was east, by road or on the Greater Winnipeg Water District Train, to Whiteshell Provincial Park and Shoal Lake, in the Lake of the Woods area, with which he was quite familiar.

On one of these early photographic trips, Bill was intent on exploring a back route into the camp, a little creek he had seen on the map that led, via Falcon Lake and High Lake, from the south end of Whiteshell Provincial Park over the border into Ontario and waters connected to Shoal Lake. They rented a canoe in town and drove east three hours to Falcon Lake and the Manitoba/Ontario border. It was a trip that Don Campbell remembers vividly:

> We got the canoe and all our stuff up the portage from Falcon Lake to High Lake. We were paddling along and it was raining. It was *miserable* weather. We got up to this creek Billy had found on the map—it was marked on the map as a river but it really wasn't; it was more of a little creek, shall we say. You couldn't float a canoe in it, or anything else for that matter. It was full of rocks, sticks, logs— you name it! So we decided, after an awful lot of flailing about, that this was as far as we were going to get. So we turned back and we camped on a little island in High Lake. We got the tent set up, and the pots and pans out, and Billy said, "Do you have a match?" And I said, "No, I don't smoke. I don't have a match. Don't you have matches?" He went through everything: we didn't have matches! So there we were, sitting out on this lake; we had cold—I forget what it was—cold beans or something out of a can. There he was, sitting there with rain dripping off his nose, saying, "This shouldn't have happened." I certainly agreed with him.

At the time, Mason earned the princely salary of $35 per month; Campbell, presumably, slightly more. Bill had bought a share in the family car, the taupe Hillman, and chipped in for groceries at home, but he paid no rent, was able to save to purchase his camping kit, and usually had funds left over to pay for gas and a couple of rolls of 120 Kodak colour film for the Rolleiflex camera. Don and Bill would play off each other's creative photographic impulses as they rambled on the weekends taking pictures, and would anxiously await processing to compare their slides. Bill invariably photographed nature, in particular, water and sky.

Don remembers one occasion when Bill spent a whole evening setting up a shot: the fire and the tent set against the night sky in which hung a giant crescent moon. Using time-exposure technique he'd learned from Campbell, Bill waited until the moon was in exactly the right location relative to the tent, stoked the fire with birch bark to make it flare, and then, using a flashlight, laboriously "painted" the tent from the inside to make it appear on the film. Understandably, Bill was devastated when the slides came back with that image cut in two. The technician in the film lab had seen the moon and the fire-and-tent combination and mounted them as two separate images.

Although they photographed together, and competed to see who would get the best image of the same subjects, there was a fundamental difference in point of view between the two. From the very beginning, Bill needed to show people what he had found in the wilderness. After his death in 1988, Campbell, obviously still affected by this quality, talked about Bill's sense of purpose:

> I had a scout troop out in Elmwood and I asked Billy if he would come and show a slide presentation. We had invited another guest speaker that night, a Mountie, who spoke first. The Mountie came up to me after he'd finished his part of the program and said, "I can only stay for the first couple of slides because I've got another appointment." Billy had a two-and-a-quarter slide projector; he was feeding the slides in by hand and talking at the same time. He kept that audience spellbound for nearly half an hour. It was fantastic. And of course he included a little bit of very subtle preaching. . . . When the show was over—I guess there'd have been about fifty people there—the lights came on in the church and I expected to see the Mountie gone, but there he was. I remember him standing

at the back of the room saying, "I never saw anything like that
before. I couldn't leave."

The hunt for ever-better images to add to Bill's slide show took
Campbell and Mason out in all weather and in all seasons as well. And
although Bill was a skilled summer camper and a reasonably skilled
winter traveller by day, winter camping was something with which he
was not all that familiar. But in the true Mason spirit, if you could
camp in the summer, you could camp in the winter. It would just be a
little colder. Campbell still remembers a bitterly cold expedition which
put him off winter camping for life:

> We hiked into Lions Lake [a small lake just north of the no-
> matches outing at High Lake, again near the Manitoba/
> Ontario border]. There were no roads there at that time. We
> just hiked in from the highway, and spent the day wandering
> around taking pictures. I think it was February. We were on
> snowshoes. We picked a nice place in the woods and decided,
> well, we'd pitch our tent. It was getting dark, and we went to
> sleep. When morning finally came, Bill poked out from his
> blanket roll and said, "You scared the heck out of me last
> night. I heard this grunting and groaning, and I thought a
> bear had come out of hibernation!" That was the sound of a
> man freezing to death, I told him. We met someone walking
> his dog later that day, and he said, "You guys didn't sleep out
> over night did you? It's thirty below!" That was one of our
> first (and my last) winter camping trips.

The camping techniques and equipment to which Mason subjected
his colleague he had learned about through Manitoba Pioneer Camp,
and the principal guide and reference for the camp were the teachings of
Calvin Rutstrum, a man who had spent much of his life in the Canadian
Shield country between Minnesota, Ontario and Manitoba, west of Lake
Superior. Rutstrum, thirty years old and already very familiar with the
Quetico/Superior wilderness when Bill was born, took a job at Camp
Lincoln, a "rich man's set-up," near Brainerd, Minnesota.[1] One of

Rutstrum's duties at Lincoln was to write a wilderness manual for children, which he entitled *Way of the Wilderness*. Published first in 1946 as a rudimentary mimeographed affair, with Rutstrum's own unvarnished prose and functional line drawings, this little book became the "other" bible for campers and staff at Manitoba Pioneer. Mason's first copy of *Way of the Wilderness*, which he received at camp, became standard equipment on all his early outings, and on that memorable February night, while Don Campbell groaned, Bill would likely have been buoyed (if not warmed) in spirit by the teachings of Calvin Rutstrum.[2]

Way of the Wilderness speaks subtly about a man's love for the wilderness and the freedom and possibility that it represents. Calvin Rutstrum, when once asked by reporter why he had been on so many canoe trips, responded:

> I had a commitment to happiness. We need the joy of living optimally, where every natural force is playing on one's being, as multi-coloured spotlights play on the actor who is exuberant with the joy of assuming his role. That exquisite pleasure of being an integral part of the natural universe, of being in its spotlight, makes one ecstatic about just living.[3]

Of special significance to Bill's way of thinking about wilderness living was Calvin Rutstrum's assumption that canoes were not for paddling around a dock, or kneeling up in, or for racing from A to B— canoes had one purpose only and that was for travelling in the wild. *Way of the Wilderness* includes a detailed section on strokes, techniques and advice, for solo and tandem paddlers, and expands this with notes on camp equipment and procedures.

And Bill also took to heart Rutstrum's views on shelter.[4] Throughout his life he would be partial to one type of tent, a wall tent with an open front he learned about in *Way of the Wilderness*. Among the ten features Rutstrum's ideal tent must possess are the following:

> It must permit freedom and diversion during prolonged rains, allowing an open view of the waterfront during a rain, at the same time giving protection.

Most tents are "dog houses" one crawls into during a rain and for a night's sleep. Come the heavy rains and cooking is usually put off just at a time certainly when hot food is needed most.[5]

Rutstrum goes on in graphic detail about the ins and outs of this reflector tent, and concludes with the following claim:

In such a tent I have stripped in zero temperatures with perfect comfort. The luxury of loafing and eating meals on cold wet days—yet remaining warm, dry and comfortable before such a tent, gives one that added assurance that living out-of-doors in any weather is not too difficult. But this largely is to be translated into one word, EQUIPMENT, with perhaps the knowledge of how to use it.[6]

The equipment Bill would use on his wilderness trips he either made or purchased to Calvin Rutstrum's specifications; the knowledge of how to use it was derived from firsthand experience. Learning was part of the great adventure. This combination of knowledge and experience resulted in the appreciation of a much deeper message from Rutstrum, a message about the natural world and the integral part humans play.

The kind of lore Mason may have taken from his hero Rutstrum is described by writer Jim Dale Vickery in *Wilderness Visionaries;* some of his observations about Rutstrum could just as well have applied to Bill Mason:

No matter what job he held, no matter what weight of obligation employers tried to lay on him, he left every August for parts little known. He came to view cities as "large trading posts," and jobs at those posts as a means to get grubstaked for the next adventure. Never was work an end in itself. Never could jobs preempt a canoe trip. This was religion for Rutstrum, as close to religion as he ever got. It was also a religion that some employers simply didn't appreciate. One boss told Rutstrum that, because of his "reckless leisure," he would blackball him so he could never get a job in that city again. Cal looked the guy in the eye and asked him if, in planning to cut off his chances for subsistence survival, he— Mr. employer—expected to remain alive.[7]

Bill thought nothing of following Rutstrum's philosophy and handing in his notice each summer to extend his one-week holiday allotment into enough time to work at the boys' camp at Manitoba Pioneer and maybe take a short canoe trip afterward. Blake James, another of the artists on staff at PGA, had already established this pattern in a much more whimsical manner than Mason, so colleagues and even Phillips and Gutkin, at least knew about the process, even if they never did learn to appreciate it. The most formidable opposition to Bill's making the decision to quit his work would have been Granny Mason, but she had passed away in 1952. Continuing the traditional view of what a man should do was Bill's mother, Sadie, who thought it was against all that was good and right, and possibly the work of the devil, to toss over a $35-a-month job in favour of rustling around in a canoe.

The aspect of Bill's wandering that Sadie abhorred perhaps even more than the fact that pre-empted work was his habit of returning from camp, or from his canoe outings, with the makings of a beard on his face. Sadie feared that the neighbours would think her son was a beatnik.

It wasn't until the summer of 1954 that Bill really kicked over the traces: quit work, went to camp and didn't return until freeze-up. Whether it was the Lord's will or his own, that was the summer he was given his first movie camera, and it was also the summer he bought his first canoe. These two items would shape the rest of his life.

Canadian Studies professor John Wadland, at Trent University, has made a wry observation about the canoe: the Americans have as one of their central informing symbols the horse, a domesticated animal; by contrast, embedded in Canadian consciousness is the birchbark canoe, a domesticated tree. Others have described the canoe as "a perfect machine . . . about as close as people get to building a part of nature."[8] For a Canadian like Bill Mason, who found such resonance with the natural world, it makes perfect sense that his vehicle, his preoccupation—his obsession—would be the canoe. He loved the craft and all that went with it, the art of paddling with its echoes of voyageurs and Native people. Though Bill likely imagined himself paddling a bark canoe on all of his trips, that was not practically possible. Instead, his first canoe was a 15-foot laminated wood Plycraft model made with bomber technology from the Vickers aircraft company in Montreal, a far cry from the Native original. But his favourite canoe—the revered Chestnut, purchased when the Plycraft disintegrated in an early rapid-running disaster—was as close as modern manufacturing technology of the time could get to the original birchbark design. To understand Bill Mason, one must appreciate, as he did, the historical development of the boats he loved.

In 1797, the Hudson's Bay Company began replacing the 36-foot, birchbark *canot de maître* and the 26-foot *canot du nord* with larger, more durable York boats that could be rowed or sailed, and this point in history marks the beginning of the evolution of the modern-day canoe. Smaller canoes remained in use for hunters, police, missionaries, surveyors and engineers who crisscrossed the country, but as the big bark canoes of the fur trade gave way to larger craft, eventually powered by steam and combustion engines, canoe-manufacturing technology began to change quite dramatically.

In 1811, as Canada's map maker David Thompson and his crew headed west over the Rockies, a dearth of suitable birch bark forced them to build a canoe of cedar planks pinned and sewn together with split spruce roots, emulating the practice of Native people from around the world, such as the Sare of the Gulf of California, who, for centuries, made canoes from strips of wood woven together with vegetable fibres. The manufacture of canoes was also influenced by the popularity of cloth as a trade good in commerce with Native people across the country. Tears in the remaining bark canoes were regularly being repaired with pieces of canvas fabric worked over the fragile bark with balsam pitch. It was only a matter of time before Natives in service to the Hudson's Bay Company were making canvas-covered canoes in the exact same manner as they had bark canoes, beginning with a sheath or skin of heavy canvas duck instead of bark, then building a cedar frame inside. By the mid-nineteenth century wilderness travellers were carrying ready-made waterproofed canvas canoe skins, patented by Adirondack surveyor Verplanck Colvin, that could be fashioned almost instantly into a serviceable boat with nothing more than some pliable white cedar, an axe and a crooked knife.

On Georgian Bay, at the garrison at Penetanguishene, tinsmith Toussaint Boucher had another idea. He soldered and riveted together a 45-foot replica of the *canot de maître* that could carry lots of goods and people without being damaged in the shallow rivers of the area; it dived through waves on the Great Lakes like a submarine, unlike its buoyant bark inspiration, which "bounded over them."[9] As silly (or revolutionary) as this manufacturing technique may have seemed at the time, the tinsmith's notion was more or less what the Grumman aircraft company did in pioneering riveted aluminum canoes after the Second World War, using the metal fabrication technology perfected in the construction of war planes.

Elsewhere in Canada in the mid to late nineteenth century, the same forces of industrialization that motorized the fur trade were creating a middle class with disposable income and time to play. Recreational duck hunting was one of several canoe-based pursuits that were all the rage for Upper Canadians in 1850, but getting at the ducks in wild-rice marshes was notoriously difficult because the sides of the broad bark canoes would be caved in by the pressure of thick rice beds. Irish shipwright Dan Herald, in Gore's Landing, observed that local Natives had much more success using heavier, narrower and more durable dugout canoes to enter the wild-rice plantations to shoot ducks and harvest the rice. But these basswood and pine dugouts were notoriously tippy. Herald set to work to manufacture a boat that would allow duck hunters to access the ducks without boat collapse and finished up with a two-ply solid wood canoe with quarter-inch boards on the outside, running longitudinally, and quarter-inch boards on the inside, steamed to run laterally, at ninety degrees. This beamy, heavy canoe was almost impossible to carry but worked exceptionally well for hunting because it could penetrate the reeds, and it was much easier to clean than a ribbed canoe after being loaded with dead ducks. It was the design of this 1860s boat, the "Herald Patent Canoe," that inspired the Plycraft that became Mason's first canoe in Winnipeg eighty years later. But wooden boats, however made, were still fragile and subject to cracking from misuse and the vagaries of weather.

Subsequent manufacturing innovations in the boat-building indus-try in eastern North America in the later years of the 1800s were di-rected to the perfection of other recreational canoe designs. The E.M. White and Old Town canoe companies in Maine, and Payne Brothers, at their lumber mill near Lakefield, Ontario, among others, crafted in-geniously lightweight dugout canoes from straight-grained basswood and cedar logs. In nearby Peterborough, John Stevenson, working with a Col. J.Z. Rogers, created a superbly finished all-wood canoe of rib and plank construction, operating out of a water-powered lumber-plan-ing mill on the east bank of the Otonabee River.[10] These canoes be-came the standard for racing and recreational use across the country.

The all-wood canoes had aesthetic appeal, they were light and much more durable than their bark predecessors, and they were used by latter-day Victorian explorers such as the Tyrrell brothers,[11] but for use in wilderness locations, for lugging rock samples, hunting equipment or survey instruments, there was a much more practical and durable de-sign—the wooden canoe with canvas skin. The Peterborough boat builders knew this technology and were using it to some degree, but some would say that, relatively speaking, they were well behind their counterparts in the northeastern United States. Builders at the E.M. White and Old Town canoe companies had been refining canvas-canoe manufacturing techniques since the 1850s, experimenting with canvas sandwiched between wooden layers in the hulls of canoes, and with painted cotton duck as a skin on the outside of cedar ribs and planking that made the boat waterproof and protected the vulnerable wooden ribs and planking from abrasion and impact damage.

The Canadian connection to these, arguably superior, New England canoes was through the owners of the hardware store in Fredericton, New Brunswick. Strict tariffs had made it advantageous for merchants in Canada to buy Canadian, which had protected the Peterborough canoe-building industry and its all-wooden boats, but the Fredericton *Daily Gleaner* reported in 1897 that Mr. W.T. Chestnut had imported a canvas canoe from a "leading and renowned boat building house in the United States, it being especially for use at Pine Bluff Camp." The article main-tained that this fine canoe would be exhibited at R. Chestnut and Sons' hardware store for a few days.[12] Shortly thereafter, the J.C. Risteen sash and door company in Fredericton (owned by a group including W.T. Chestnut and his brother Harry) started making a canoe identical to the imported American model and, in 1905, the venerable R. Chestnut and Sons canoe company was incorporated.

A curious aspect of this importation of an American canoe was that W.T. Chestnut secured a Canadian patent for the canvas-covered canoe design, despite the fact that the technology had been in use elsewhere in the country in one form or another for decades. Armed with this new patent, Chestnut launched a lawsuit against the Peterborough Canoe Company, alleging violation of its canvas-covered canoe patent. According to canoe historian Roger MacGregor, "Peterborough's reply . . . was lengthy, detailed, and devastating. Chestnut did not even file a counter-reply." And, MacGregor notes, as if to add insult to injury, another company, the Canadian Canoe Company of Peterborough, seeking entry into the canvas canoe market in 1907, simply acquired a Chestnut canoe from Fredericton and copied it exactly as Chestnut had done earlier with the American canoe.[13]

Perhaps the central human force in putting these boats to widespread recreational use in North America, moving beyond static lake and river paddling to the idea of a canoe *trip*, was one John MacGregor, a Scot living in London, England, who came to Canada in 1859 in pursuit of "muscular Christianity, an evangelizing philosophy that sought converts through the example of sportsmanship, physical training, and athletic competition."[14] On the Ottawa River during that visit, MacGregor was invited to try out a variety of canoes and, on return home to London, designed a canoe he called the "Rob Roy" that looked like a cross between an Inuit kayak and a birchbark canoe made using the all-wood Peterborough style of construction. MacGregor then took this boat, which he packed full of bibles and religious tracts, on a three-month journey through Germany, France and Switzerland, thereby becoming the father of modern-day canoeing in Europe, and producing a book about his adventures, entitled *A Thousand Miles in the Rob Roy Canoe*, that became very popular on both sides of the Atlantic.

The peripatetic Scot's popularization of the canoe as a recreational vehicle spawned clubs and organizations devoted to canoe "cruising," in the northeastern United States and Canada. Perhaps inspired by

MacGregor's exploits in Canada and abroad, and in the spirit of true explorers like John Franklin and David Thompson—and certainly aided by the many improvements in canoe construction and design— so-called Gentleman Adventurers of the late nineteenth century turned from peregrinations around the European continent—in the manner of medieval pilgrims[15]—to grand adventures in the Canadian Northwest. People like Warburton Pike, Frank Russell, the Tyrrell brothers, Henry Toke Munn, Caspar Whitney,[16] and many of the heroes of substantial fads like the Klondike gold rush, took to canoes, crossing the country, going west and north, touching all the major watersheds, and generally returning to tell of their adventures in books or periodicals of the day. The tales of these canoeists added to the more functional stories of the mappers and Dominion surveyors who also used canoes to access the frontier. And, of course, by the years leading up to the First World War, artists like A.Y. Jackson and Tom Thomson had added an aura of real romance to the legendary building around the Canadian canoe.

By the time Mason was born, all-wood and canvas-covered canoes were in common use at places like Mimico and Grand Beach. With magazines and books celebrating the romance of canoeing the Canadian wild, and vigorous railway advertising campaigns to "explore Canada by canoe," it is little wonder that a boy with a vivid imagination and a love of boats would dream of one day living the life of a voyageur. Riding the train to Grand Beach, he was already part of the tradition. Although at Manitoba Pioneer Camp he paddled all-wood Lakefield Canoe Company canoes, kneeling up on half-rounded ribs in the manner of the regatta racers of the day—probably emulating publicity photographs of Canadian Francis Amyot, who won a gold medal for canoeing in the 1936 Berlin Olympics, the year canoeing was first accepted as an Olympic sport—he crossed over to more wilderness-oriented traditions when he experimented with the cruising style of canoeing, and branched out from Manitoba Pioneer Camp into the Whiteshell with Don Campbell and on his own.

Although in later life Bill vehemently defended the virtues of his beloved Chestnut—his personal fleet included three, a 16' Pal, a 16' Prospector and a 17' Cruiser—he could have been paddling any number of canvas-covered canoes built in the 1930s, 1940s and 1950s. In fact, there were on the market, for all intents and purposes, dozens of nearly identical models made by various manufacturers in the United States and Canada, many of which even had the model name "Prospector." But, even as a class or type of canvas-covered canoe, the Prospector that became his favourite was entirely consistent with Bill and his view of the world. It was mostly made of natural materials—steamed white cedar ribs and planking; brass tacks and screws; cotton-canvas skin; and white ash or oak seats, thwarts and gunwales. It was solid; it was durable; it could be repaired in the field; and it moved quietly and responsively in all types of water. But, before Bill could purchase his first Chestnut, he had to smash up the Plycraft—all in pursuit of truth and beauty in the wilderness of Whiteshell and Lake of the Woods.

7

HEAVEN ON EARTH

BILL'S WEEKEND RAMBLES with Don Campbell and others took him more often than not to Betula Lake campground in the heart of Whiteshell Provincial Park, from which they would jump off by canoe across Betula Lake and downstream on the Whiteshell River to a place Campbell later called "Bill's Domain." The place they liked was a broad expanse of flat rock, sloping off into a shallow rapid that riffled the river as it made a sweeping bend to the west. From Betula Lake, they would have to portage through the reeds and cottonwoods around a cement weir and two other short rapids to access this Shangri-La. And had they ever chosen to come upstream to Bill's Domain, they would have had even more portages around another series of rapids and falls.

The place was scenic—excellent for photography—but what Bill liked best about it was the isolation. Neither fishermen nor other Whiteshell visitors had the energy or the inclination to lug their gear upstream or downstream. It was a place in the wilderness that Bill and Don could call their own, protected by whitewater at either end. Here Bill would cook, camp, photograph and swim. Here he was in his element and largely oblivious to the rest of the world. Don remembers that more than once Bill would announce he was "going for water" for tea or to cook a meal, only to be found hours later scooping up frogs with the pot or photographing in different ways the reflections at the spot where they used to draw water.

That he loved this place is evident from the first and only systematic record of his wilderness activities. On May 8, 1954, he began a little red 3½- by 5-inch Five-Year Diary in which he kept a more or less complete record of the next four years of his outings. Milestones were recorded briefly in hastily scrawled pencil script on the tiny pages. Bill paid no attention to the discipline imposed by the book's designer, scratching out the printed dates, as required. Beside a pencilled-out January 3, Mason writes:

> June 5/54   Left Friday night with Frank Kunz [another colleague from Phillips/Gutkin]. Camped at Granite Lake. Saturday morning went to Clearwater Bay. First trip with my canoe. Paddled south almost as far as Echo Bay.

What this journal entry does not convey is the fact that, after years of wishing and renting, Bill had finally been able to purchase his first canoe, the Plycraft. Bought from the Hudson's Bay Company catalogue, it was a bright red, beautifully shaped 16-foot canoe made from a wooden laminate, trimmed with plywood seats, two stout hardwood thwarts and mahogany gunwales. This is the canoe that sat beside the walk at 209 Oakwood, outside the kitchen window; the canoe he mentioned years later in his book, *Path of the Paddle*; the one he gazed at from the breakfast nook like a love-struck teen.

The little red diary records the first outings in the red Plycraft, trips with Don Campbell, trips with his cousins, trips with the Elim Young People's Group, and his first encounter with the idea of actually paddling in rapids:

> May 24/54   I went with Moses Kaljean to Granite Lake on Friday night. On Saturday we went through Kenora to the Black Sturgeon River. Rented a small rowboat and went as far as rapids near Winnipeg River. We saw an Indian family

shoot the rapids. Camped on a high ridge on north side of river for two days. On Monday afternoon we went to Redditt. Returned Monday night.

This entry is significant because it shows how skills and circumstances combined to produce his first big river trip. The Winnipeg River was a tangible, geographic connection to his heroes, the voyageurs, and formed a natural line between Manitoba Pioneer Camp on Shoal Lake and the site of the old cottage at Grand Beach. Journals and stories of the fur-trade era he had read or heard as a boy told him that, each year, until the amalgamation of the Northwest and Hudson's Bay companies in 1821, brigades of his beloved voyageurs took bundles of fur from inland western posts to Fort William in spring and returned with trade goods in later summer. Great explorers like Alexander Mackenzie, Alexander Henry and David Thompson had plied these waters too. Fur-trade historian Eric Morse describes it this way:

> The Winnipeg River was unquestionably the grandest and most beautiful river the Montreal Northmen saw on their whole journey from Lake Superior to Lake Athabasca. Running often through tortured rock and dropping fast, it was a river of spectacular rapids and falls. Twenty-six historic carrying places marked its course. . . . For thirty-three miles below Kenora, to about where the C.N.R. crosses at Minaki, we have a fresh, free-flowing, often dancing river, still unspoiled.[1]

But before getting onto the rapids of the Winnipeg River and realizing his dream of becoming a modern-day voyageur, Bill had yet to have his first whitewater experience. The diary quietly records this event:

> Sept 2 Went camping to White Lake [next lake upstream on the Whiteshell River from Betula Lake] with Blake Herman [a friend from Winnipeg] and Don [Campbell]. Set up camp and fished. Caught several and ate one of them for supper.
> Paddled Blake back to car and dropped him at Rennie [whistle stop on the CPR at which Whiteshell Park Headquarters is

located—from here, Blake Herman could take the train back to Winnipeg].

Don and I returned to campsite at night. Got off course once but found our way. Next day, Sunday, paddled down Whiteshell River and shot my first rapids.

Continued down Whiteshell River, portaged over a long shallow stretch of rapids and shot another short fast rocky stretch. That night we camped at mouth of Whiteshell River on Betula Lake. Rained all day Monday, and we returned across Betula Lake.

After a busy spring and summer of outings, he had yet another summer stint at Manitoba Pioneer:

Aug 6   Went on canoe trip with 8 fellows at Pioneer Camp. Paddled south into Shoal Lake. Ran into heavy seas and one canoe tipped, losing all our canned goods. We ate fish, tea bisk and berries for the next two days.

Aug 15   Took 8 intermediates into Bag Bay. On return trip had to buck strong head winds and heavy seas so lashed two canoes together. They rode well but shipped water. Canoes should have at least 1 ft between them, and should be toed in slightly.

Aug 18   Took out a senior canoe trip for 3 days. Travelled southeast to dead man's portage, then south down to the States. Camped on this side of the border for the first night then headed for States in morning. I got completely lost that day and after we decided the States was too far away and we had better head for home, some Americans informed us that we were in the States and had been for most of the day. We had paddled up the North West Inlet without knowing it. We then visited Fort St. Charles. About 3 o'clock we headed for home and camped just past first camping spot. We arrived home about 5 o'clock, just in time for a banquet. We travelled about 90 miles in the 3 days.

Although not documented in the little red diary, records show that Bill earned both his Intermediate Certificate and Award of Merit from the Royal Life Saving Society of Canada at camp that summer. And, at the end of camp, at the age of twenty-six, Bill Mason took the first extended canoe trip of his life. After almost a year of planning, he and fellow staff member Peter Buhr left Pioneer Camp on Shoal Lake on the *Pioneer II* (the camp launch) and were taken to Kenora, where they did last-minute shopping and ran into two camp friends who offered to tow them west along Lake of the Woods to Portage Bay, past the Keewatin Bridge, where they portaged into the Winnipeg River.

David Thompson's original map of this area, published in *The Shoe and the Canoe*, a travel book by Dr. J.J. Bigsby, Secretary of the Canada/U.S. Boundary Commission, shows that the route Bill and Peter took to access the Winnipeg River was one of three possible portages from Lake of the Woods. Bill followed the diaries of Thompson and Bigsby, and may well have had with him knowledge or a record of Bigsby's original description of this carry:

> The Rat Portage, we reach by a narrow cul-du-sac, 600 yards long, ending in a grassy swamp, the portage lying between two eminences. . . . This cul-de-sac is 120 yards broad at the portage, and is made offensive and foul by dead insects . . . and the plague of mosquitoes. The portage is a neck of land fifty paces across, between the dirty cover in the Lake [of the Woods] and a magnificent sheet of water [Darlington Bay on the Winnipeg River].[2]

With that, Bill and Peter were over the divide, heading downstream in the direction of Lake Winnipeg. The diary records steady progress on the river, and a regular camp schedule, with meals of dried potatoes, chipped beef and fish they caught along the way. At Minaki they stopped to write postcards and dry out, having been badly soaked and nearly swamped by large waves just prior to arrival. Notes then show Bill's lifelong affinity for waterfalls and how, to engage them fully, he must explore them photographically and with his paints:

> The Winnipeg river forks into two rivers, one a large body of water and the other quite small. There are falls at the mouth of both rivers, so we visited the falls on the big river first, had lunch and did some sketching. We then paddled to the mouth of the smaller river and were met by a beautiful falls rushing through a narrow gorge. We decided not to shoot them because of a huge razor-edge rock in midstream. We made the portage and continued on our way. The beautiful scenery ended abruptly as we came to a place where a forest fire had swept through about 10 years ago. The foliage was small and dense, very unsuited to camping. We went down a few small rapids without any trouble. Then as we rounded a bend in the river, we came upon some that were a little more difficult but we decided to run them. We started out fine, but then we swung sideways and couldn't make it through the shoot I had chosen so I picked another on the other side of a rock, but we couldn't make that either so we hit the rock dead on. However no damage was done as the current wasn't too strong. We back-paddled and got into the correct channel and continued on our way.
>
> It began to get late and we couldn't find a suitable camp because of the heavy underbrush. At this point we came to a huge falls which descended in 4 cascades to a drop of about 20 feet. We had to portage again and as we were loading the canoe at the end of the portage we noticed that we could scarcely see more than half a mile. We looked up at the sun, which was a brilliant red, then at times it would disappear completely.
>
> Then we realized that smoke from a forest fire was causing this strange effect. The wind which had been blowing hard all day had increased in strength. We decided to camp where we were as the visibility was getting worse. We decided not to put up the tent because of the wind. We rolled out our

beds under the canoe, then found a sheltered spot on the rocks for our fire and cooked supper. We went to bed, keeping an eye on the direction of the fire in case it blew our way. However, we reasoned that it couldn't be close because there was no glow on the horizon and the strong wind could have blown all the smoke from miles away.

Sept 6   We got up about 8 o'clock this morning and there was no sign of the fire. The smoke had cleared completely and the sun was shining. We had a leisurely breakfast of bacon and pancakes. Some clouds moved in and obscured the sun, so we killed some time breaking camp as I didn't want to leave without getting some pictures of the falls. I finally got my pictures and we decided to push on. There was a beautiful little rapid by our camp where the water rushed through a gorge about 20 feet wide. I ran the rapid with an empty canoe and Peter took a picture for me. I slid sideways onto one rock but no damage was done. We loaded up and set out at 10 o'clock. We only went about a mile when we came out of the area which had been burned many years ago. Soon we were met by another rapids which we found to be ideal for camping. In fact it was a camper's dream come true. It was a long rapids with a waterfall at one end. One side was a sheer cliff and the other side sloped up from the water, leveled off at the top and the rocks were covered with moss. Huge white pines towered above us. We pitched camp and decided to stay here a couple of days. The moon is just coming up and I guess it's time to go to bed.

Sept 8   We awoke to a beautiful day this morning. We took several pictures before breakfast. In fact it took all morning. I wanted some pictures of this campsite from across the rapids so I had to take Peter across above the rapids, set up the camera, come back across, track the canoe down the rapids to the camp then Peter took the picture. Then I had to track and portage the canoe to the bottom of the rapids, pick up Peter, then we had to do it all over because the camera fell open. However, we figured out a way to get across the rapids by our campsite. We rigged up a ferry with the canoe and a rope which turned out to be a little precarious as the canoe always tipped considerably, shipping a little water. However, we got our pictures of the campsite.

We packed a lunch and started out to find the mouth of the river. We turned only one bend in the river before we came to some rapids. The water was forced between a narrow opening but there were no rocks, so we shot them. They were very turbulent and we shipped some water, so we paddled into shore to empty the canoe. While I was tying the gear back in, Peter tried a couple of casts and caught a nice jack. We continued on our way and shot another small rapid. We came onto the main channel of the Winnipeg River and paddled up to the falls and had lunch. I did a little sketching and Peter caught more beautiful pickerel. We headed back home and on the way we stopped to take pictures at the rapids.

Absent from this trip account is any technical language of whitewater or canoeing technique, but in many respects this feature of the diary signals a pattern of emphasis for Bill. For his entire life, it was the places the canoe took him that were always more important than the act of canoeing itself. Another interesting feature that emerges in this first trip chronicle is Bill's setting of the agenda. He had the interest, the knowledge and the camping skills, and he liked to be in control. The diary makes it clear that this was Bill's trip. His companion, Peter, was welcome, but it was taken for granted that he would play along with Bill's dalliances with photography and art:

Sept 12   Today was a beautiful, warm, calm day. We had pancakes again this morning and made enough for lunch. We haven't had any bread for about 6 days and our hard tack ran out about four days ago. We paddled up to the first falls and I took some pictures of snails and flowers. Then Peter found a snake and I was able to, at last, get some pictures. I've been trying for 2 years to get a picture of a snake. . . . We set up camp at the mouth of the river right above the rapids. Then I shot the rapids and Peter took a picture for me. Then Peter and I went down them together. It sure was thrilling. We didn't hit any rocks but sure came close. Tonight is a beautiful starry night. The northern lights are flashing overhead. Tomorrow we head back to Minaki.

Peter and Bill parted company at Minaki. Peter took an evening train west, back to Winnipeg and Bill waited a couple of hours for a train heading east to McIntosh, where he slept the night in the station and headed out the next morning for the Canyon River. As was the case on the night on the banks of the Red River under cover of the River Speeder, Bill seems completely at ease on his own in the bush. But the issue of loneliness and the tension between solitude and kinship on the trail do arise, if only in passing. He's conscious of the risk in being out alone, but the exhilaration of being out tends to push the practical issues of safety into the background, with matters of canoe technique. When one is alone, the smallest things become subjects for journal entries:

Sept 16   I went to bed at 9 o'clock last night and had a good rest in spite of the fact a mouse kept running across my head and thumping around. Every time I turned on my flashlight he was never there.

I got up at 8 o'clock this morning, had a good breakfast, then I packed a lunch and paddled down to see what the Canyon River was like, and how the portage would be. The river is small but the portage was very good so went back and broke camp. I arrived back at the first portage at 1:00. It was a very long hard portage but it was well worth it. At the end of the portage which I made in three trips was a beautiful little lake. I [took] some pictures of a frog then paddled down to see the next falls. They were beautiful but there wasn't any place to camp so I returned to the other falls and found a beautiful spot right above the fall. I put up the tent carefully and made a good fireplace because I plan to stay a few days before pushing on. I'm warm and comfortable in my tent with everything neatly arranged. I just looked over my film to see how much I've got left. I guess I'll do a little reading and turn in. Tomorrow I want to do some painting and take plenty of pictures.

Sept 17, Sat   It was a dreary overcast day so I got up later than usual. I had breakfast, did some washing, and boy they sure needed it, then I got in some firewood. About twelve I started doing some painting but later it began to rain so returned to the tent to read for awhile.

Today I noticed the loneliness, I guess I'm not on the trail and busy. The only noise I can hear is the constant roar of the falls which are right beside my tent, down in a gorge about 30 feet deep. I guess I'll write some letters, do a little reading, and then turn in. I hope my candles hold out. I've been using $\frac{1}{2}$ a candle every night and I've got $4\frac{1}{2}$ left.

Sept 20, Tues   I portaged the canoe over to the bottom of the falls so I can get an early start in the morning. I have to be extremely careful when carrying the canoe as an injury would be very serious. I haven't seen anyone or heard an airplane since I started out. There are now 3 tough portages between myself and civilization. I had a nice campfire at the door of my tent tonight and I took some exposures by firelight and candle light. The fire has died down and it's getting cold. I guess I close up for the night.

Sept 21, Wed   Today was the most miserable day yet. It was very dull and it rained continuously all day. . . . I kept the fire going for warmth and spent the day painting. I didn't leave the tent all day and was warm and dry and cozy. The only drawback was not to be able to be out taking pictures. I want very badly to make it to the mouth of the river but if it's raining tomorrow I guess I'll have to give up and start heading for home. It sure is cozy with the tent all sealed up and a nice warm sleeping bag with cheery candle for light.

Sept 24, Sat   This morning when I looked out of the tent there was one encouraging blue spot in the sky. I jumped out of bed and got dressed but halfway through breakfast rain clouds moved in and drizzled most of the day. I painted until 4 o'clock, then the sky started to break up and it rained and shone every half-hour. I managed to squeeze in 3 pictures. I started supper at 4 o'clock and really had a banquet tonight: soup, then boiled rice, fried ham and parsnips. Then I had tea and hard tack and jam, then rice pudding. The sky has completely cleared and the moon is shining. I sure hope the sun shows up tomorrow as I will be breaking camp and heading for home.

The following June, Bill would have his first major canoeing mishap, the closest he ever came to getting killed. The entry for June 1 understates the seriousness of the event:

Just bought car [a Nash Rambler]. Slept at Betula. Let out with canoe (the old Plycraft) loaded very light. Shot first and second rapids, portaged falls. Portaged gear over 3rd rapids, then proceeded to shoot them as customary. Got on wrong side of rock in middle of rapids and canoe was swamped then smashed to pieces. Left it on shore and walked home a little wiser.

In *Path of the Paddle* there is a photograph on page 75 captioned "a deceased laminated wood canoe," but Bill does not let his reader in on the fact that this is his first canoe, ripped mercilessly from gunwale to gunwale and held together only by its keel, unceremoniously left for dead on the shores of the Whiteshell River, forcing him to walk 10 miles through the bush to safety and his new (used) Nash Rambler at the Betula Lake campground.

What one sees looking back on these sparse accounts of Mason's travel in Whiteshell, in Lake of the Woods, on the Winnipeg River and in the Shield Country west of Lake Superior is the establishment of patterns that would last the rest of his life, significant among them, of course, the artist and woodsman quitting his job every spring to roam alone in the wilderness until freeze-up, in his beloved red canoe. The diary documents that he did in fact do this in the early 1950s—later accounts of his doing it "every" summer might have been a little overblown—but it formed a pattern nonetheless, most vividly in Bill's imagination. The little red book also documents the persistence and ingenuity of a fundamentally unskilled and unschooled canoe-tripper and paddler who, with Calvin Rutstrum's *Way of the Wilderness* in hand, essentially invented technique to suit circumstances as he went along.

Another of Bill's life patterns that emerged on these trips was the enduring fascination with film and the way in which this interest suborned his desire to paint. Later, in an unfinished, handwritten memoir, he would write: "I didn't completely forsake my painting, but the photography was ideal for me at the time because . . . my wanderlust was in constant conflict with my love of creating. I loved to paint but found it difficult to sit still for long."

Above all, the little red book highlights the durable independence of the man, and the profound peace and joy he found in his own company. It wasn't that he did not like companionship; in fact, he did get lonesome and did enjoy travelling with his camp friend Peter Buhr. But having grown up under the ideological thumb of his grandmother, having been the master of his own creative devices in his own little world upstairs at 209 Oakwood, and having tasted a way to celebrate God's word in the natural world, he records, beneath the notes in the little red book, a powerful subtext of escape to a place where he could be in control and able to practise faith his way, in the wild. Later, in the unfinished memoirs, he would write: "It is impossible to describe the sense of total freedom that came over me as I loaded my canoe and gear on the train and headed east."

The last series of entries in the red diary register the purchase of a new red canoe to replace the "deceased" one—this time, a 16-foot canvas-covered cedar Chestnut Pal, which Bill and a friend picked up in Kenora on April 12, 1958. The friend, whom Mason identifies as "Joy" in the diary, is Lorraine Joyce Ferguson, a woman he met through Elim Young People's. Unknown to his parents (or anyone else, for that matter), Bill had been slipping up to the Winnipeg General Hospital nurses' residence for clandestine dates. As a student nurse, Joyce was on a highly structured schedule, working shifts around the clock and going to classes during the day. Just getting a phone call through took more than casual persistence, there being only one phone in the residence, at the main desk. Once or twice Bill asked Joyce to a concert or a movie, but, more often than not, he would bring a Thermos of coffee and a piece of cake to the residence, where Joyce took the risk of slipping out, with floormates covering for her, meeting Bill outside, and slipping back in before anyone found out she was gone. The importance of this budding relationship is acknowledged in the diary, as Bill's scrawl is replaced by Joy's neat handwriting:

> June 16-20   We (Joy and I) paddled around on the Bird River. Shot millions of slides—turned out nicely. Beautiful day. Portage to Tulahie. Home + tired!!!!!

Before long Bill would marry the woman he nearly exhausted to death on the Tulahie Lake portage.

The photographic images Mason brought back from his trip on the Winnipeg and Canyon rivers were added to a slide show called "God Revealed" that he had been working on since his first year at Phillips/Gutkin. On every outing since those early instructional forays with Don Campbell, the photography had more or less ruled Mason's movements in the outdoors. "Getting the shot" was almost always more important than getting home and, without question, more important than getting back to work, except perhaps to show his transparencies to Don Campbell or other colleagues at PGA. By the time he had purchased the Plycraft canoe, tales of his adventures in Whiteshell and around Manitoba Pioneer Camp were told at the slightest provocation in living rooms, church basements, classrooms, libraries and anywhere else people asked Bill to speak. Very soon after the first rendition of "God Revealed" was assembled, Mason took advantage of audio-recording facilities at PGA and cut together a soundtrack for the show. He would play the tape, push the slides one at a time through a projector and talk all the while about his adventures, interspersing ad hoc commentary with pithy quotes from the Bible. Writing about this process of learning and development in his creative life in his unfinished memoirs, Mason acknowledged, "It was the slide show that honed my skills as a photographer and storyteller."

Scripture references read to accompany the slides were drawn predominantly from the New Testament—Matthew, Mark, Luke, John, Romans, Colossians, to Hebrews and Revelation—although he did dip into the Old Testament books for quotes from Genesis, Exodus and Job. In fact the title of the show, "God Revealed," appears to have come from the Old Testament book of Isaiah (40:4–6): "Every valley shall be exalted, and every mountain and hill shall be made low; and the crooked shall be made straight, and the rough places plain: and the glory of the Lord shall be revealed, . . . and all flesh is grass, and all the goodliness thereof is as the flower of the field."

On the surface, the combination of pictures, music, commentary and earnest Bible references sounds like daunting fare, closer to indoctrination than entertainment, for a group of schoolchildren or unruly boy scouts. It is certainly easy enough to imagine where Bill found these elements, especially the Bible references, having grown up with the likes of Granny Mason and Dr. Mitchell. In many ways his was a narrow and cloistered intellectual and spiritual milieu, filled with Christian virtue and restricted by the expectations of Christian behaviour. Growing up at home, attending Elim Chapel on Sundays and Young People's through the week, and camp in the summer, Bill was a product of his environment, an unwavering Christian. His friend Wilber Sutherland later described Bill's faith as "neither vague nor rudely aggressive, but simply the reference point in his life; the base from which all his work flowed in the most natural and almost inevitable way."

Nevertheless, the slide show was a resounding success whenever and wherever it was delivered. Mason's innate charm and enthusiasm instantly transcended the Christian dogma; his wonderful and engaging abilities as a storyteller and his pictures from a canoeist's point of view swept people with him into the wild, leaving them moved and fulfilled by the experience, and hungry for more. However, Bill's audiences were largely city folk unfamiliar with wilderness, neophytes in the world of audio-visual presentations—the unconverted, as it were. And he didn't go out of his way to share the slide show with his photographer/film maker colleagues at work after his friend Don Campbell had squirmed in response to the religious narrative that Bill felt must accompany the pictures.

In later life, when he was surer of his work and before he had a library of films to show in the living room at Meech Lake, Bill was quick to play "God Revealed" for friends, neighbours—anyone who would sit in front of his projector—and solicit feedback. The typewritten script from subsequent slide shows, stuffed away with his large-format slides, illustrates an evolution of the music, the commentary and the quotes, drawing much more heavily in later shows from secular material. However, anyone who saw these shows would say with enthusiasm that Bill's commentary never sounded wooden or scripted. He had an innate ability to understand the interests, needs and mood of an audience, and to deliver what he had to say, often departing from the written script in a way that left people feeling he had crafted the presentation just for them. Because everything he spoke of during the slide shows was from firsthand experience on the land—taking the pictures, dealing with the waves and weather, contemplating a breathtakingly beautiful vista— there was an immediacy and authenticity to his storytelling that brought people as close to wilderness as they could possibly go without leaving the comfort of the Masons' living room.

On another piece of paper with "slide talk" scribbled on the top in Mason's hand are these pieces of text that provide a feel for what he was doing, where he was going and how he was evolving with his slide show:

> This is voyageur country. Only 150 years ago voyageurs manned birchbark canoes along these same waterways. Sounds are the same. Smells are the same. Inhabitants are the same. Mile-thick glaciers carved out the lakes.
>
> Professor Arthur Lower expressed himself thus: "Only those who have had the experience can know what a sense

of physical and spiritual excitement comes to one who turns his face away from men [and] towards the unknown. In his small way he is doing what the great explorers have done before him and his elation recaptures theirs." Wilderness is timeless. Blessed is the wilderness.

Life. Is it merely a sentimental delusion, a "pathetic fallacy", to think that one sees in the animal a capacity for joy which man himself is tending to lose? We have invented exercise, recreation, pleasure, amusement, and the rest. To "have fun" is a desire often expressed by those who live in this age of anxiety and most of us have at times actually "had fun". But recreation, pleasure, amusement, fun and all the rest are poor substitutes for joy; and joy, I am convinced, has its roots in something from which civilization tends to cut us off. . . .

Cried the angel in Revelations: "Hurt not the earth, neither the sea, nor the trees." For nature is a part of the glorious fullness of God's creation no less than man.

Of these, the Lower quote is especially revealing because of the mantra-like way in which it resonates with Bill's approach to wilderness: "Only those who have had the experience can know what a sense of physical and spiritual excitement comes to one who turns his face away from men [and] towards the unknown." In his own way, Bill was doing what the great explorers had done before him, and his elation was at recapturing their sense of adventure and discovery; he was, in his way, turning away from people to a place where he could create in solitude. There was no question that it was the *experience* of being in the wild alone in his canoe that left him with so much more than sun-drenched skin and sore muscles. Turning towards the unknown in the physical world—the wilderness—was turning towards the "glorious fullness of God's creation" that energized him in ways he could only begin to comprehend and express. Lower's notion of "spiritual excitement" was embodied by Bill Mason and, in the end, it was this that drew people to Bill when he began to reach a wider audience through film.

In 1953—the year television came to Winnipeg—Mason was lent a

Kodak Ciné Special movie camera by Henry Reimer, a family friend from Elim Chapel. Compared with the animation cameras he was seeing at Phillips/Gutkin, the Ciné Special was a primitive fixed-focus clockwork unit that ran only at silent speed, sixteen rather than the more conventional twenty-four frames per second. Nevertheless, the Ciné Special was a 16mm movie camera and one Bill could call his own, more or less; and it was a natural extension of his creative thinking to wish for a ciné camera to capture the wonders he had found in the Whiteshell wilderness.

The problem was that movie film was expensive, and it took something like four 50-foot rolls to yield just four minutes of viewing. Bill did take the Ciné Special with him initially on canoe outings, but before long he'd figured out that animation cinematography requires shooting movie film only one frame at a time and that, if he were to begin some kind of animation project, he could learn about film and film making without breaking the bank. Within just a few months of borrowing the camera, Bill and Don Campbell had built a sophisticated animation stand in the basement at 209 Oakwood Avenue.

The topic of Bill's first efforts on the basement animation stand— and later of his first bona fide film—was the Tabernacle as described in Exodus. How he came to focus on Exodus may have had something to do with a curious teenage communicant asking questions about where the name "Elim" for the family church had come from. He would have been told by Dr. Mitchell about Moses leading the Israelites out of Egypt, crossing the Red Sea, spending three days in the wilderness without water, and, thinking the Lord had forsaken them, coming to Elim, where there were "twelve wells of water, and threescore and ten palm trees: and they encamped there by the waters" (Exodus 15:27). And later Bill would have learned the rest of the story of Exodus: manna from heaven, water from the rock, the defeat of Amalek, Jethro advising Moses, the Ten Commandments and God's instructions for the construction of a place to keep the covenant and worship saying, "let them make me a sanctuary that I may dwell among them." (25:8) and "thou shalt make the tabernacle [a tent] with ten curtains of fine twined linen, and blue, and purple, and scarlet: with cherubims of cunning work shalt thou make them" (26:1).

Bill was fascinated by Exodus 26:14–18; being a practical person, he was drawn to details of lengths, widths, materials and construction:

> And thou shalt make a covering for the tent of rams' skins dyed red, and a covering above of badgers' skins.
>
> And thou shalt make boards for the tabernacle of shittim [acacia] wood standing up.
>
> Ten cubits [an archaic measure of length equal to a fore-arm] shall be the length of a board, and a cubit and a half shall be the breadth of one board.
>
> Two tenons shall there be in one board, set in order one against another: thus shalt thou make for all boards of the tabernacle.
>
> And thou shalt make the boards for the tabernacle, twenty boards on the south side southward.

Exodus goes on in graphic detail, outlining every dimension, every appointment for this makeshift spiritual camp in the wilderness for the people of Israel. Whatever the charm of the tabernacle in the story, Bill had a subject for his camera and animation stand, and set to work with a 3- by 4-foot piece of plywood, glue, sand, matchsticks, Plasticine, wire and material remnants to follow the home-build directions in Exodus. He built a 2-by-4-foot base and lugged in buckets and buckets of sand to the basement of 209 Oakwood from which he fashioned a likeness of Mount Sinai and the surrounding desert. Sadie remembers Bill's absorption with the project: "Billy whittled a little priest and the little priest had to stand in a certain spot in the tabernacle. He whittled all the little people, dressed them all in different garb and painted them all. It was quite a work of art."

Slowly, methodically, frame by frame, moving his little characters an eighth of an inch at a time, Bill began the process of making a film about the tabernacle. Of course, the whole story could not be told on the "set" he had constructed; alternate shots were taken on the great pile of sand in the basement. And when he needed to branch out be-yond that, he used handpainted backdrops and acetate animation cells and the techniques he had learned from the artists at Phillips/Gutkin.

Don Campbell, who helped in the construction and in some of the filming, to this day has a rather imposing cell of Moses, white hair aflutter, gazing down at the Campbells' bed with the most disconcerting stare. Shooting with the animation stand took place inside at night and on weekends, using bright lights. But, when the weather was good and the light was right, Bill would take the model and the animation stand outside and shoot in the backyard at 209 Oakwood.

The tabernacle model, and the subsequent film sequences, took Mason as a young man to the front of Elim Chapel to sermonize on the Children of Israel's exodus from Egypt, and later to Sunday schools and churches across Winnipeg to tell the story.

One of the lessons Bill learned from the tabernacle project was that neither the model nor the silent film sequences could engage an audience by themselves; the storyteller needed to be present. And what he knew, conceptually at least (because he had not the skills, equipment or money to bring the idea to life), was that the film medium, suitably dressed up with commentary and music, could be used without the storyteller actually being there, and thus reach a much broader audience. As Bill built, refined and tinkered with the soundtrack and imagery for his slide show, he began to realize that the same principle applied to his sharing of God's creations in the wilderness as well. If he were to replace the static imagery in his slides with movie footage supported by a soundtrack of music and the right commentary, he could reach a much wider audience. His life, in fact, was about to be changed by the viewing of a film that represented all he had dreamed of. In 1955, he was invited to a screening of a film called *The Seasons* at Phillips/Gutkin.

When Tom Thomson first saw A.Y. Jackson's *The Edge of the Maple Wood*, he said it made him see Canadian landscape for the first time. Bill experienced a similar revelation on seeing *The Seasons*:

> That film changed my life. It was the most beautiful film I had ever seen. There was no commentary. Just scenes of nature accompanied with music that matched the action perfectly. There were beautiful transitions from scene to scene like aspen leaves blowing in the wind mixing to waves breaking

on a shore. And the camera pans! I had never seen anything like it. Long slow pans that slowly revealed one beautiful sight after another. I knew then that was what I had to do but I would do it all from a canoe. I knew of many places that were more spectacular than what was in the film but could I do it with such artistry?

Unknown to Bill that day, as fate would have it, the maker of *The Seasons*, Toronto-based Christopher Chapman, had already heard of this keen canoeist in Winnipeg, the one with the fancy slide show. He would soon be knocking on the door of 209 Oakwood with a proposition that would eventually take Bill away from commercial art, away from Winnipeg, and into his lifelong career as a film maker.

8
——

QUETICO

"THE SINGING WILDERNESS," Sigurd Olson wrote, "has to do with the calling of the loons, northern lights, and the great silences of a land lying northwest of Lake Superior. It is concerned with the simple joys, the timelessness and perspective found in a way of life that is close to the past. I have heard the singing in many places, but I seem to hear it best in the wilderness lake country of the Quetico–Superior, where travel is still by pack and canoe over the ancient trails of the Indians and voyageurs."[1]

In the landscape of rock, green and shining water that became Bill Mason's home away from home, no expanse was more influential than the Canadian Shield, west of Lake Superior. In his 1988 book, *Song of the Paddle*, when he writes: "Some people hear the song in the quiet mist of a cold morning; others hear it in the middle of a roaring rapids . . . ," the echoes of Sigurd Olson are obvious. Bill's thinking about wilderness in general was grounded in Quetico.

By the 1950s, Quetico, Olson's "singing wilderness" that touched the jurisdictions of Ontario, Manitoba and Minnesota, was already a veteran of thirty years of development skirmishes, on both sides of the international border. In Canada, this superb canoe country had been protected by the establishment of Quetico Provincial Park, and in the United States the act to set out the Boundary Waters Canoe Area Wilderness did more or less the same thing; however, echoes of Illinois landscape architect Paul B. Riis's call for "a road to every lake" and plans to dam a chain of lakes right in the heart of Quetico–Superior persisted. The fiercest fight raged in the mid-1940s over an airplane ban in the area. In 1946 there were fly-in fishing camps and resorts built or being built on almost all the major canoe routes; the little town of Ely, Minnesota, had become the largest inland seaplane base in the world. On December 17, 1949, when President Truman signed an executive order to prevent planes from flying over the Superior National Forest—the first time in U.S. history that air traffic had been controlled for reasons other than public safety or national defence—the land developers vowed to get their way.

At the heart of this protracted development skirmish was Sigurd Olson, the American writer and naturalist who spent his life fighting to understand wilderness and to educate people about the value of nature undisturbed. Although schooled in the natural sciences at Northland College in Ashland, Wisconsin, and later at the University of Wisconsin at Madison, Olson was a pioneering conservation voice, asserting that wilderness was not just a matter of scenery and land to use for this or that, or some kind of scientific abstraction; but a cultural matter linked deeply to the human spirit.[2] Olson led the way for Bill, putting into words in his books the many sensations of wilderness travel, not least of which was the central message that nature was something to be treated gently and with respect—something worth fighting for.

Among those in Canada of similar ilk was film maker Christopher Chapman, who, after attending vocational school in Toronto and working for six years in advertising, was hired by the Quetico Foundation to make a film to take the wilderness fight to a wider audience. Like Bill, members of the Quetico Foundation had seen his first film, *The Seasons*, and knew that this was the film maker they wanted to promote the wilderness values of Quetico Provincial Park.

In the winter of 1956, as Mason traipsed around with his slides, telling people about his wonderful trip on the Winnipeg and Canyon rivers, Chapman took the train into Quetico to get his bearings and do some winter shooting. From there he journeyed west to Winnipeg to meet the enthusiastic canoeist he had heard about. It was a meeting that would establish a lifelong personal and professional connection for both men. As one of a half-dozen speakers who eulogized Bill at his memorial service in Ottawa in November 1988, Chapman remembered turning up at the front door of 209 Oakwood:

> I knocked on the door of this house; the door opened, I didn't see anybody! I looked down, and here was this BOY! And I thought—I was expecting some old trapper-canoeist that I was going to put in my film! Well. This guy was *so* enthusiastic; he was *so* excited and so I thought, "There's nothing I can do but have him along!"

On this first visit, Mason showed Chapman "God Revealed" and took him down to the basement to see the tabernacle set-up. Chapman remembers being a little overwhelmed by Bill's detailed recollections of *The Seasons* and his rapturous praise for the film. In among Bill's chattering, Chapman was able to wiggle in a word or two of his own and explain what he was trying to do with the Quetico film. He was trying to capture the spirit of wilderness. Hearing that, Mason was more keen than ever, hopping all over the place, talking, talking, talking. Following this initial meeting, Chapman wrote to Bill to ask formally for his help with the film.

In his best artist's scrawl, Bill wrote to Christopher Chapman on June 6, 1956, to confirm his interest in the offer:

> Dear Chris,
>
> I was overjoyed to receive your letter and I am definitely interested in working with you in Quetico. I will arrange to be free for as long a time as you need me whenever we decide is the best time to shoot the film. . . .
>
> As far as salary goes I believe I told you I was making $50 a week, I am now making $65, but anything around $50 is perfectly all right with me, Chris.

As you mentioned there are many plans to make and things to discuss and there are lots of questions I would like to ask you but I will make this letter short so I can get it in the mail.

Just to give you a rough idea of when the colours change around the Kenora district which should be about the same as Quetico I would say about Sept. 20. From your letter I gathered that you would like a couple of weeks of summer foliage and a couple of weeks of fall. To play safe I would think that August 24 to the end of Sept. would be the best period of the year. However I will send some slides to you with dates on them and you can see for yourself how they changed last year.

I am going canoeing this weekend and I thought I would take along the camera to experiment with camera movements from the canoe. If there is anything you would like me to try I would be only too happy to do so.

I have good news to report on my biblical film. We finished shooting the model of the tabernacle and just got our work print back, and are quite pleased with the results. The camera movements, which we did by sliding the camera on Masonite guides, are reasonably smooth. The effect we got by moving the camera towards the tabernacle, past tents, people, rocks, foliage etc., is really amazing. I am glad it's finished and in the can, next I will shoot the animation but I won't do that until next winter. I grew some more grey hairs for a couple of weeks because they lost the film in the mail but found it after 3 weeks.

Well, Chris, I guess I'll say goodbye for now and get this in the mail. Thanks for the Land Fellowship bulletin, I found it very interesting and I would like to look into it further.

Mason took leave of his job at Phillips/Gutkin in time to assume his customary place on the staff of the boys' camp in August that summer. For the first week, he was leader of Cabin 13; the second week, he counselled another group at a more rustic outpost camp that had been established on Cache Island, slightly east of MacKinnon Island and the main camp. Later in the summer he led canoe trips with some of the more senior boys on trips he had pioneered for the camp, loops in the Shoal Lake/Lake of the Woods vicinity called the "Short Circuit" (three days) and the "Long Circuit" (five days). But, come August 28, as he had done the previous year with Peter Buhr, he took the *Pioneer II*, the camp launch, to Kenora with his Plycraft canoe, spent the night, and the next day boarded an eastbound train for the Lakehead, where he met up with Christopher Chapman.

Chapman was shocked by the vision that stepped off the train. Somewhere between camp and Port Arthur, Bill had stopped at a barber's and had a haircut so severe that it left his tanned face, neck and ears ringed with a fluorescent strip of white skin:

> Here came this young, excited young boy, and . . . to my *horror* he'd just had a haircut and was absolutely pure white all the way around! It *shattered* me because he didn't look anything like the image of the canoeist I wanted in the film. I remember for a long time we used to have to get ashes out of the fireplace and darken all the areas that had been cleared of hair! Fortunately, he had his hat on most of the time! God, it was a blow.

Hair or no hair, three weeks in Quetico with Chapman amounted to a crash course in film—Bill's only formal training, a twenty-one-day apprenticeship with a real film maker. The two of them travelled in a rented Plycraft canoe. Mason was quick to learn that, with a stripped-down crew like this—one film maker, one "actor"—there was time to do very little else than tend to the business of the film. He had with him his little red diary but managed only a two-page summary of this pivotal period in his life:

> August 30   Arrived in Quetico with Chris Chapman. We rode on the same train in Fort William. We spent a couple of days at Roger Thew's planning trip. Flew over most of Quetico.

Plane set us down on a lake where we started our journey. We were travelling on the Maligne river system. Passed three beautiful falls and portage into Agnes Lake by middle portage. It was murder. Worse portage I ever made.

Camped on Agnes, photographed huge cliffs.

Caught 15 lb. northern. Ate it for three days.

Picked up by plane dropped on Tanner Lake. Paddled up stream on Maligne River, then downstream. Saw many evidences of historic trail, Dawson trail. Picked up on Lac La Croix.

Spent couple more days at Roger's.

Time spent in Quetico involved lugging equipment, helping Chapman set up, paddling in various sequences, setting up and taking down camp, holding this, getting that—glamorous, not. Chapman was intent on making his film and is sure that no actual teaching went on between them. "It was just Bill's observation of the way I operated. It was as simple as that. At the time the camera was *incredibly* simple, and you didn't have through-the-lens viewfinders or anything. You were very limited in what you could do filmically or photographically." Still, if the congruency between *Quetico* and all of Bill's later films is any indication of what Bill learned on this shoot, this time together was of profound significance in Bill's development as a film maker.

Quetico opens with a relief map—more like a plaster-of-paris model than a two-dimensional depiction. On the soundtrack are the echoes of French-Canadian voyageur songs. The commentary is very sparse, leaving music and visual imagery to carry the burden of the film's message. There are many detailed close-ups of ice, water, plant life, rocks and reflections on water. Scenes of the brilliant red canoe—in mist, in white-water, from cliff top—are balanced by scenes from the canoeist's point of view as he makes his way through rapids. A slow pan caresses the side of an empty bobbing red canoe, passes the bow and moves out along a drooping painter tied to Bill's moccasin-clad foot as he relaxes in the Canadian Shield sunshine. And twice in the film a majestic osprey appears, circling in a cerulean sky, plaintively calling. The film closes with a pull-focus on the 3D map, giving the impression that the film maker and the canoeist are leaving the area on some magical rocket, no tire track or whiff of exhaust remaining. Every one of these devices would recur in Bill's future films.

The paddler one sees in *Quetico* kneels in a manner that would make only Manitoba Pioneer Camp canoe instructor Chuck Tipp proud. The paddling technique looks awkward and unpractised, and the way in which Mason negotiates whitewater could charitably be described as "tentative." But the character of Mason-the-paddler in his lone red canoe is essentially the character he would become in his own canoeing films: the hat, the plaid shirt, the bandana, the Calvin Rutstrum belt knife, the jeans, the moccasins and the red and white–topped grey work socks (which so predictably ignite as they dry by the crackling fire). The only exception is the hair, which is dark; the beard, which is absent; and the face, which is fresh and young. A monastic sweatshirt hood covers Bill's head in the opening canoe shot, but, other than that, the severe haircut is adeptly camouflaged by blacking from the fire and strategic use of silhouette exposures when the white-walled head looms large.

Being with Christopher Chapman in the field for this brief period had an air of excitement for Bill that was eclipsed only by his first viewing of the finished product. As the deep voice of a narrator intoned, "Northwest of the Great Lakes, between Superior and Lake of the Woods, there is a vast network of smaller lakes and rivers. A region once famous as the water highway of the singing voyageurs, whose birchbark canoes carried explorer, trader and traveller across the continent in search of trade and discovery," Bill was overcome with emotion. His euphoric letter to Chapman after seeing it for the first time caught his raw zeal:

> I scarcely know how to begin this letter. I just saw "Quetico" and I haven't the words to describe the sensation it gave me. . . . Since I saw it night before last, I've been walking in a daze as scene after scene passes before me. I spent most of last night reliving each scene. Never have I wanted to see anything again so badly. . . .
>
> The things that stick in my mind are,

— The mist scenes
— The echoing cry of the loon
— Tremendous mixes red leaves to red canoe
— Canoe blocking out screen then night scene. Fabulous
— Music and cutting of rapid sequence was fantastically tremendous and looked much more exciting than it was. Fishing sequence great cutting
— Just enough narration? I'm not sure. I would like to see it again before I say.
— Script was really great.
— Voyageur songs! I darn near paddled my chair down the aisle.
— Winter scenes and music was breathtaking
— And so on and so on.

Bill eventually ran out of words and he moved on to his main criticism of the film: it was too short. "It seemed to end right in the middle for no reason at all," he wrote, quickly countering: "they say it's better to quit while the audience want more." The letter concluded by sharing with Chapman his restlessness with life as a commerical artist in Winnipeg, and his desire to find again the fulfilment he'd experienced in Quetico.

Between the summer of 1956, when *Quetico* was shot, and the spring of 1958, when Bill viewed the completed film, much had happened. Bill's sights had gradually turned outward, away from Winnipeg and away from his work in commercial art. He had come down from the high of working with Chapman and found himself re-employed not at Phillips/Gutkin but at Brigden's, the competition. When that palled, he briefly tried working at Eastman/McConnell, another Winnipeg advertising firm, and finally ended up at his old desk at PGA, with a promotion and a raise! But he was far from satisfied with his work as a commercial artist.

With Chapman's encouragement, Bill wrote an unsolicited letter to Colin Low at the National Film Board, enquiring about the possibility of work and about their interest in a cross-Canada canoeing film. Meanwhile, Christopher Chapman wrote to Budge Crawley of Crawley

Films—"Film Producers for Industry, Government, Education, Television" (according to their letterhead of the day)—introducing Mason and asking about the possibility of work. At the time, other than PGA and the NFB, Crawley Films was about the only film game in the country. It was Chapman's letter that would eventually take Bill east to work for Crawley Films in Ottawa.

Never one to sit still for long, and always pushing himself to new challenges, Bill produced a photojournalistic account of his time in Quetico that was published in the August 30, 1958, edition of the *Star Weekly*, featuring a dozen of Bill's colour slide images of Quetico, its vistas, animals and flowers. A biographical sidebar to the photo-story contains a black and white photo of Mason, hair slicked back, with bandana and plaid shirt, over the headline: "Petrified by Skunk." In the following text, Mason describes leaving open the front flap of his tent and being joined in the night by an errant Pépé le Pew. In this first published article he writes:

> Visions of paddling home in my bathing suit danced through my mind as the skunk explored the foot of my sleeping bag, soon began a "nose-to-toes" relationship which struck terror to my heart. With iron-nerved gentleness, I eased from the bag and tip-toed toward the door. I kept my courage through four careful steps which took me almost to safety, then fled into the night in stark panic. Unbelievably, no odor of skunk came to me as I stood shivering in my skivvies. I stood cautious watch for a frigid half-hour until the skunk emerged and ambled quietly into the bush. I slipped back inside, barricaded the door, finally found sleep—and dreamed of skunks.

Clearly, even in this early piece of writing, Mason has learned the value of editing and selective recounting in the telling of a story. If in fact the skunk encounter did happen in Quetico, his partner in the venture, Christopher Chapman, seems mysteriously to have disappeared, at least in this part of the tale. A last paragraph in the sidebar makes this parenthetical addition:

My most concentrated dose of canoe adventuring came when I worked with Chris Chapman of Toronto while he made his widely lauded film, Quetico. It was also my first venture into the acting department—I'm the canoeist in the film. Quetico was shown at the Stratford film festival in July, will have general distribution in Canada this autumn. It helps explain why I'm an enthusiast about canoe trips—and Quetico.

The publication of this story was just one of many moves that repositioned Bill for a career change. Since *Quetico*, he was thinking differently about who he was and what he might do. Throughout his whole life, careful treatment of the natural world was a religious imperative. To denigrate the natural world was to defy God. To love nature was to love the Creator, for God's hand created the natural world. That was reason enough to treat the wilderness with the utmost of care; and reason enough to spend his whole life as a film maker celebrating the wilderness. But Christopher Chapman focused Bill's attention on the ecological, as opposed to the religious or spiritual, consequences of destroying nature.

In his unfinished memoirs, Bill acknowledged this important moment in his life:

> One other thing happened to me while I was with Chris. Around the campfire at night Chris shared his concern for the natural world and the wilderness. Up to now I had been a perfectly normal, happy person. For the first time I heard about the detrimental effects of herbicides, fertilizers and in general our ruthless treatment of the land. It was as though I had come of age and the knowledge took some of the simple joys out of nature watching. But at the same time it launched me in the direction of environmental concerns. With my new knowledge, I could never go back. One of the organizations I joined was Land Fellowship. Chris had been one of the originators and [a] driving force behind the organization. Their research and knowledge was impressive but they were like a voice crying in the wilderness. Very few people were listening.

Wanting to move forward in his life, Bill travelled to Ontario, met Budge Crawley in Ottawa, filmed with Chapman on the French River, and pretty well made up his mind that a move east was what he wanted. Back in Winnipeg he restlessly made the rounds of Brigden's, Eastman/McConnell, and Paul, Phelan and Perry. Finally, his dream came true. On the recommendation of Christopher Chapman, and very likely a nudge from Wilber Sutherland as well, Budge Crawley offered Bill a job in the Animation Department at Crawley Films. In late spring Mason wrote to Chapman in a letter headed with a cartoon character (in plaid shirt) jumping for joy. "WHOOPIE!," it said in bold block letters; "I start at Crawleys on July 2."

9

EARLY DAYS AT MEECH LAKE

ON A SMOKY GATINEAU MORNING, Bill opens the top of his sleeping bag, props himself up on an elbow and peers out, his eyes following the smooth surface of Meech Lake to a point where the silver of water and the swirling whiteness of the air meld into one. Just visible is the steeply banked west side of the lake, with its luminous spring greens texturing the fog. Bill rises and heads to the water to wash. A startled loon trips the silence, then, like a circus clown, comically runs and flaps its way into the mist. Circling overhead, the bird leaves only the squeak of its wings against still air over the campsite. With a splash of cold fresh Meech Lake water and a quick bowl of oatmeal, Bill crosses the lake in his red canoe, changes into slacks, shirt and tie he has stored in the car, and makes his way down the road to work at Crawley Films. With campsites like this so close to town, who needs an apartment?

For the first few months in the East, this was the life Bill led, working as an animator by day, and living in the manner of his heroes, the voyageurs, by night on an outcropping on the east shore of Meech Lake. It didn't dawn on him to worry about getting a place to stay with a solid roof. He was doing what he really wanted to do, and he could not resist taking advantage of the fact that the rugged Canadian

Shield country, which had been three hours' drive east of Winnipeg, was right there, just north of town. Bill had visited Christopher Chapman at Meech Lake soon after shooting *Quetico*. Now the place was *his* home. Parking his car on the road opposite Mel Alexander's rental cabins, where Chapman had stayed, he put his canoe in the pristine waters of Meech Lake and paddled across it, beneath the prime minister's formal summer house that sits like a castle to the south, to a campsite on a point on the opposite side of the lake, just out of sight. Here, surrounded by what little material wealth he had brought with him from Winnipeg, Bill would rise early, swim naked, as he'd learned to do at camp, eat simply, savour reflections, paddle the morning mists, and work days in town, often returning by starlight. It was a heady time in his life—hard for him to believe he was here since so much was changing, so quickly. He had moved from Winnipeg and was working in film. And back home, before leaving, he had proposed to Joyce Ferguson, his friend from Young People's. There was marriage to look forward to as well as more days like this. When he was alone, on the shores of Meech Lake, in the mist or under a pincushion sky, his life had a dream-like quality. And, although the work was routine, it too, at least in the beginning, was hard to believe.

His first assignment was to animate a script about molecular theory, a job he later called "the worst possible boring animation" one could conceive, yet it was *his* project, and the people around him were super. Through Crawley's he met many kindred spirits, both in the studio and elsewhere. And what he missed in the way of nourishment for the spirit during long hours of animating, he made up for on the first of many forays onto the wild rivers of eastern Ontario and western Quebec. With Pat, the eldest of the Crawley children, he would chug up to Glasgow Station, between Arnprior and Renfrew, on Highway 17, in the old Nash Rambler with the red canoe on top, drop southwest on Highway 508, and paddle the gentle rapids of the lower Madawaska River from Calabogie back to Arnprior, with one night in between. For an artist and an accomplished dreamer, these were magnificent days. On Madawaska weekends, and in the quiet and solitude of his canvas home on Meech Lake, Bill's imagination soared freely, unfettered by the judgment of home or anyone's schedule but his own.

Principal among these dreams was a plan to make a film about Manitoba Pioneer Camp. Wilber Sutherland, now the general director of Inter-Varsity Christian Fellowship, the camp's parent organization, had visited the camp the previous summer. Wilber had known Bill since his visit to speak to the ISCF at Kelvin High School a decade earlier; he had seen "God Revealed," Bill's slide show, several times. He had even spent time with Dr. Mitchell and the Elim Young People's Group in the basement rec room at 209 Oakwood, during which time he saw the artwork, model and set-up for the tabernacle project. Mason and Sutherland had settled down under a massive cedar tree on a point jutting out into Shoal Lake. They talked about Bill's interest in film, and Wilber shared with Bill his dream of one day making a film that would give parents a clear idea about the religious instruction their children received at camp.

In the filtered light beneath the big cedar, they talked. Reflexively, Sutherland the administrator turned to the pragmatics of the idea. Thinking out loud, looking out over the lake, he said, "I have no idea where we'd get the money for a project like this. I know for sure that Inter-Varsity has nothing in the budget right now for something like this."

Mason heard nothing about the money. His mind was off on another grand adventure. "I could come out here in the early spring to shoot break-up, and camp. Or maybe snowshoe in for a day in the winter. And then, in summer, I could just work around the kids and teens who would already be here." Then he paused and remembered that this was as yet a dream, but somehow closer to reality than the dreams he'd had in his room at 209 Oakwood or at Grand Beach. Coming down to earth again, Mason asked, "Hey, how serious are you about this idea?"

By the time the conversation was finished, the plan for Bill's first film commission was hatched. The two men shook hands as they rose and walked back towards the centre of camp. Mason's head was reeling with all of the things he would have to do—and learn to do—and how good it would be to tell his friend Christopher Chapman about this surprising turn of events. Sutherland, on the other hand, while convinced from the outset that Mason was the right person for the job, was awash with uncertainty about how he was going to execute the project financially. The camp was struggling. However keen the camp director would be on the idea of a film, there just was not a lot of spare cash for extra projects. The board of Inter-Varsity was another matter altogether. But as general director, Sutherland had the opportunity to sway board opinions, to some extent, in decisions about what the organization might do. He knew in his bones that this film was a good idea, and that Bill Mason had the faith, the talent and the passion to get the job done. Believing in the project would make it easier to sell.

In November, Christopher Chapman came to visit, just as things on the Meech Lake campsite were getting a little too chilly for comfort. Chapman introduced Bill to his old landlord, Mel Alexander, who rented cabins near the place where Bill parked his car. Fortuitously, the little cabin that Chapman had rented when he had worked for Crawley's a couple of years earlier was vacant. Mason rented it on the spot. And as the two of them broke camp, paddled Bill's tent and supplies from the other side of the lake, and then unloaded the animation stand and everything else out of Bill's jam-packed Nash Rambler, they talked incessantly about the Manitoba Pioneer Camp film. By now, Bill had a budget, such as it was, and he'd been dickering back and forth with Wilber about the content of the film. He showed his sketches and notes to Chapman over cups of tea in Mel Alexander's four-room log cabin. A blaze crackled in the leaky fieldstone fireplace. The two of them talked film—shots, angles, exposures—Chapman the two-film veteran, Mason the artist with a dream.

Back in Winnipeg, Bill's fiancée, Joyce, was caught up in prenuptial excitement. She had fallen madly in love on those clandestine cake-and-coffee dates, so much so that her classmates in the nurses' residence would come to help her dress in the complicated starched white nurse's uniform of the day to make sure that she didn't appear on her hospital floor with pieces crooked or missing altogether. While Bill was planning for a filming honeymoon, starting in a canoe at Manitoba Pioneer Camp on Shoal Lake, followed by travel west and east to other Pioneer camps across the country, Joyce was working with her mom and Sadie Mason, organizing matters of matrimonial protocol. She was ecstatic about the prospect of marrying this artist adventurer and heading off into the blue.

As late as a week before the wedding, Bill was nowhere to be found. The *Winnipeg Free Press*, under the headline "Mother Entertains For Bride Elect," informed the city of Winnipeg that Mrs. Duncan J.

Ferguson, Fleet Avenue, entertained Friday afternoon and evening in honour of her daughter Joyce, whose marriage to William Mason was to be held the following Saturday. The paper detailed who was received by Mrs. Ferguson and her daughter, who presided over the teacups, who assisted, and who was in charge of the gift rooms, but it gave no clues about the activities of the errant bridegroom elect, who was dashing around Winnipeg in jeans and T-shirt, picking up film and other last-minute supplies for the commencement of the camp film.

For the important trousseau tea, the only prenuptial event for which Bill was issued an ultimatum to appear, he turned up late, bearded, and in his greasy old clothes, claiming that his car had broken down. He walked into the tea in this state, took one look at the expressions on the faces of his mother, his future mother-in-law and his horrified betrothed, and blurted, "I'll come back later."

Uncomfortable as he was with fuss and fancy clothes, Bill did go through with the wedding on May 16, and the *Free Press* noted that the bride wore

> . . . an original floor length gown of ivory silk peau-de-soie designed on Princess lines. The fitted bodice featured lily point sleeves and a bateau neckline decorated with small inserts of Swiss guipure lace. The full skirt drifted to a slight train. A small coronet of matching lace held her elbow length veil of pure silk illusion and she carried a cascade of Joanna Hill roses and ivy.

By the time the wedding announcement was published, Joyce had packed away her peau-de-soie and coronet of matching lace, trading them for boots, raingear and a paddle. The paper's cryptic reference to "a wedding trip to points East" masks the real nature of the honeymoon (about which both sets of parents were a little embarrassed), which began in a canoe on the Manitoba/Ontario border destined for Manitoba Pioneer Camp on Shoal Lake. By this time, arrangements to make the film about Manitoba Pioneer had been ironed out with Wilber and the board of Inter-Varsity. Bill had been hired on as an IVCF staff member for as long as it took to shoot the film, and the plan was to spend their summer-long "honeymoon" filming at Shoal Lake and at Pioneer Camps in Alberta, British Columbia and Ontario, before going back to work at Crawley Films sometime in the fall of 1959.

With the red canoe atop Bill's Nash Rambler, they headed east to Kenora. The only real canoeing and outdoor activities that Joyce had done by that time were with the Elim Chapel Young People's, with Bill as leader. She trusted him implicitly but remembers being amazed that Bill could find his way through the island labyrinth in Lake of the Woods. They took their clothes; the camera, tripod and some film; and a little bit of dried food and flour, expecting to be fed when they arrived at MacKinnon Island. To their surprise the camp was deserted, still completely boarded up for winter. "We didn't want to break into the kitchen," recalls Joyce. "My new husband was going to provide us with fish. Well! What a laugh! Bill never was much of a fisherman."

By this time, Bill—or "Paddles," as he was now known at camp— was starting to develop a reputation as a seasoned and experienced wilderness canoeist, even though his fishing still left something to be desired. He and Joyce pitched a tent and made do with bannock, tea and the small amount of dehydrated food they had brought with them, until the regular summer staff arrived. In later years, Manitoba Pioneer Camp lore had it that Paddles and his new bride had been found starving on the end of the dock, too weak to lift their heads. "We were hungry, and we were really glad to see people when the work crew arrived," admits Joyce, "but it wasn't all that bad."

Nevertheless, Joyce's surprise on arrival at the camp with this man to whom she had committed herself for the rest of her life was recorded in her diary notes:

> Camped on a small island in Canoe Lake (Wow!) Lots of firewood and ideal camping spot. Slept wonderfully well (thank goodness) Broke camp about 10am Thursday and arrived at Pioneer at 4pm. No one on island. No food no nutting! Boy this is living!

The Masons were assigned to "Stuga," a cozy little frame cabin off on its own beyond the last camper cabin, looking south across Shoal

Lake. In the days before the campers arrived, the two of them lugged the tripod and Bill's Ciné Special all over the island, just as Christopher Chapman had done in Quetico, filming frogs, snakes, bugs, birds, crayfish—anything that moved—in the hope that this footage could later be cut into the finished film. Bill used Joyce's hands if anything needed to be held on camera, knowing that they could pass for a young camper's hands in the finished film. By night, they sat chatting by the fire in Stuga, on the three-legged overstuffed couch, as yellow light from the fire flickered on the varnished wooden walls and back to the polished fieldstone fireplace and chimney. And as the evenings warmed into June, provided the bugs weren't too bad, they would sit on the great sloping rock at the water's edge, watching stars reflected in the calm surface of Shoal Lake as, behind them, candlelight from inside the cabin illuminated three twelve-paned windows across the front of their first shared home.

When the campers arrived, Bill disappeared, leaving Joyce a little bewildered. While Bill lined up a counsellor and cabin group to paddle in his movie, Joyce—always the willing one—found herself helping in the kitchen. Then, when the nurses arrived, she assisted in the camp infirmary; and when it became clear that the camp was one counsellor short, Joyce took on the position for a cabin of young boys for the session. Bill single-mindedly began shaping camp events to suit his needs, disrupting meals and campfires with his photography. Joyce cringed from time to time, but never more so than the night Bill "borrowed" a set of lights without asking:

> I remember being *so* embarrassed because he stole these lights, because they needed them for a campfire or something. Bill stole them for his filming. I couldn't believe it! I remember feeling so upset. I felt *so* responsible. It took me a while, but it was right then and there, that first summer, I realized I wasn't responsible for these things he did—otherwise I would have been in a state all the time.

This decision Joyce made so early in her life with Bill would be her operating principle for the rest of their time together. She supported

102

Bill, and loved him, but, in her mind, he, and only he, was responsible for what he chose to do. The love and support she was able to provide her husband, as a result of this decision, was unconditional. To outsiders the freedom Bill enjoyed within the family to pursue his career was often misinterpreted; he was seen to be a man out of control, taking advantage of the good graces of his mate. In fact, the freedom he had was in large measure given to him when Joyce made that decision during their first summer together.

As the camp session got under way, Bill set out in canoes with counsellor Wolfgang Phillipi, five teenage campers, and another junior leader, who paddled with Bill and served as his assistant. Later Bill would say that this first filming trip, over which he had charge, was done without training of any kind—it "just sort of happened." The truth was he had had more training than he was aware of during his time in Quetico with Christopher Chapman. The shooting Bill did was patterned substantially on observation of his mentor in action three summers earlier. Bill's natural inventiveness added to those tricks. In the course of a month on Shoal Lake, travelling from campsite to campsite, the group circumnavigated MacKinnon Island, stopping among the pines on Cash Island and Indian Pipe Island, and filming a cliff-jumping, swimming sequence on Long Island. Often Bill would hike to points of prospect on rocky outcroppings high above the lake, leaving the young crew to while away time until they got the shirt-wave signal or heard a hoot from on high indicating that they were to make their way on some predetermined lake path in their red canoes.

With the Ciné Special camera, Bill had no idea of the exact images that were being recorded on film. But following Chapman's filmic lead and his own creative impulses, he ran himself ragged, rising before dawn to catch the mist and magic of early morning, working to get ahead of the crew all day, canoeing out on the lake after everyone else was tired and settled in for the evening, and staying up late into the night scouting or planning his shots for the next day. And even without extensive film training, Mason intuited enough on this first film outing to cover his angles—to shoot the campers landing and getting out of their canoes from a water vantage and again from the campsite perspective, and maybe from far away and from close in as well. He knew

103

enough to zoom in and out on whitewater scenes that caught his eye. When he was struck by the beauty of a static image, such as a lichen-encrusted rock in the evening sun, he panned first one way and then the other, to give him latitude at the editing stage. Exposures, especially when shooting into the sun or with low-light situations—around the campfire, for example—were a matter of guesswork based on his experience with still photography. The exposed film was packed away and, in due course, shipped to Crawley Films in Ottawa for processing. A phone call from a Crawley technician assuring him that the footage was okay from a technical standpoint was all he had to go on that what he was doing was on track.

The crew was finally excused from their service with the zealous film maker, and the boys returned to camp. Joyce finished her counselling job. After Bill filmed a few pick-up shots around the camp, they packed up their belongings and paddled back out to their car, in Kenora.

Joyce and Bill car-camped their way west for a short-lived visit to Alberta Pioneer Ranch Camp, where Bill's virulent allergy to horses forced a hasty return to the road. They continued to Pioneer Pacific, a similar children's camp on an island, much like the MacKinnon Island set-up, just off Vancouver Island. These visits were not so much for filming as for gaining an appreciation of the Pioneer Camp ethos as embodied in these other summer operations. They then headed back to the Lake of the Woods for a visit to the Inter-Varsity installation of university-age young people called "Campus in the Woods," and then farther east, to Ontario Pioneer Camp near Huntsville, north of Toronto. If Joyce thought arriving at Manitoba Pioneer Camp in May with no food or accommodation was "living," that definition was further stretched when they arrived on the shores of Meech Lake to begin their life together, tired after their cross-country honeymoon, to find that Bill's cabin at Mel Alexander's had been rented, in the absence of notice from Bill about his future plans.

Fortunately, Budge and Judy Crawley, who lived on a farm in the Gatineau Hills not far away, offered Bill and Joyce the use of Christopher Chapman's modest house trailer parked in their back pasture. In his unfinished memoirs, Bill recalls Joyce's frightening introduction to farm life:

One morning as she lay in the sun in front of the trailer she was awakened by a vibration in the ground. She looked up to see a herd of stampeding cattle thundering down on her. She leaped into the trailer and watched as they lumbered by. Soon the cause of the stampede appeared over the brow of the hill. It was Budge Crawley himself driving them. He could have passed for one of the bulls himself with his great hairy chest. When Joyce told him that he had nearly gotten her killed, he laughed as only Budge could. He said, "I can see the headlines now back in Winnipeg. 'Local girl killed in cattle stampede.'" Then he disappeared with the cattle.

Tents and trailers and cattle were finally behind the newlyweds when the snow flew that fall and they were able to move back into Mel Alexander's log cabin with their scant worldly goods and seventeen cans of film from their summer of shooting. Not least of those relieved to see Bill and Joyce finally settled in the East was Sadie, who was furious with the way Bill had dragged his bride all over the countryside when they should have been nesting. Joyce's parents weren't too impressed either. Neither set of parents, in fact, was all that pleased with the marriage. The Fergusons were suspicious of this character their only daughter had fallen for, who had changed jobs so many times, to say nothing of whisking their only daughter off into the wild. Sadie and Bill Sr. didn't have anything in particular against Joyce, but were prone to judge everything and anything the children decided to do. Thinking back on this, Joyce remarked:

> Leaving Winnipeg was the only way we could have survived because we would have had too much interference. We weren't doing things the way they were supposed to be done. If we'd been closer in miles, it wouldn't have worked. We had to move. One set of parents told the other about what we were doing, and everything we did was wrong.

For Bill and Joyce, nothing they could have done would have been better for beginning their life together. This first summer of adventure, their movements shaped by the force of Bill's desire to film, tested and confirmed their compatibility and love for each other. And this foundation, combined with the Meech Lake base of family operations and Bill's love of his work, established the template for their life together. The last element fell into place as they unpacked their boxes in the cabin overlooking banks of autumn colour on the opposite shore of Meech Lake: Joyce quietly decided, perhaps influenced by Bill's enthusiasm for the film life he saw before him, not to continue her career in nursing. For better or worse, Bill and his career became Joyce's life; it was a decision that she took willingly and with great expectation, one that would tie her to the highs and lows of an artist's struggle, one that would take her to Hollywood and to dinners with Queen Elizabeth; it was a decision she would ultimately have to defend to friends, neighbours and family, but which she would never really regret.

The greater Ottawa community in which the Masons found themselves in the autumn of 1959 was a place of great prospect. They had moved to the centre of the private Canadian film universe, Crawley Films having the edge on industrial, commercial, government, instructional and animated film making in Canada, with open connections to New York and California. Ottawa was also the home of Eric Morse, the man who would become dean of recreational canoeing in Canada and another, if unsung, mentor for Bill.

About the time Bill was born, Eric Morse was twenty-five years old and studying for his Master of Arts degree at Queen's University. As a graduate student, Morse read Harold Innis's *The Fur Trade in Canada: An Introduction to Canadian Economic History*. Using a basic commodities approach to understanding economic history, *The Fur Trade in Canada* examined the ecology and ethology of the beaver but, as he did in all his works—whether exploring the cod fishery, forestry, agriculture, mining or the fur trade—Innis, like Eric Morse who followed, celebrated the canoe as a central and grounding element in almost all aspects of Canada's economic development. When not studying, Eric Morse was paddling in eastern Ontario and western Quebec, honing skills that would take him to Lake Superior and Quetico, and eventually to first recreational descents on many of Canada's north-flowing rivers.

Passion for fur-trade history and canoeing inevitably led Morse to long and exotic canoe journeys along the river trade routes of Canada, and, as he published articles about these (and eventually a book, *Fur Trade Canoe Routes of Canada/Then and Now*), many young dreamers, including Bill Mason, hung on his every word, eventually setting out on extended canoe adventures of their own.

At a dinner party in 1951, Morse, then national director of the Association of Canadian Clubs, teamed up with friends and diplomats and formed a group of paddlers the Ottawa press dubbed "the Voyageurs." This group included Blair Fraser, Ottawa editor of *Maclean's* magazine (who would die in a rapid on the Petawawa River); Omond Solandt, chairman of the Defence Research Board of Canada; and, later, Minnesotan Sigurd Olson. Together they paddled Quetico through the early 1950s, and the Churchill River (the trip about which Olson wrote his epic canoe story *The Lonely Land*), and worked their way to the Northwest Territories on the trails of the original voyageurs, surveyors, engineers and clergy. In doing so, they established themselves as the first recreational paddlers on many of these historic routes.

In the winter of 1959–60 the Voyageurs were making plans to paddle the Parsnip and Peace rivers in the footsteps of the explorer Alexander Mackenzie, but, as it happened, all of the crew except Morse and his wife, Pamela, were otherwise committed. Not wanting to be down in a "deep ditch" crawling with surveyors and engineers preparing for the Bennett Dam, as they would have been had they stuck to their original Peace River route, Eric and Pamela Morse prepared instead for a one-canoe traverse of Lake Superior's north shore, from Fort William to Sault Ste. Marie. It was Eric Morse's published account of this trip that inspired Bill a couple of years later to take the north-shore trip, thus starting his lifelong relationship with Lake Superior.[1]

At Meech Lake, still on a minimal staff salary with Inter-Varsity, Bill and Joyce converted the tiny front bedroom in their cabin to a makeshift studio and were sorting through the seventeen cans of film. One of the first projects was the construction of a map like the one Bill remembered from Chapman's film *Quetico*. To get the three-dimensional effect for the map, he painted in thick oil paint on a sheet of glass, and then, using a technique that is largely a Mason innovation, he painted cloud scenes on another pane of glass that he affixed above the first. Using the lights on the tabernacle animation stand from 209 Oakwood, he could cast cloud shadows on the painted landscape and create an even more dramatic effect. An animated zoom shot down into a lake area on the map could be dissolved to a live overhead shot of a lake, creating a powerful geographic effect in his film. For the editing, Budge Crawley gave them permission to work at Crawley Films.[2] Joyce and Bill, or Bill alone, would carry in the marked-up work prints of their summer footage, edit through the night on Crawley's professional equipment, and then slide out and back home in time for the Crawley staff to return to their stations in the morning.

Speaking to people later about the early days of his film career, Bill was quite candid about his lack of knowledge about film and film editing, and about how the compulsive cutting and recutting of his camp film taught him everything he needed to know:

> I knew nothing about proper procedure, so developed my own, which I would use through my film career. I broke all the material down into subject-matter and put each on a reel. I then hung the reels on nails driven into the walls of the cabin. Everyone in the industry said a cameraman should never edit his own footage. On the contrary, a cameraman who wants to and has the ability has every advantage over an editor. Even as I shot, I knew instinctively where stuff was going to go.

From time to time, his co-producer on the camp film, Wilber Sutherland, would travel to Ottawa from Toronto to check in. By now he had invested heavily of his own time and energy in the film, largely because of his personal interest in Bill and in the project, but also because he had the daunting task of keeping the Inter-Varsity board of directors at bay while Bill's estimated cost for the film escalated from its original $3,000 towards its final cost of about $10,000. Wilber was the only person who had any idea of the endless variations of the footage with which Bill and Joyce had been experimenting as Bill learned through experience the art of film making. Wilber remembered the endless arguments:

Bill with his mother and his sister at Grand Beach on Lake Winnipeg in 1941. Elizabeth is newly five years old and growing. In four years, she will be as tall and heavy as her sixteen-year-old brother Bill.

Thomas and Elizabeth Mason, Bill's paternal grandparents, dressed for church. A stern and powerful woman, Granny Mason had a profound effect on Bill's upbringing.

The 1943 graduating class on the front steps of Riverview Elementary School in south Winnipeg. Bill *(top left, second to back row)* is fourteen and noticeably smaller than his grade 8 classmates. It will be several years before his parents will get so concerned about his size that they will take him to the Mayo Clinic in Rochester, Minnesota, for hormone treatments to make him grow.

After being dubbed "Kelvin's gift to art" at his high school in Winnipeg, Bill went on to study at the Winnipeg School of Art. Taken in 1948 during his first year at commercial art school, probably a self-portrait, this photograph shows Bill in his first studio, a small room adjacent to his bedroom upstairs at 209 Oakwood Avenue where he spent long hours painting, drawing and dreaming.

Bill's first trip on Lake Superior was in 1962, along the coast from Marathon to Michipicoten Harbour, stopping along the way to fish, paint and photograph himself and his surroundings. By this time, Bill's self-portraiture was an art, involving careful setup of a canoe, water and sky, followed by a frantic scamper to get into position looking relaxed and natural.

Cutting the cake on 16 May 1959, flanked at the head table by best man Don Campbell and maid of honour Eileen Hildebrand.

After years of trying, Bill finally got a budget from the NFB in 1963 which allowed him to load up the Land Rover with his pal Blake James and all their camera and camping gear, and travel from location to location, filming as they went.

Bill and Blake James put the finishing touches on the dummy to take Blake's place in the canoe that is dropped from a helicopter into Meech Lake during the shooting of *Rise and Fall of the Great Lakes*. The canoe was a square-backed clunker purchased locally that Bill and Blake reshaped with fiberglass and paint before annihilating it in the high-flying stunt.

Paddling his first favourite canoe, the 16' Chestnut Pal, Bill with tripod and rolling camera in the boat begins a point-of-view sequence in whitewater for *Rise and Fall of the Great Lakes*.

Lifelong friend and collaborator, Blake James, in full flying regalia—leather helmet, goggles, fur coat—with Mason-rigged mount for a 35mm movie camera to get point-of-view sequences for the flying film *Blake*, which earned Mason his second of two American Academy Award nominations.

Bill with Blake James, shooting an early scene for *Blake* in Blake's rented log cabin at Meech Lake, just up the hill from the cabin that was Bill and Joyce's first home in the east. Beside Bill is the hearth where the cabin sequences from *Paddle to the Sea* were filmed.

I would visit Ottawa and sit up all night with Bill debating over his latest version. I would argue vigorously for some scene and against another. Bill would agree. But the next time I saw the footage his choice would be in and mine out! We fought and argued night after night over every conceivable aspect of the film until gradually a sense of an editing philosophy emerged.

They see-sawed back and forth about the making of the film. Various working titles coalesced into the final title for the piece. At Wilber's suggestion, the film came to be called *Wilderness Treasure*. But there was much work yet to do. The project was already far over budget, and there was no possible way for Inter-Varsity to maintain their financial support for Bill and Joyce, no matter how modest.

Fortunately, about this time, Budge Crawley got a contract to produce *The Tales of the Wizard of Oz*, the first animated series for television. He was in dire need of artists and animators, and was prepared to pay $125 per week, excellent money by standards of the day. Bill, who in his first incarnation as a Crawley employee worked in the regular animation department, churning out commercials, titles and animated industrial films like the dreaded molecule movie, was hired to help set up the *Wizard of Oz* animation studio. It wasn't long before this exciting project drew to Ottawa Blake James and Barrie Nelson, from Phillips/Gutkin in Winnipeg. With these three lively Manitoban cartoonists at the centre of this massive project, the animation loft at Crawley Films became legendary for its antics.

Blake James, Barrie Nelson and Bill had known one another in Winnipeg, but it took the common project at Crawley Films in the rarefied air of the Crawley animation loft to allow them be both creative and crazy. They would head out on weekends to paddle the rivers around Ottawa, returning on Monday with grossly exaggerated tales of daring intrigue on the water. Colleagues at Crawley's dubbed them "the Madawaska River boys." An early issue of the Crawley in-house newsletter, *The Credit Union Crier*, features a typewritten article by Bill entitled "Down the Madawaska" describing their first two-day run from Calabogie towards the Ottawa River. Four of them—the three

Winnipeggers and the oldest Crawley son, Pat, Bill's previous partner on the Madawaska—spent as much time jumping off cliffs and bridges and swimming in falls as they did paddling. And when they moved downriver, they portaged, tracked or waded all rapids, to protect their canoes. Mason describes their "wading procedure," which is one whitewater technique that never made it into any of his subsequent books or films on canoeing:

> The bow man would drape himself over the bow with his feet hanging in the water. The stern man would pay out the rope attached to the stern as the bow man guided it around and between the rocks. In this way if the bow man stepped over his depth or lost his footing the stern man could pull him back or ease him downstream to the next rock. The whole purpose of wading was to keep the canoe from going so fast as to lose control and smash headlong into the rocks. Sometimes the water was only knee-deep and we could make good time. The width of the river determined the depth. Sometimes you could hardly float a matchbox through while at other times the *Queen Mary* could have made it nicely.

It was during the preparations for one of these wild paddling weekends that Barrie Nelson, Mason's friend from Phillips/Gutkin and Crawley's, happened to be in the boat house on Meech Lake where Bill kept his canoes and camping supplies. Looking at hardwood paddles hung on nails driven between the studs on the boat-house wall, he focused on one with a worn "NBL" stencilled in black letters across the blade. "Hey"—he poked in Bill's general direction—"where'd you get this paddle?"

"I found it at Grand Beach," Mason boasted.

"Found it!" Nelson said incredulously.

"Yeah," Mason said. "I found it. Actually, I found it in the reeds by the trestle to Victoria Beach in the lagoon. I stood it up by a tree and left it there for a couple of days. No one claimed it, so I brought it back to the cottage."

"Do you know what 'NBL' stands for?" Nelson barked.

"I don't know. Somebody's initials?" Mason guessed, grinning.

"No!" said Nelson triumphantly. "It stands for *Nelson's Boat Livery*! My parents owned that place where you could rent canoes and row boats."

Nelson plucked the paddle off the wall, cranked it under his arm and taunted Bill, "You're a paddle thief, Mason!"

And so began a rivalry that added to an already strong friendship between Mason and Barrie Nelson. The stolen-paddle story became part of every canoe trip the two of them took from that moment on.

And of course, like all good Winnipeggers, when the rivers froze, the boys turned to hockey, dragging much of the rest of the Crawley staff with them to outdoor skirmishes on ice surfaces around Ottawa. In the March 1962 edition of the Crawley Films *Credit Union Crier* there is much talk (and excellent pencil illustrations by Blake James) of the official line-up for the 1961–62 hockey season. At centre (predictably) was Number 11, "Mad-Man" Billy Mason. That year, Crawley's hockey team had a record of seven wins, five losses and three ties, for a total of seventeen points, thumping teams from Runge Press, TMC, Hudson's Hornet, CJOH and the men from Dustbane, the second-place team accumulating a miserable six points. The *Crier* reports that the executive of the league had a lot of trouble voting for the all-star team for 1961–62 but were able to carry out the task: Goal—Blake James; Defence—Ron Haynes and Jack White; Wing—Neville Smith; and Centre—Billy Mason. A note below the announcement indicates that the people who voted for the all-star team were, of course, Blake James, Ron Haynes, Jack White, Neville Smith and Billy Mason.

Tommy Glynn, the beleaguered production manager at Crawley Films and the man charged with the responsibility of getting these animators to produce to tight deadlines, learned to dread hockey nights. Invariably, on mornings following hockey, the all-stars' work stations in the animation loft would be spottily filled, with places left empty by animators who were too tired, too sore, or both, to struggle in to work.

When they did make it in, the work was exacting and repetitive. The best and fastest of the animators did about five or six 5- to 6-minute cartoons in a year. Story ideas were developed, and "pencil tests" were done in 16mm black and white film to show the producers at Rankin/Bass in

New York for approval. Once the go-ahead was given for a cartoon, the animators would begin the laborious process of drawing the cells that would be transferred to 35mm colour film for broadcast. Running speed of the 35mm film was 1,440 frames per minute, meaning that, even with so-called limited animation in which movement occurred in only every second frame, Bill and his colleagues would still have to produce in the order of 4,000 separate drawings for one program. The Rankin/Bass people were so pleased with the work of the Crawley animators that, in the middle of the series project, they offered a contract for the same crew to produce a feature-length animated film of the whole Wizard of Oz story. In a span of four years in the early 1960s, with people drifting in and out at different times, Crawley animators produced the Wizard of Oz feature and 120 episodes in the series.

In the middle of this whirlwind, Christopher Chapman called. In seconds, Bill put in his notice at Crawley's and left to visit Chapman at his parents' farm on Lake Simcoe for a couple of weeks to do the titles for a film Chapman was making about an archaeological dig at an ancient Iroquois village. Adding even more hype to an already bursting life, a call came in for Mason at the Chapman farm from Budge Crawley, not to chastise him for unceremoniously leaving the animation project, but to offer him a film assignment in the Arctic. Budge's wife, Judy, would be attending the Anglican Synod in Aklavik, and then travelling across the full span of the Canadian North with Bishop Marsh, visiting communities along the way. Judy was making a film about the Arctic for Shell Oil, and was offering Bill film stock, a much improved rendition of the Ciné Special movie camera, food and accommodation, and a seat on their bush plane in return for access to anything he filmed. After babbling "Yes," Mason got off the phone and breathlessly told his friend Chris the momentous news. Chapman smiled at Bill's good fortune. It wasn't until years later that Mason would learn it was his sly friend Chapman who had recommended him for the assignment in the first place.

He returned to Meech Lake in a flurry to tell Joyce of his good fortune and to gather together his kit for this dream-of-a-lifetime as-signment. When Bill had calmed enough to listen, Joyce had news too. She was pregnant. The baby would arrive just weeks after Bill's planned return from the North. Bill, of course, was elated to hear the news but

112

was unswerving in his one-track effort to get everything ready for the next big adventure. Life was a manic flurry from one project to the next, with no time to think about doings in the margins, and, besides, it would be months before the baby was born. He'd think about that later. For Joyce's birthday in November 1960, Bill gave his pregnant wife a massive Woods down-filled parka that fitted him, to go with his army mukluks, five-star sleeping bag, and fur-backed gauntlets. Joyce hugged and thanked him, especially for the hand-drawn cartoon card, and continued to assist with preparations. But in her inimitable way, when Bill's birthday rolled around in April, just before he set out with Judy Crawley, Joyce presented him with a shiny new woman's bicycle!

Amid the flurry of activity before Bill departed, they moved from Mel Alexander's up the road to another more spacious house owned by Dave and Moiya Wright, proprietors of The Snow Goose Canadiana shop in downtown Ottawa. The Wrights had built a new house closer to the main road, vacating their original frame bungalow higher up the hill, at the end of a steep driveway. The Wrights' rental house was much bigger than Mel Alexander's cabin, but, more to the point, it was right inside Gatineau Park, where the Masons could camp, paddle and ski, and it commanded a very pleasant view of the lake they had come to love. In one of the bedrooms, Bill set up his animation stand and pounded in nails to hang his precious reels of film. Life was full. Joyce wondered when something was going to give way.

In May 1961, Judy Crawley and Bill made their way from Ottawa to Edmonton on Trans-Canada Airlines, and then north, to the Aklavik Synod in the Mackenzie Delta, in a venerable DC-3 aircraft, where they met with Bishop Marsh and began their pan-Arctic tour in a Norseman on skis. From the moment pilot Rocky Parsons first threw a canvas shroud over the nose of the Norseman and lit the firepot under the big piston engine to metamorphose the crankcase oil from cement to molasses in the minus-forty-degree temperatures, Bill was entranced by the romantic image of this daring aviator. "Rocky and his Norseman were one," wrote Mason; "they were part of each other."

The four of them made their way east from Aklavik, stopping first at Inuvik to film the winter carnival, then on to Coppermine, Holman Island, and Cambridge Bay, sleeping in Anglican missions, as billets in the community, or as guests of the Hudson's Bay Company. At Holman Island, the HBC factor heard that Mason was interested in igloos and lined up a local Inuk to build one for him to film. Much to the consternation of the builder, with whom Mason had been billeted on that occasion, Bill watched the construction of the igloo with rapt attention and then moved in, leaving the Inuk to return home without his guest. Bill said that this was the best sleep he had had during the entire trip. It was absolutely soundless inside the igloo and not nearly as cold as outside. This knowledge and experience gained on Holman Island proved invaluable later in his career when he returned to the Arctic to film wolves. Igloos not only would be his solitary home for weeks on end but also would provide a hidden place from which to observe and film the elusive arctic wolves.

When the group arrived at Baker Lake, at the west end of Chesterfield Inlet, at the mouth of the Thelon River, Bill got the chance to film one of the last great igloo villages in the North:

> There must have been forty of them. Many of them were interconnected. I went down into what I thought was one igloo to find it was a huge igloo with many smaller igloos running off it where each family lived. There were wooden boxes for shelves. There was a wonderful eerie light that came in through the ice windows in the roof. It was tough to film because the humidity condensed on my camera and lenses. Outside I filmed way into the night. It never got completely dark at that time of year so there was always something interesting going on. Children practised with their dog whips or slid in the snow. Their faces and clothing were great subjects. I almost starved on the entire trip because I loved the evening light and would be out filming from afternoon well into the night. By the time I returned to where I was lodging, supper was usually long over and put away. I missed many a caribou dinner. I would have to settle for a Spam sandwich. Night after night it was the same. The hardest part about the shooting in these amazing conditions was rationing film.

This experience in the Arctic with Judy Crawley had a profound effect on Bill. He coddled his equipment in cold conditions and learned experientially about cold turning oil into paste, and pliable celluloid film into glass ribbons that would shatter with the slightest provocation. He confronted the problem of condensation—inside and outside the camera—when cold equipment was brought inside. He learned to make do, to improvise, to guess exposures when the light-meter reading was not to be trusted, and repeatedly had reaffirmed by the experience the importance of patience and ingenuity in carrying out the work of a film maker away from the controlled conditions of a studio. In Baker Lake, in particular, the nights he spent with the Inuit families in the igloo village found a place instantly in his imagination beside the storybook imagery of voyageurs and hardy adventurers. Besides providing technical education in igloo construction, which would later be used when he was on his own on Baffin Island filming wolves, the Baker Lake igloo experience taught him that arctic living was not so much about "survival"—as southern equipment manufacturers led people to believe with their advertising—as it was about people living comfortably and happily in a way that was compatible with the strictures of their land and climate.

During the six weeks Bill was away in the North, Joyce filled her days by looking after the Wrights' five children as her pregnancy progressed. Physically, Joyce blossomed in Bill's absence. When she went to meet her bold hero husband at the Ottawa train station, Bill disembarked and marched right past her, without a flicker of recognition. That night, when they celebrated their reunion with a quiet paddle on Meech Lake, Mason quipped, as he was in the habit of doing when people didn't move quickly enough, "Step lightly from the canoe." Without even looking, an eight-months-pregnant Joyce growled back, "Step lightly yourself."

The cycle of separation/reunion that had been a fact of their life together was, with very few exceptions—notably the canoe incident—a circumstance that both partners took in stride. As soon as Bill was back from the North, they were back on track taking life day by day. About that time Bill's old boss from the Paul, Phelan and Perry agency in Winnipeg asked Mason to be Art Director, and the Masons were off again on another adventure in Bill's career. Bill could remain in Ottawa, come up with ideas and art for the various accounts, and communicate with the Winnipeg office by mail, phone and telex. It was the perfect arrangement. And, of course, Bill, always frenetic, and perhaps driven by the realization that he was about to become a parent, responded to the push to continue work on the Wizard of Oz series, and went back to Crawley's nine to five as well. On July 7, 1961, when Paul David Mason arrived, Joyce and Bill were on as stable a footing as they had been in their lives, with a roof over their heads, money to pay the bills, and attractive future work prospects for Bill.

Joyce busied herself with the baby; Bill continued his work. Back in Winnipeg, parents were proud, pleased and more than a little relieved to see the Paul, Phelan and Perry announcement on the business pages of the Winnipeg papers, celebrating Mason's appointment as art director with a glowing biographical note beneath a black and white portrait of an ultra–respectable-looking, clean-shaven Bill in a suit jacket, collar and tie. Even the worst imaginings about what Billy was doing—to say nothing of what he might look like—in the Gatineau woods, having spirited Joyce out of the respectable ambit of her parents, were offset, at least temporarily, by this public announcement of mainstream success. This illusion was dashed, however, when Bill and Joyce and the baby arrived in Winnipeg for sister Elizabeth's wedding sometime thereafter, with one side of their vehicle all bashed up and muddy, having rolled the car on snowy roads as they journeyed west. As measure of the doubt she felt towards Bill, his bride and their exploits, Sadie, with apparent disregard for its shaken occupants, asked that the damaged vehicle be parked for the wedding reception in such a way that only the good side showed.

Back in Ottawa, Bill busied himself with his animation during the day and his advertising work at night. From his colour-stained plywood work table in the rented house on Meech Lake, over which still hung the dusty working reels of *Wilderness Treasure*, Mason produced full-colour print advertisements for, among other accounts, Paulins Crackers, United Grain Growers, and Vulcan Machinery and Equipment, makers of skidders for the logging industry, and designed a variety of full-size billboards promoting Manitoba vegetables, the Yellow Pages, and other products and services that towered Bill's creative artwork over the streetscapes of Winnipeg and the wheatfields of Manitoba. And for an account for which he had a special affinity and total creative control, he produced dozens of pamphlets and print ads in a national campaign for Reimer Express Lines, a Winnipeg trucking firm. Many of these ads, especially those for Reimer Express, evoked images, maps, letters and ideas of the voyageurs and of the natural world. Trucks, for example, wouldn't be shown on any highway; they would be drawn as situated on the shores of Lake Superior. The work was more important than any wilderness morality he might have held at the time. Art is what he did to make a living; the environmental ethic he had learned from Christopher Chapman existed in a separate compartment of his mind. For Bill there was absolutely nothing inconsistent or contradictory about drawing ads for logging equipment or producing a corporate Christmas card for E.B. Eddy and Sons, showing a proud woodsman in a plaid shirt standing beside a felled tree on the front, and, on the inside, a chopped-out "Merry Christmas" in big block letters along the length of the trunk. As was the case for many other creative people, the more mundane world of commerce paid the bills while Bill developed his craft.

The Morses' account of their traverse of Lake Superior had been published by this time and, following the annual pattern established when he was single, despite the new baby, in the summer of 1962 Bill quit his job and headed out to Lake Superior with his canoe. Taking the new leg of the Trans-Canada Highway through the rugged Shield country between Wawa and the Sault, he paddled solo from Marathon to Michipicoten Mission, etching in his memory forever the sights of Cascade Falls, Denison Falls and, on the way home, Old Woman Bay. In the evenings, writing by candlelight, he found time to draft an article about this journey that was published in December of that year, his second photo-story in the *Star Weekly* magazine.

Joyce kept the original drafts, rewrites and letters associated with this story, and it is interesting to note the systematic effort of the editors at the *Star Weekly* to make the piece palatable for a secular readership. In the original submission, Mason captioned a black and white photo of himself writing as follows: "Calculating distances on the way by candlelight inside the tent. The voyageurs' notes and the Bible make good reading in such a setting with loons echoing out on the lake." The edited version of the same caption says, simply, "By candlelight, Mason studies old journals." But the essence of Bill's fertile imagination and his reverence and respect for wilderness were well established in this early writing. Here was a camper who, instead of huddling for cover in his tent during a storm, sits with the front flaps open and takes advantage of the blasts of light in a night storm to appreciate the force and power of the waves on the lake:

> In the evening, as I sat before my fire, my mind was free to wander back into history, for in this setting time ceases to exist. Possibly the voyageurs sat on the same spot and laughed and joked and sang their songs. It was at such times that the great David Thompson, Canada's map maker, would bring forth his well-worn Bible and read out verses.
>
> Not all of my evenings were spent so peacefully. One night the wind swooped down from the north between the hills. I scarcely had time to tie down the canoe and weight the tent with rocks before the storm hit. During the lightning flashes I could see the white-capped waves of Superior towering high into the air. The roar as they battered the shore was deafening. . . .
>
> During my 23 days on Superior I was windbound for about half the time. Not always because the waves were too big to paddle, but because there was no way to launch my canoe from the shore. However, the delay is a lot to be said for loafing in the sun.

As exciting as it must have been for Bill to see his words and images in print again, one must not forget that this was just one of a multitude of projects that were on the go at the time, not to mention a relatively new marriage and an infant son. Still in development, of course, was *Wilderness Treasure*. By now, he and Wilber Sutherland were wrestling with the commentary that would go with the film. Sutherland had soothed the Inter-Varsity board's nerves about the fact that not *a single* camp building appeared in the movie, and helped them come to terms with the fact that

Wilderness Treasure was a film about a canoe trip. But, thanks to Wilber's convictions about Bill's talents as an artist, everyone more or less agreed on the final edit of the film. All that remained was the commentary and the music. Sutherland struggled constantly to rein in Bill's penchant to quote huge passages of Scripture in the film. Fortunately for Sutherland, Bill always deferred to Christopher Chapman, who preferred sparse commentary: *The Seasons* had had none at all, and *Quetico* had had just a few words. If Mason and Sutherland could not agree on the content of commentary—and they were often at odds over this—they were of one mind that no words were better than the wrong words to accompany the imagery and music.

Using moments snatched from a harrying schedule, Bill began editing the great visual storm sequence in *Wilderness Treasure* to the storm sequence in Beethoven's Pastoral Symphony, and learned almost immediately the facts of life about music and film—that it is much easier to establish the visual sequences first and then add the music. It was at this point in the evolution of *Wilderness Treasure* that the Crawleys and Christopher Chapman viewed a print and urged Mason and Sutherland to use a live performance of music specially written for the film. With the requisite time-out for Wilber to raise yet more money to cover this additional expense, Budge Crawley introduced Mason to his son-in-law Larry Crosley, who wrote a score and conducted the orchestra. This collaboration between Mason and Crosley began a professional friendship that would last for more than a dozen future films.

At this late stage in the making of *Wilderness Treasure*, Bill and Wilber were also able to hire Sally MacDonald, a jack-of-all-trades who worked in Production Services at Crawley Films. At first, Sally looked at the edited version as it stood and said, "Bill, you can't do that. You've crossed your angles." But rolling the film back and looking at it again, she uttered, "Darn it, it works. You've crossed your angles, but the way you've put it together it works! As a matter of fact, it is the only way it *will* work. What you've done is right, but according to the rules it's wrong." At this point in production, Mason stood back and watched in awe as Sally MacDonald supervised the laying-down of soundtracks and prepared the film for negative cutting. After four years of looking at the film without sound, Bill could not believe what was happening the first time Crosley's music was run in time with the film. Four years of effort coalesced when, under the able direction of Sally MacDonald, they entered the mixing theatre at Crawley's and put the whole film together, once and for all. One of the most intriguing aspects of the making of *Wilderness Treasure*, and a theme that built in intensity during his film-making career, was that Bill's artistic impulse (which he always chose to follow) led him *away* from what others, by choice, experience or convention, thought he should do and towards what, for him, was the essence of the film. Sticking to what he called "objective film making" ran contrary to his creative instinct, and the success of *Wilderness Treasure* confirmed that intransigence on this line had merit. It was an aspect of his film making that would get him into many more fights before his film career was over. Mason wrote of seeing *Wilderness Treasure* as a finished product and the way in which the wisdom of his approach to instinctual film making was confirmed:

> To this point I had enjoyed my work as a photographer, painter, commercial artist and animator but nothing equalled the thrill of that day. It was the highlight of my life to see many years' work come together into a finished film. Wilber and the Pioneer Camp trustees were ecstatic with the film even though the entire film was about the canoe trip and there wasn't a single shot of the camp itself. So much for objective film making. Objectivity would never be one of my great strengths.

Wilderness Treasure was submitted to the Fifteenth Annual Canadian Film Awards, Travel and Recreation Division. To Bill's utter amazement and Wilber Sutherland's relief, it won first prize in its class, receiving nine out of a possible ten points in every category, with one judge giving it ten points for visuals. From the music to the opening map, the crossed camera angles and pans, the circling osprey in a cobalt-blue sky, *Wilderness Treasure* demonstrates Mason's debt to his friend and filmic mentor Christopher Chapman. Despite the angst it had caused them up to this point, Inter-Varsity board members loved the finished film, even though it ran contrary to just about every original

120

hope for the project. What they wanted was a film that would convey to parents the well-rounded Christian education their children were getting at Pioneer Camps. What they got was a film about a canoe trip. And yet, when they saw the finished product, they couldn't argue—Bill had caught the essence of the camp experience.

There is no doubt that *Wilderness Treasure*, like all films, was a collaborative effort from its inception. But in it are the hallmarks of Bill's films: first, the film maker is in love with his subject—canoes in the wilderness—and viewers get a feel for what it's like to be in the boat, paddling through all types of water, and at the same time come to appreciate the canoe and the act of canoeing in the wilderness context; second, there is humour in the mundanities of life on the trail—a camper is shown carefully hanging and rehanging his wet moccasins on a slippery tent guy-line, only to have them fall off, onto the ground, each time as the boy turns to walk away. Finally, most evident in *Wilderness Treasure*, although in nascent form, is the message that one must approach the natural world with reverence and regard. The ensemble impression created by cinematography, editing, sound and script gives the work an unassuming air of significance and a certain numinosity that lingers long after the house lights come up—the Mason touch. A film career was launched.

10

PADDLE TO THE SEA

A SHORT ITEM IN THE *MONTREAL STAR* of May 9, 1963, headlined "NFB Film Called Best in Canada," reports that *Lonely Boy*, a half-hour film on the career of Ottawa-born singer Paul Anka, had been named Canadian film of the year. Farther on there is mention of a win for *Wilderness Treasure* by unknown Canadian film maker Bill Mason. Whether or not winning this Canadian film award in fact made any difference in any one's mind but Mason's about his ability to perform as a film maker, the success of *Wilderness Treasure* gave him better luck with his advances to the NFB.

When the NFB was formed by act of Parliament in 1939, its mission was "to make and distribute films designed to help Canadians in all parts of Canada to understand the ways of living and the problems of Canadians in other parts."[1] In the early days, NFB film production was directed towards patriotic wartime propaganda; after the end of the Second World War, its agenda for documentary films largely continued to be set by the anonymous ambitions of government of the day. It took until 1947 for film makers to win the right to be mentioned in screen credits. This change signalled a larger shift on the part of the NFB and its film makers from film making as a "public service" to film making as a means of creative and artistic self-expression, but, all the same, the tourist and travel films of the late 1940s and early 1950s show that a hefty political motivation remained.

There was no tradition in the early decades of the NFB of making anything like "nature" films, or, for that matter, films about any non-human subjects. Film makers were heading into the inhospitable Arctic to document life there—in 1951, *Canada's Awakening North* received the first prize for best geography film at the Venice Film Festival—but nature filming, as such, did not have any real presence on the Canadian film scene until 1954, when Christopher Chapman's *The Seasons* won film of the year at the Sixth Annual Canadian Film Awards in Montreal, where a photographer, Yousuf Karsh, presided as host.

In those days, the typical NFB film maker was an urbane creator who went about the business of making films from a base at NFB headquarters in Montreal, with a technical crew and plenty of help to lug all the equipment around. It would not be until Bill was retained by the NFB that the idea of working alone, or with minimal crew and equipment, would gain credence. He would lead the NFB to places it had never been and to subjects it had never tackled when he began his wilderness filming of children's stories, wolves and canoes.[2]

Since writing to the NFB about work in the buoyant aftermath of his starring role in *Quetico*, Bill had got it in his head to make a film that he *knew* was right for the Film Board. It was based on *Paddle to the Sea*, a children's book he had seen as a teenager in Eaton's in downtown Winnipeg. It was a simple story by an American writer, Holling Clancy Holling, about a carved wooden Indian in a canoe who makes his way from meltwater in Nipigon on Lake Superior all the way through the Great Lakes to the Atlantic Ocean, having all kinds of adventures. While he was working at Crawley's, and assembling *Wilderness Treasure* at home, Bill's interest in *Paddle to the Sea* grew. With Joyce's continued encouragement, he went to a lumberyard in Ottawa, bought a piece of tulipwood, and on the second try with knife and sandpaper carved a respectable likeness of the main character. And from the moment he started shooting scenes in the creek beside their house at Meech Lake, he began promoting the idea to anybody and everybody at the NFB who might support the project.

With the same competitive spirit he had on the hockey rink, Mason was determined to get the funding before someone else scooped the project. With the idea out in the open, and without money to fund the film himself, he felt vulnerable. As money and time became available, he would buy another hundred feet of film and shoot another sequence or two from the book with the help of his pal Blake James. Activity invariably ended with Blake getting soaked on Bill's behalf.

Using the skills he and Joyce were learning while assembling *Wilderness Treasure*, they spliced these sequences into the beginnings of a film. Over three years, he pitched the project numerous times to the NFB in Montreal but, though a variety of producers expressed interest in the idea, there were no bites. In the fourth year of trying—by now he had more than 600 feet of *Paddle* footage and cells from an animated film about voyageurs he had been working on at Crawley's—Bill was finally offered a contract in the animation department at the National Film Board, drawing what he termed "boring maps" for other people's films. Boring or not, this was Bill's foot in the door at the NFB.

In a Land Rover just like Christopher Chapman's, purchased when the Nash Rambler gave up the ghost, Bill drove the 120 miles from Meech Lake to the Film Board office in Montreal. To save money and time, he ate out of paper bags and slept either under his editing table or out in the Land Rover in the NFB parking lot while he was in Montreal. He would clock in Monday, Tuesday and Wednesday; by working into the evening on each of the first two days, he could complete a forty-hour work week on the third day and be home late Wednesday night, to carry on with his commercial art and other projects. Whether or not he liked to drive the Land Rover, or found it comfortable for overnight accommodation, Mason thrived on the idea that it *looked* like something a real film maker would drive. The frenetic life wearied him and took its toll physically, but Bill was damned if he was going to let that get in the way.

He wasn't at the NFB long before his talent as an animator was recognized. Under the direction of NFB producer Derek Lamb, but using his own animation style, Bill produced two television commercials—one on preventing forest fires, another encouraging employment of the handicapped—that were well received. Daily he walked the halls among world-famous film makers: Colin Low, Norman McLaren, Wolf Koenig, Tom

Daly and Bob Verral, and as these directors brought films to completion, he would sneak into the tiny viewing theatres along the long hall on the second floor of the main NFB building, and watch and listen as the creative process on each of these projects was concluded. Every time there was a director or producer whose ear he might bend, Mason trotted out the *Paddle to the Sea* footage to see if anyone was interested. Still no takers.

Then, one day in the winter of 1963, Mason heard a rumour at the Film Board that a film on the voyageurs was going to be shot that year. In the last of the pencil scratches that constitute his "unfinished memoirs," Mason describes what happened next:

> I was envious to say the least. I knew everything there was to know about the voyageurs. I found out the director was regarded as a heavy-duty outdoor film maker around there, probably because he had a cottage up in the Laurentians. He also certainly looked the part. He was big, handsome and rugged-looking. I had always thought I would like to make a film on the voyageurs but I would have been happy just to be one of the paddlers. I saw the voyageur era as a very romantic part of Canadian history. One of my goals had been to paddle the entire route, but over the years I always ended up just roaming around photographing and painting.
>
> One day at the Board I got a message that the director of the voyageur film wanted to see me. I rushed excitedly to his office, where he offered me the job of second cameraman. I would be shooting from on board the canoe and I would get to wear a voyageur outfit. When we weren't shooting I would be one of the paddlers. This was definitely another momentous event in my life.
>
> Stepping into my voyageur outfit was like stepping back 200 years. First thing I did was head for the cafeteria so I could strut around in it. The feeling was like "Yeah, we're just heading out for Ft. William with a load of trade goods, then we might be heading up to Lake Athabasca to pick up a load of furs. I'll be back in a couple of years!" I actually wish I had been born 200 years ago.

When I returned to the costume department I met the rest of the crew and a rugged-looking bunch they were. They were real bona fide woodsmen from way up in Quebec. All except one who was a racing canoeist from the U.S. He had a body that would make Tarzan look like a whimp! All the men from Quebec were also racing canoeists, so it looked like the director was off to a great start. He had personally chosen the men.

He also did a good job selecting the canoe. It was a wood [and] canvas canoe about 25 feet long and looked just like a birchbark voyageur canoe. I could hardly wait to get into it and start paddling.

The camera department outfitted me with what would be the first professional camera I had ever used. All my shooting until now had been with the Kodak Ciné Special. I would be using an Ariflex. I was in the big time now. This was real film making, Hollywood style. We had a director, location assistant, location manager, two cameramen, and a sound man. And most important a cast of seven in the canoe, counting me.

My first clue that all was not well was when I was handed my paddle. It was a great wide racing paddle and it was painted a pastel peach colour. The other guys had paddles in powder blue, yellow, pink, and a bilious sort of green. One lucky paddler actually got a red one.

I took the director aside and explained that voyageur paddles were long with narrow blades and they would be just natural wood or bright red. He replied that he read that the paddles were very colourful. I said, "Yeah, colourful like red." As for width he explained that the men were all racers so wanted wide blades. I mentioned the fact that some of the men were smoking modern pipes, the leader was wearing non-period glasses and all were wearing heavy bush boots.

He suggested that maybe we should go have a drink and talk it over. As we talked it became clear that he had read very little about the voyageurs. He realized that he had a problem and suggested I be the advisor on authenticity. I agreed and began by saying it was common to have passengers in the centre of the canoe such as a Hudson's Bay Factor, a priest or even a woman travelling west to join her husband. He said, fine, you be the passenger. I replied that I couldn't because I was wearing a voyageur outfit and didn't look the part anyway. Then he said okay, I'll be the passenger and we will just make a film about an authentic-looking canoe and a bunch of authentic-looking paddlers retracing the old route in modern times.

The director was outfitted from head to toe in U.S. Army gear. Around his waist he was carrying a machete. With his rugged handsome face he looked like he had just stepped out of the jungle in a World War II movie. My whole movie-making world came tumbling down on me. I wanted to be back at my animation desk. I didn't want anything to do with this fiasco.

Bill's experience on this film went from bad to worse. A major upset occurred in Culbute ("ass over teakettle") Rapids on the Ottawa River that was later given prominent play in the "what not to do in a canoe" section of Mason's first paddling book, *Path of the Paddle*.[3] But there were other uncomfortable episodes in this experience, from which Mason derived memorable and long-lasting lessons, none more humiliating than a situation that developed while they were shooting near the mouth of the French River on Georgian Bay.

Bill maintained throughout that the costumes made them all look more like voyageurs than the voyageurs did, but that the most authentic aspect of the rest of the crew was their love of alcohol. At the least provocation, they would stop in taverns along the way, with the director as chief provocateur. On this occasion, however, they were camped outside, at a Georgian Bay location Bill had been at before with Joyce and baby Paul, a site Bill loved. He suggested the place, and they did some shooting there, in big waves on the bay and on tranquil waters at sunset one night. The director was very pleased with the sequences filmed at this location, so much so that he gave the crew a day off to paddle to

Highway 69, drive to the nearest Brewers' Retail, and return with a canoe-load of beer. Bill stayed behind and spent the day sketching.

Bill took his share of ribbing from the burly voyageurs about his size and Puritan ethics. At this juncture in the shooting schedule, however, they began to mock him with the nickname "Seagull," for the way he sat out on the rocky points with his meal or his sketchbook. Whenever Bill took the axe to chop firewood, they called him "Le Castor," the beaver. On this occasion, when the party began, Bill joined in with the fun around the fire, singing songs and telling jokes along with the best of the raconteurs, Bill with his tea, the crew with their ale. But things got coarse around the fire, and Bill politely took himself off to bed.

As moods expanded, the lads began whistling beer bottles into the rocks and trees near the campsite, and laughing as they smashed in the darkness. Quietly, Bill got up, went out and told the director that breaking beer bottles on this campsite was not a good thing to do. What would happen, he asked, if he brought his family back here, and someone cut a foot on broken glass? The director gave the crew a cursory dressing-down, and Bill went back to bed. And the beer bottles continued to fly. The next time Bill went out to speak to the director, he said that he would be staying at the campsite until every single piece of glass was picked up. The director told him that they didn't have time for that; they had to be moving on the next day. "Fine. You'll be moving on without me," Bill replied. "You can do without your second camera."

Bill was up with the birds the next morning, fuming, and made lots of noise as he threw shards of glass into the empty cardboard cases. The director rose and rallied the hungover crew. They breakfasted, broke camp and loaded the canoe. When it was clear that Bill was going to make good on his promise of the night before, the director ordered the men to help with the clean-up, which they did reluctantly, cursing all the while under their breath at "The Seagull." Two hours later, when Bill was finally satisfied, a pile of cardboard cases full of whole or broken beer bottles stood on the Georgian Bay rock beside the canoe. The director took one last look at the pile and said, "Get in," to Bill and the rest of the men. "What about the beer bottles?" Bill inquired. "There's no room. Someone will come by and pick them up and make a little money on the side" was the director's sarcastic reply. Bill stood firm: "If the bottles stay, then I stay."

After a moment of eye-to-eye silence, the director ordered the boxes loaded into the canoe. The whole way back to their van, along the mouth of the French River and up the lower part of the Pickerel River, the men took turns hanging their arms over the side of the moving canoe, filling the whole beer bottles with water, and sinking them, one by one, smiling in defiant silence at "The Seagull."

That trail of beer bottles on the bottom of Georgian Bay, for which Mason felt wholly responsible, was just one of the several symbolic lessons that emerged from his first experience as an NFB cameraman. Perhaps the saddest of all outcomes from his participation in the film was the way in which the drinking and carousing—which he knew were part of the authentic voyageur experience—burst the romantic bubble that had surrounded the idea of the voyageur in his imagination since his childhood. After the film, voyageurs were no longer his heroes. As well, watching big, skilled men chop down trees and throw a second 90-pound pack on their back—feats that he was physically powerless to emulate—led to the realization that smaller crews, in every respect, would make things easier to take, and that travel companions would have to be chosen with great care. And, finally, he realized that, if he was ever to be happy in the making of films outdoors, he needed to be behind the main camera; he needed to be in control. He vowed never again to suffer the humiliation he did that day on Georgian Bay.

Fortunately, his voyageur footage, including the segment processed wet from the $5,000 Ariflex camera that swam with him through Culbute Rapids, was praised by NFB colleagues. And at home, on his return, all was well too, with Joyce coming to term in her second pregnancy. On October 1, 1963, the second of the two children, Rebecca Joy (Becky) was born. And about that time, Bill was stopped in the hallway at the Film Board by Stanley Jackson, one of the best-known writers and narrators at the NFB. Jackson informed Bill that he had just been placed in charge of film for children and wanted to have another look at the pilot film for *Paddle to the Sea*. With so many disappointments, and still a little cowed by the voyageur experience, Bill complied, but without enthusiasm. Surprisingly, Julian Biggs, head of

English Production at the NFB, called to say that Bill could have a budget for *Paddle to the Sea*. Finally Bill had control; he was off on his own as a freelance director with the National Film Board.

Bill hired his old friend Blake James to assist with the production. The two were very much alike—small in stature, big in enthusiasm, and bursting with creative energy. Together they set out in the winter of 1964 to begin shooting. When the streams started to run, they played in the creeks at Meech Lake. And when they'd lose a model under the ice, Blake had the skills with his hands and the artistic touch, just like Bill, to carve and paint replacements identical to the original. Eventually they devised a scheme involving an old fishing rod and reel with transparent line that could be affixed to Paddle's under-side to reduce losses. As they walked down the road at Meech Lake in their jeans and rubber boots, Blake with Paddle hanging like a stiff trout off a rod over his shoulder, and Bill with some crazy inner-tube contraption for floating the trusty Ciné Special camera stuffed under this arm, they looked for all the world like characters in a Norman Rockwell painting.

Once they had done all the shooting they could around Meech Lake, James and Mason loaded up the Land Rover with the red canoe on top and did some shooting on Lake Superior around Michipicoten Mission and Old Woman Bay. By July, they had passed through Ottawa again, restocked and headed east, this time to film Paddle in the lower St. Lawrence and "in the sea" from locations in the Gaspé, New Brunswick and Nova Scotia, working long days and sleeping in the ve-hicle. On their return journey, they came back through the Gaspé peninsula and Bill took a moment to write to his friend Chapman:

Dear Chris:

Blake and I are sitting in the Rover staring out at Percé rock near Gaspé. Rover has proved to be worth His or Her weight in gold. No trouble and goes anywhere. The other day we took a wild road out to Cape North in Cape Breton and man what a road. I swear it goes like this

Were you ever on it?

It goes out to the <u>lighthouse</u>. I guess those little short wheelbase jobs would have a difficult time of it at that. Man this long job is sure great for living in. It is a wonderful convenience not to have to bother with a tent. It is quite comfortable for two short guys. We pack all the extra stuff under the canoe on top.

Well the filming is coming along not too badly. We are sure going through a lot of film trying to get that little son of a gun in frame. He drifts everywhere and in every direction but where we want him.

. . . I hope you are well. Joy and the children are fine. Boy I miss them. The good part about filming is that it makes me appreciate them more. . . . Well I better sign off for now.

Bill

[On the back page of the letter, beside the handwritten message, is a cartoon of a Land Rover with canoe on top moving vertically up the page with the caption: "Say Jamesy I guess we better stick it in bull low if it gets any steeper."]

Looking back on his career late in his life, Bill always maintained that there was a crucial segment in every film: "every film has its impossible sequence," he would say. In *Paddle to the Sea*, the sequence involved the depiction of Paddle going over Niagara Falls. Shooting the little wooden boat in the surf of Cape Breton Island and against the massive lakers in Beauharnois Lock, near Cornwall, had not been easy, but how to get the same point-of-view effect at Niagara had Mason stumped. With the tourist season winding down in early September, Bill and Blake loaded up the Land Rover with a fishing rod, Paddle,

Ciné Special, a lot of film stock, a waterproof housing for the camera and a variety of other supplies, including hand tools, rope, wire, inner tubes, bits of plywood, and plenty of the film maker's and canoeist's ubiquitous heal-all, duct tape.

The first sequence they worked on was the Paddle-eye-view of turning at the brink of the falls. In theory it was a simple-enough task; all they had to do was float the Ciné Special over the falls in its waterproof housing, tied to and supported by an inner tube. The first problem had to do with retrieving the rig after it had done its job. Originally, they had intended to use the fishing rod and line, but quickly realized with a few test runs from the sidewalk at the edge of the Horseshoe Falls that the combined weight of the tube and camera, especially if they were buffeted by the downward force of the water, was too much for even their heavy-test fishing line to bear. That meant they had to use rope, which of course would be pulled and affected by the fast-moving water in ways different from the tube and camera. And dropping the tube and camera into the fast-moving water above the falls would offer no guarantee that the camera would be facing the right way as it approached the falls. Eventually, however, with take after take, each one with a little different variation of keel, tube, rope, camera and overall set-up, Mason was satisfied. Now it was time to shoot Paddle himself in exactly the same place.

They could shoot the brink sequence close up on any other less hazardous falls. The challenge was to place Paddle obviously at Niagara. If all turned out as expected, the camera in the housing, actually going over the falls, would give viewers a sense of the size and power of the place with very little risk to Bill or Blake. But now, to shoot Paddle, one of them would have to swing out on rope from the railing at the brink of the Horseshoe Falls, endeavouring to get low enough and close enough to the brink to pick up tiny Paddle in motion. The other would have to cast Paddle upstream on the fishing line and concentrate on reeling him in after each take. Bill chose to be behind the camera, and Blake stuck to his post as the keeper of Paddle's lifeline.

With plenty of delays for adjusting ropes, changing film and heading off to the public washrooms in the park across the street to release the adrenaline from their systems, they eventually started to get what they wanted. Because both Blake and Bill were over the railing, and more or less out of sight, much of what they were doing had gone unnoticed by passers-by and spectators. In the middle of this round of shooting, however, they had to stop and take a moment to explain when a woman looked down over the railing and saw Blake with his fishing rod at the brink. "Someone please take care of that poor little old man! He's never going to catch a fish there. And what if he falls in? Would someone *please* take care of that poor little old man!"

By the time they had finished shooting, quite a crowd had gathered around the two film makers. As they loaded the Land Rover, they got to chatting with an American about the problems they had had with losing Paddle and the delays caused by carving and painting new ones. By chance, the man was an engineer with the Ford Motor Company, just across the river in New York State. He told them about a new process Ford had developed for making moulded floor mats using a buoyant hard-rubber compound, and invited them across the river to join him at the plant to have a look. Mason and James took him up on this invitation, and when they eventually headed east again for Meech Lake, they did so with enough materials and instructions from their Ford Motor Company friend to make a mould of their existing model and begin "mass-producing" hard-rubber Paddles, as required.

The day Bill decided to try out the moulding process, Joyce headed back into town for groceries, leaving him to watch toddler Paul and baby Becky, as he went about his work. It never dawned on Bill to manipulate these mysterious chemicals anywhere other than right at the kitchen table, and so he began, following the directions as he remembered them from the Ford man, mixing up the rubber for the mould and packing it around Paddle and, of course, speeding up the process by putting the curing rubber on an electric heater. By the time Joyce arrived home, the house was so full of noxious fumes that Bill and the kids had been forced outside, where she found them playing happily on the lawn.

Happily no harm was done, and the floor-mat materials turned out to be perfect for making Paddles on demand. The hard-rubber compound took paint in much the same way the original tulipwood did, and with a little ballast, floated in much the same way as well, only without the bothersome and time-consuming process of melting lead into Paddle's keel. Now, if Paddle happened to go astray, a new one could be moulded overnight and, in the deft hands of Bill or Blake, could be painted up and back on "set" in a day or two.

Sequence after sequence, following Holling Clancy Holling's original story, Blake and Bill shot *Paddle* into the fall of 1964. One of the last scenes they filmed that year was another tricky one that, like Niagara Falls, was much easier to write about than it was to set up and commit to film: the forest fire. Bill went back into Gatineau Park behind the house and collected a goodly number of dead trees and dragged them down the hill to Meech Lake. With the indulgence of their neighbours down the lake, the Wardens, they stood these up in a marshy spot. Using a borrowed gasoline-powered fire pump and hose for safety, and with the help of the Masons' neighbour and landlord, Dave Wright, Bill and an assemblage of curious friends and neighbours waited until dusk, doused the standing trees with kerosene, and positioned Paddle in the water just off shore, and the trusty Ciné Special in a canoe a little farther out. On a signal from the man hunched over the camera in the silent red canoe, a match was struck in the shadows on the shore, and the still night air of Meech Lake was broken by the light, whoosh and roar of an instant forest fire.

Good planning yielded magical silhouettes of Paddle outlined against flickering reflections and the powerfully contrasting blacks, reds and yellows of the fire. Good fortune allowed Blake to paddle Bill and the camera near enough to the fire for shots of Paddle illuminated by the blaze. Blind luck and a man with a camera in the right place at the right time allowed Bill to capture in the same frame a burning tree falling into the water while stoic Paddle looked on.

It was a night the neighbours did not soon forget.

Along the way in his apprenticeship as a film maker, Bill had learned not only to listen to his hunches about what would work filmically, but to leave the camera rolling when something unplanned was occurring. What turned out to be the most popular scene in *Paddle to the Sea* began as a result of the Masons' recalcitrant golden Labrador retriever, Buff, *not* performing for the camera. Bill had son Paul at the shore of Meech Lake while he tried to film a scene in which the little boy finds Paddle, and then, in the course of playing with the tiny wooden toy, loses touch with it as it floats beyond the reach of a twig in his hand. At this point, the dog, who had been watching with interest, was supposed to bound into the water at the boy's bidding and fetch the canoe. Buff, who had been in and out of the water all morning, playing havoc with the filming by stealing Paddle and prancing down the beach with him, was nowhere to be found. When he did answer Bill's call, it became clear that there was no way in the world he was going to cooperate. No matter how much urging he received from Paul or Bill, the dog simply wagged his water-soaked tail, barked and laughed, tongue out of his mouth, as only a retriever can. This was not at all what Bill had in mind, but he left the camera rolling anyway and captured the most charming of scenes.

Throughout the following winter, as Bill drove up and down to Montreal to edit *Paddle to the Sea*, Joyce had been having nasty stomach pains that just wouldn't go away. By the time Bill's birthday rolled around on April 21, it was clear that she would have to have her gallbladder removed. The shooting schedule had Bill filming *Paddle* in the Nipigon area, north of Fort William, and he also had taken on a small contract to assist with some filming associated with the Centennial Cross-Canada Canoe Pageant in the Lake of the Woods area, so Joyce opted to take the kids and drive with Bill to Winnipeg. While visiting, Joyce had another attack of stomach pain and saw a doctor, who decided she should have her gall-bladder removed. The path of least resistance for accommodation in Winnipeg while this went on involved Joyce and the children staying at her parents' place—the Fergusons could look after their grandchildren while Joyce was in the hospital—while Bill carried on with his shooting, staying at his parents' place when he was in town. The surgery went smoothly and Joyce was recuperating at her parents' home when the years of frenzy finally caught up with Bill.

As always, Sadie was mortified when Bill turned up sporting a beard. What *would* the neighbours think? Succumbing to Mother's harping, he took himself into the bathroom at 209 Oakwood and shaved, on the promise of a nice breakfast of bacon and eggs. Sadie busied herself in the kitchen. Bill and his dad took a football across the road to Fisher Park and had a rough-and-tumble game of catch, just like the old days. They arrived back in the kitchen with a rush of fresh May morning air, out of breath, but seemingly healthy and happy. Bill Sr. was smiling for the first time in months. The two of them sat down at the kitchen table and carried on with their kibitzing by having an arm wrestle across the placemats. Suddenly Bill's arm lost all resistance. His dad's forearm slammed his on the table, sending the salt cellar skittering across the linoleum floor. Bill took a short breath and slumped over the table. At thirty-six years old, his face tanned and his body fit from a winter of skiing and hockey at Meech Lake, Bill Jr. was having a heart attack.

Sadie was sure it was nothing a good breakfast wouldn't cure. Bill was such a joker. Maybe it was just a bad case of indigestion. Bill Sr. was a little slow on the uptake as well, refusing to believe that anything serious could be wrong, but when it was apparent that their son's condition was definitely not a joke, he called an ambulance. Within moments of arriving at Grace Hospital, Bill went into full cardiac arrest. Physicians at Grace knew that Mason needed the services of the Coronary Care Unit at the Winnipeg General Hospital, but before he could be moved across town his heart stopped a second time. Defibrillation again restored his heartbeat. By the time he was hooked up on the heart monitors at Winnipeg General, his condition had stabilized somewhat, and he had regained consciousness, but doctors were very worried about strange arrhythmias in his electrocardiagram.

Cardiologist Ted Cuddy was called to take over the case at Winnipeg General. He remembers struggling to control the "nasty fluctuations" in Bill's heartbeat, while Bill cheerfully prattled on about the film he was making about *Paddle to the Sea*, as if nothing had happened. Mason told him that, just as soon as he got out, he was going to be heading back out to Lake of the Woods to finish his voyageur canoe pageant shoot, then back up to Nipigon country to do some more shooting for *Paddle to the Sea*. Says Cuddy, "I'd looked at this guy, thirty-six years of age, who'd just had a heart attack, had cardiac arrest and severe arrhythmia, difficult to control, and he's going up to the north woods! I literally thought he was out of his mind!"

Meanwhile, back at the Fergusons', Joyce had been trying all day to phone the Masons. The plan was that she and Bill would take the kids to the zoo that day. By mid-afternoon she was beginning to wonder if everything was all right, but was amply reassured by Sadie, who phoned to say that Bill had finally shaved off that terribly scruffy beard and that he had been admitted to hospital that morning with the stomach flu. About this time Joyce heard from the hospital, but the seriousness of Bill's condition did not register. In no particular rush, she dressed, still sore from her surgery, left the children with her mother, and made her way to the hospital. Having trained as a nurse, she immediately saw the critical-care colour flag on Bill's chart hanging on the end of his bed, and knew that there was a lot more going on in her husband's body than stomach trouble. What was Sadie trying to do? This misinformation had disturbing overtones of jealousy and a mother's neurotic possessiveness of her only son. If Bill had died, Joyce would have been left sitting at her parents' home, blissfully unaware that he had been sick!

During the three weeks that Bill remained in the coronary-care unit, Joyce stuck close to him. She spoke with Sadie, but nothing was ever said about her being misinformed about Bill's hospitalization. Fortunately, Bill was a hit with everyone around the hospital, telling stories about his exploits in the wild and drawing cartoons, including one that showed a character trying to break through the bars of a prison window that he stuck on the tiny wire-reinforced portal of his hospital door. People—especially family—felt better around Bill, even when he was sick. A slightly more realistic version of how he felt about the heart attack is contained in a letter written from his coronary-care bed to his old friend Chapman:

May 26/95

Dear Chris:

I guess you have heard by now but if you haven't I nearly packed it in with a heart attack. Did you ever hear anything so ridiculous? It happened in Wpg so I am caged up in a boiler factory they call a hospital. Believe me it isn't really a hospital, it's a survival course.

If I don't catch something (everyone around here has lung trouble and hadn't heard of a handkerchief), or if I don't die of exhaustion from lack of sleep or if I don't pack it in from the food it will be a miracle. Joy has been bringing me raw vegetables and fruit. Good grief it's fantastic me having a heart attack! You know there's so many possible reasons isn't there. I could honestly believe it could be from the huge quantities of insecticides I devour because I eat so much fruit and veg. I am a heavy eater but I eat virtually nothing that is fattening. . . .

Well so much for all the beefing. Actually I am coming along phenomenally fast. The heart attack was as serious as it can get but the day after I felt like a tiger and that's what makes it so difficult. I could run 10 miles but they won't even let me out of bed (I would rather be in jail). And of course it's horrible thinking about the Wpg to Montreal canoe trip this summer that I won't be able to go on. . .

Upside down temporarily

Bill

Beneath this bravado was a very frightened man who had nightmares night after night in the hospital—nightmares about not being able to portage his canoe. The ultimate fear was that his weakened heart wouldn't allow him to play hockey, he thought, but if he couldn't portage his canoe, he could not get to the wilderness, and without that, he told Joyce in strict confidence, he could *never* get completely better. She recalled those dark and frightening times:

He said it was almost as if he had to escape; he felt he could really get well if he could escape and get out. He was deathly afraid that he wouldn't be able to escape and go to the wilderness. Wilderness for Bill began when he carried his canoe around the first falls or rapid. This meant he could be alone. If he could not portage, it was like he was trapped, for the rest of his life.

Since leaving Winnipeg, Bill and Joyce had toyed with churches in the Ottawa area, participating by and large through support of young people's groups, but they had found no lasting spiritual fulfilment in institutional aspects of Christianity. By now, Bill's faith was embodied almost completely in nature; his God was the God of Creation, the maker of all that filled his heart in the back country, the misty mornings, the sunset and sunrises, and most especially the Creator of the falls and raging rapids that kept out anyone unwilling to face the challenge and physical torment of the portage. If this heart attack were to cut him off from portaging and wilderness, it would be cutting him off from his connection with the Creator, denying him ultimate salvation. He could believe in Jesus Christ with all his might, but to stop communing with the Almighty in the wilderness was a reason to die or to get well enough to once again carry a canoe.

After six long weeks in the hospital, Bill was finally discharged and almost immediately headed back to Meech Lake with Joyce and the children. It had been a harrowing period for Joyce, who had constantly bickered with her parents about getting out to the hospital to see Bill when they argued that she should be resting and recovering from her own surgery. Not one to let a heart attack slow him down, and burdened in his soul by the powerful fear that he had lost something essential to his being, Bill began portaging a canoe up and down the hill at Meech Lake to get back into shape, much to the bemusement of the Wrights and other neighbours.

That summer, he requested minimal equipment from the NFB in Montreal and continued editing *Paddle to the Sea* in the tiny middle bedroom in their house, but he was still not a well man. In the space of only six years, he had been through a tumble of change: he had married, moved, had two children and changed careers; he had added film directing to his freelance portfolio of commercial art, acting, camp counselling, animating, photography and public speaking. In that sense the heart attack was completely understandable. But why an apparently healthy, physically fit thirty-six-year-old had had a heart attack continued to baffle Dr. Cuddy and the staff at Winnipeg General. It wasn't until years later that they would learn about the Mayo Clinic therapy he had undergone, which caused them to speculate about the connection between some types of therapy for smallness and heart disease. Bill had undergone a very unusual cardiac event, from which he would eventually recover, but he was losing weight rapidly. By the end of the summer, he had inexplicably lost 20 pounds, 15 per cent of his total body weight. The editing stopped that fall when he was readmitted to Ottawa Civic Hospital for a comprehensive set of tests to see what was going on.

While in hospital, he again charmed all of the staff with his infectious humour and, despite the fact that he was now a very scrawny 100 pounds, he found the energy to sneak out of the hospital to exercise or head down Carling Avenue to a greasy spoon on Bronson Avenue for a hamburger. Joyce knew all was not well. This round of hospitalization was far more frightening than the heart attack, a known problem which the doctors seemed well able to treat. This mysterious weight loss was much more sinister. No one seemed to know why her husband was fading away right before her eyes. All she could do was respond to Bill's complaints about the hospital food by spiriting in baked potatoes in her pockets—and hope. They checked for cancer, they did nutritional-balance tests (that were badly skewed by Bill's secret menu), they did blood work. To keep Bill sane, the hospital allowed him to work on *Paddle to the Sea* from his hospital bed, and on one occasion they let producer Stanley Jackson sign him out of the hospital for a day. Bill was feeling a little better by then, and didn't want to go back. Although Jackson knew from Bill's emaciated form that he needed hospital care, he played right along with his wishes, saying, "Phone them up! Phone them up and tell them you can't make it back because you're not well!"

Finally, doctors at Ottawa Civic determined that Bill could not tolerate wheat and had a variety of other food allergies and vitamin deficiencies that were confounding his body's ability to digest meals. With a strict dietary regime that was begun in the hospital, he was sent home, but not before Joyce had undergone a major turning-point in her thinking about life:

> I grew up when he had the heart attack. While I was waiting out there in Winnipeg, I realized that I was not out to please my parents and his parents. From that point on I was

going to do things for our family. But that was nothing like what happened in September.

In September I became very aware I could be a widow at that point, and I became very aware of all the wonderful things we had done together and was quite upset within myself, thinking, "I can't ever continue on with this tradition. I can't do it by myself."

Bill did recover, so much so that, when the water pipes at the Meech Lake house froze the following February, they loaded up the kids and the dog in the Land Rover and drove to visit their old friends Barrie Nelson and Don Campbell, who by this time were living and working in California. Along the way, and much to Joyce's chagrin, Bill took time out in his recuperative plan to hike to the bottom of the Grand Canyon and back. They were back in time to participate in the final mix and release of *Paddle to the Sea*. And, by summer, perhaps as a way of securing in his own mind that portaging was still possible, Bill was back out at Manitoba Pioneer Camp. Camp documents from the summer of 1966 indicate that Bill "Paddles" Mason worked with paddling instructor Stephen "Polo" Osterhus to revise the entire camp canoeing-certification program. Almost as a footnote to the medical tumult that accompanied its completion, *Paddle to the Sea* was an instant success, winning Bill praise from outside and inside the NFB, and awards—eventually an Oscar nomination—that helped establish him at the NFB as a talented and creative freelance film director. One of the elements that caught people's eye about *Paddle to the Sea* was its subtle messages about stewardship and the importance of caring for the natural world. Quietly and unobtrusively, Bill had found ways to divert attention from Paddle's journey to issues of water quality in the Great Lakes, thereby setting his story in the environment as a whole and compelling viewers to appreciate the significance of this in Paddle's life and, by extension, to the lives of every living creature.

Before *Paddle to the Sea* had reached its final form, Mason had been contracted by the Film Board to make a film for schools about the evolution of the Great Lakes. Blake and Bill were back on Superior, back at the locks at Beauharnois, back puddling with canoes and film, only this time Blake was not only the "assistant"; he had replaced Paddle as the "star" in another classic Mason film that came to be called *Rise and Fall of the Great Lakes*. The subtle environmental sub-text—Bill's "message," as it were—found its way into *Rise and Fall* as well, only stronger and more obviously. He was getting back on track. The fear of not being able to reach his beloved wilderness receded and his life returned to its normal fervid pace.

11

A RISING STAR

BILL'S LIFE WAS GOVERNED by a very simple philosophy. "If a little is good, then a whole lot's better," he would say, as explanation for what had just happened or as portent of future events. In the case of activities like painting or spending time with the family, of which he did very little from the moment he began making films for the NFB, that explanation became more like a heartfelt wish. Nevertheless, with the possible exception of sleeping, the axiom was applied to most everything else: angel-food cake with seven-minute icing; popcorn; duct tape; canoeing; editing; cartooning; inner tubes; roof racks; running around; and, of course, hockey, his favourite.

Some neighbours thought it was effrontery, others were sure it was the strange and uncompromising act of a displaced Westerner, but everyone along Meech Lake watched in awe as Bill carved into the hill beside the house at Meech Lake a "small" outdoor skating rink with boards and lights. Lining the rink with plastic sheets, welded together by a friend in the local school auditorium to stop the water from running down the hill, across the road and into the lake, he flooded the rink as soon as it got cold in November and was playing hockey long before the lake surface was frozen thick enough for winter sports. Of course "small" to Bill meant that it wasn't as big as the outdoor rinks at the Riverview Community Club he'd played on as a kid; the Meech Lake rink was a minuscule 40 by 150 feet!

Creating the rink each fall was an adventure. New plastic would be painstakingly stapled around the perimeter, Bill and Joyce and the kids would pad around in their stocking feet to avoid puncturing the liner on the stones below while it was smoothed out. When everything was set, Bill would borrow the Wrights' gasoline-powered fire pump—the same one that stood guard over the great *Paddle to the Sea* forest fire—and with a couple of hundred feet of fire hose and at least twice that amount of duct tape to affix the malleable hose to iron pipe passing under the driveway and elsewhere en route, the board-encircled rink would be filled with water from a nearby creek. On freezing, and over Joyce's protestations about the cost of electricity, the rink would be flooded and resurfaced on a daily basis with hose and hot water from the kitchen.

This same extended length of green garden hose would be pressed into action for another purpose when the winters got cold enough to freeze the water pipes in the Masons' rented house. In the early years, the plumbing lay too close to the surface of the ground and frequently froze. To get drinking water during these times of drought, and to do the occasional emergency reflood or repair on the rink, Bill stretched the hose down the hill and into the Wrights' kitchen. A phone call to the landlord got someone to turn on the tap, which had just pressure enough to push water up the hill. As the tap ran, Bill or Joyce would fill a series of huge plastic chemical storage jars brought home from the NFB. Another phone call would see the tap turned off and the downstream end of the hose disconnected. As a final act Bill would attach his vacuum cleaner in reverse and blow out the remaining water to stop the hose from freezing.

It was on this rink that Bill really connected with son Paul, mimicking the way his father had interacted with him years earlier in Winnipeg. Hockey was something they could do together, and they skated for hours, chasing dreams of NHL greatness through clouds of their own condensed breath. Together they wheeled and took shots, the hollow sound of frozen pucks on plywood boards echoing into the Gatineau darkness. Rivalry between them about goals scored and prowess on the ice began. At first Paul thought his dad was in a league with Jean Béliveau, Tim Horton, Bobby Orr and Gordie Howe; he was bigger and had moves that could dazzle the neighbour kids who would come to play. It wasn't long, however, before Paul and his friends were as big as, and then bigger than, his dad. As the years progressed, Dad looked less like hockey poetry in motion and more like a reckless flailer on ice. But games would always end in much the manner depicted in Bill's early painting *After the Game*, with Bill and Paul arguing about who got how many goals. Bill would claim five. Paul would claim five too, but say he remembered only three of his dad's. Bill would eventually relent and say, "Yeah, well, I got two in the warm-up when nobody was in the net."

With an en-suite rink, even closer than the one at the end of Oakwood Avenue when he was growing up, Bill could become as obsessive about hockey and broomball as he was about working. "If a little's good . . ." translated into pick-up games of hockey with kids and Meech Lake friends almost every night of the week. On the weekends there would be "organized" games of hockey on Saturday, involving mostly men and boys, and on Sundays there would be raucous games of broomball in which the girls and women jostled along the boards with the boys and men.

In the early years on Meech Lake, Bill and Joyce went to the United Church in nearby Chelsea, Quebec, where Bill started a boys' club. Bill and the boys played games in the church hall, canoed in the summer and, of course, skated at the Masons' rink in the winter. Whether it was Granny Mason's suspicions about the United Church, or the minister at Chelsea United Church, or being tied down to this club that he had started, there was a restlessness about Bill and religion that took him away from Chelsea United. They moved to St. Paul's Presbyterian in Ottawa, to a Baptist congregation in Hull for a while, then to a little Presbyterian church in Aylmer, and eventually back to St. Paul's where the family maintained a loose affiliation for the rest of Bill's life. St. Paul's pastor, William Duffy, with whom Bill became fast friends—although not anything like the spiritual mentorship he had enjoyed with Dr. Mitchell—remembered the first Sunday he came to St. Paul's. After the sermon, Mason stood in the vestibule of the church, leaning back with his hands jammed in his pockets. In a voice for all to hear, he puffed, "Did you shoot your bolt this morning, Bill? Or do we get more like *that*?"

Bill was happiest and most comfortable celebrating his faith and supporting the church by having a steady stream of young people's groups up to the house. St. Paul's Young People's Group had what they called "Mason Nights" in which thirty-five to forty teens would head up to Meech Lake for a rousing game of broomball. Of course, even though Bill had been playing broomball or hockey for hours before they arrived, at any given moment in the Young People's broomball game, you could stop the action and find him right at the centre of the fray. Afterwards, everyone would troop in, leaving twenty to thirty pairs of wet boots inside the door and piles of outer clothing on the floor, use the bankrupt plumbing system, and settle in for an evening of slides, films and stories from the man himself. Even though there was never much spare cash from Bill's freelance wages, Joyce always managed to cook up a huge pot of hot chocolate and cake or popcorn or something tasty for the cold, tired and hungry gang. Often the Mason household was more like a restaurant than the quiet and tidy domicile of a family of four. Joyce would do the washing up, leaving Bill to tuck the kids into bed.

Mason Nights left a lasting impression on many people from St. Paul's. Alan Whatmough, a thoughtful musician who would later play a guiding role in Bill's struggle with his last film, *Waterwalker*, vividly remembers meeting Bill at one of these IVCF Mason Nights:

> The thing I found so attractive about Bill was that he was playing the ukelele and singing, you see, and he's tone deaf—he's just awful, "I had an old dog and his name was Blue. Betcha five dollars he's a good dog too!" He was just an awful player and singer. He'd joke about it all the time. But he loved music. He *loved* music. That came through loud and clear. And at that time I was a violin player of many years, but *that* weekend I went home and bought a baritone ukelele. I had to learn to play the uke. I started playing the uke—I had a guitar within a year. Played guitar for years—ended up being a professional musician.

146

St. Paul's pastor, Bill Duffy, saw through the buffoonery on the rink, and in the living room afterwards, and appreciated the simplicity and authenticity of Mason's faith:

> One of the things that greatly impressed me about Bill Mason is what one might call his "theology of creation," which is just a way of describing his great love for God's world. He respected it; he appreciated it; he sensed he was a steward in it. He had such a great love for God's creation because he *knew* the God of creation. That was the key. And that came through to those young people like a passion. And he could preach that. It came through in every aspect of his being. He was like Jeremiah; his faith was fire in his bones.

To Bill, having grown up in the Christian faith, there was no other way. Christianity was a fact of his life. But the extent to which he struggled within the limited confines of his faith was known to very few people. Words did not come easily to him. He was fundamentally a man of action. It was always easier to lace up the skates or paddle away in a canoe than to sit and ponder the universe from the comfort of an easy chair. He was not an obvious contemplative, but in his heart he did turn and turn again to the essential building blocks of his faith. His uncertainty went back to those early days on Granny Mason's knee in the rocking chair when she dinned in the muscular doctrine of the Plymouth Brethren. The false sanctity of his grandmother emerged only occasionally in his comments on himself, and, surprisingly perhaps, the person to whom he confided in such matters was Alan Whatmough. Bill had always found natural kinship with people much younger than himself, perhaps because he was the eternal boy in his own life. Whatmough too had grown up in the shadow of the Plymouth Brethren and remembered the struggle:

> The thing Bill and I had in common was that we both came out of a fundamentalist Christian environment. And we both found it a little oppressive. Bill fought that all his life, and so did I. For me it took twenty-five years of hard struggle to really make the break. Like Bill, I was raised in the Plymouth

Brethren church. By the time Bill got to Ottawa, he had moved into sort of mainstream evangelicalism—he was hanging out with the Presbyterians by then.

Bill was a driven man. Keeping up with people half his age and younger, and living the frenetic working life, took its toll on his body, especially his knees (to say nothing of his healing heart). Gaps between hockey games in the winter were filled with chaotic cross-country ski runs down the pitched switchbacks of the McCloskey Trail that led from the Gatineau Park plateau high above Meech Lake down through the mixed-forest glades to Mason's back door. And, of course, when the spring freshet began each year, long before the ski season had ended, interstices in the skiing schedule would be filled with canoe crashes down Meech Creek and the whitewater rivers of the greater Ottawa area. In February 1967, Joyce and Bill and both children were sick with colds and flu. Joyce remembers lying in bed with Bill, taking each other's temperature, the deal being that the one with the slightest fever would get up and tend the children. Later that month, Bill was back in an Ottawa hospital, not for heart or digestion problems this time, but to have cartilage removed from an injured knee. The pace of life with *Paddle to the Sea*, which was just starting to take off, *Rise and Fall of the Great Lakes*, which was in production, and all the other aspects of his busy life, was evident in another letter he wrote to his friend Christopher Chapman. At the time Chapman was finishing up his epic film *A Place to Stand* for the Ontario Pavilion at Expo 67:

Dear Chris:

Seems like ages since we last saw you guys. . . . We are fine, apart from my knee, which I am having fixed up tomorrow which is why you are getting a letter in the first place. The only time I ever get around to writing letters is when I am in the hospital. Seems to me the last one you got from me was when I was in 2 years ago. . . .

I wrecked my knee playing hockey, then finished it off skiing, and put the final touches on it two weekends ago halfway down Meech Creek. We were running rapids in spring flood. Man it was a neat run. Anyway it's a cartilage problem which keeps recurring so I am having a piece removed. . . .

In regard to my heart it's in great shape. Absolutely no restrictions, for which I am most thankful. A heart attack is a great thing to make you appreciate living. It's changed a lot of my attitudes. Now instead of saying let's go canoeing as soon as I get this or that job out of the way in a week or two, I just go the first sunny day, and strange as it may seem the stuff still gets done. I find that the joy used to be in the job completed. Now I find I can really enjoy the work itself, and am not in the sweat to finish it like I used to be.

I've been working mostly at the board lately. I enjoy the people but I go insane at the pace. Been trying to shoot 5 days work in 2 or 3 all winter. I've had about 7 trips to Montreal in the last two months.

Evolution of the Great Lakes is coming along. Just a few more shots. It's a crazy sort of approach to a teaching film and so far reactions are quite good, but for a while I was scared it would flop. It's that kind of film. . . .

Hey! finally got a birch bark canoe. What a masterpiece of skilled design. Truly the most beautifully functional thing man has ever or ever will create. We have 3 ½ canoes now with another on the way. That's *canoes* not kids!

Bill

The pace continued. Before *Paddle to the Sea* was released, Bill was hard at work on *Rise and Fall of the Great Lakes*, and before that film was "in the can" he committed to make yet another film with his buddy Blake James, their third for the NFB. This next project would promote Blake from production assistant to star, in a film about flying. *Blake*, as the flying film came to be called, would be shot in 35mm format, which required larger, more complicated cameras and equipment on top of an already chaotic shooting schedule.

As Blake and Bill planned the flying film, they contrived to set up and shoot the final sequences for *Rise and Fall of the Great Lakes*, the last of which was the scene in which an old red canoe, like the one Blake had paddled throughout the film, would be dropped into Meech Lake from a helicopter hovering at a thousand feet off the water. The effect Bill wished to create was an illustration of the instantaneous removal of mile-thick glacial ice sheets from the surface of Canada. Having paddled the various geological epochs through which the Great Lakes evolved, pitting Blake against roaring rivers, alligators, precipitous cliffs and dry lake beds, this final scene would show Blake and the canoe falling through space into liquid water. Mercifully, Bill agreed that Blake didn't need to be in the canoe for the shot. The two of them constructed a dummy painted to look like Blake, set it in the canoe and called the helicopter. The canoe would undoubtedly be destroyed by the fall, and the cost of the helicopter would finish the film budget, making it clear to everyone involved that this was a one-time effort. To cover his bases, Bill enlisted the help of a second cameraman to film the event. The helicopter approached the drop site with the red canoe swinging below it; unfortunately, as the canoe swung one way, it caught the down draft of the rotor, which caused it to swing with enthusiasm in the opposite direction, until it caught the rotor wash on the other side of the machine. By the time the pilot got to about half the planned altitude, the canoe was swinging so violently that he was worried it might cause the helicopter to crash. Without warning (Bill was never one for walkie-talkies) the pilot let the canoe go, and had it not been for the second cameraman, Grant Crabtree—an experienced hand from Crawley Films who thought something like this might happen and had his camera running from the moment the helicopter appeared—the shot would have gone unfilmed, with Blake behind the main camera mesmerized by the swinging canoe.

To Blake's relief, Bill purchased footage of alligators in the Louisiana bayou from Walt Disney Corporation and cut this into footage of the hapless *Rise and Fall* canoeist in more hospitable Canadian swamps, but there were other film situations Bill dreamed up that pushed his friend's patience and tolerance to the limit. Teetering the red canoe at the brink of the 300-foot deep Barron River canyon in Algonquin Park was nothing compared with the day that Mason filmed Blake in sequence after sequence at minus thirty degrees in a snow storm on Meech Lake, with his friend dressed only in summer paddling garb. And purposely falling headlong into the rocks on the shore of Old Woman Bay on Lake Superior, simulating the changing water levels in the evolution of the Great Lakes, had its painful moments too. But, for Blake, who hates water, the worst set-up of all was the scene in which a rapid rise in water level was simulated, requiring the canoe, the canoeist and an entire campsite, tent and all, to be weighted down underwater in Meech Lake so that Bill could film it all slowly rising to the surface. It was a great effect, but took its toll on Blake's good humour, of which Mason was, apparently, blissfully unaware.

Blake and others began to notice an emerging pattern in Bill's dealings with producers and other people at the Film Board. Any time he had to relinquish control for any aspect of the film, he got very uneasy. Whether it was editing, script writing, narration or music, if it was out of Bill's hands, friction tended to build. Mason's idea of music was the plinking guitar and harmonica he had put on tape for his slide show, the same kind of voyageuresque music Larry Crosley had written for *Wilderness Treasure*. And when it came time for Louis Applebaum to write the score for *Paddle to the Sea* and Bruce McKay to do the music for *Rise and Fall of the Great Lakes*, heat inevitably built between Bill and the other creative forces working on his film. One skill he had not developed working in isolation at his rustic Meech Lake studio was the ability to collaborate; he was fiercely possessive and single-minded about his film properties.

As Blake describes the genesis of the biplane project years later, this film was to be a short and simple depiction of flying, part of the "ing" series of films the NFB was producing in the mid-1960s—skiing, swimming, rowing, golfing and so on. But, in Bill's inimitable style, he could not simply shoot an aeroplane in the sky without personifying the character of its pilot, his friend Blake. What began as a one-reel short for the Film Board became a longer and more complex film about freedom and a man's love for adventure. His maniacal determination to realize his own personal vision for this film was not without risk and cost to himself and other people.

Without radio contact, Blake flew his tiny 65-horsepower linen-covered biplane, with its yellow birch propeller and twenty-foot wingspan, through clouds, over fields and against fall colours in the Ottawa River valley as Bill shot from the ground and from the air, using an overwing Cessna as a platform for his camera. Using his "if a little's good" maxim and his conviction that the secret ingredients in any great invention were duct tape and inner tubes, Mason taped, stretched and sandbagged his way to ingenious camera mounts on Blake's plane and on the following Cessna. And as always, he pushed Blake's limits as a pilot, asking him to fly past sunset and, on one occasion, to land the plane at the end of an Outaouais field—to get as close to the camera as possible—resulting in a high-speed turn to avoid hitting the fence at the end of the field. On that occasion, centrifugal force pulled the balloon tire off its rim, the starboard wing tip touched the ground and the plane pitched on its nose, very nearly killing Blake and totalling the plane.

And with a 35mm camera mounted behind the open cockpit on the 17-foot fuselage of the little white biplane, Bill would send Blake up with a shot list as the afternoon sun got low on the horizon. Being fanciful and a little absent-minded, Blake once forgot to open the valve to his auxiliary fuel tanks and was forced to land in an out-of-the-way location, or he would fly around in the clouds for hours, leaving Bill pacing like an expectant father on the tarmac at little airdromes in Carp or Aylmer, Quebec. When Blake would finally land, Bill would be outraged, though he quickly got over his anger. He couldn't appreciate that Blake, the freewheeling, easy-going character in the film, was also that in real life.

Bill was never angrier with Blake than the day they were shooting in Montreal. The idea was to film Blake flying carefree over stop-and-go traffic on the Decarie Expressway in morning rush hour. Blake (as he admitted much later) was not too fussy about flying a single-engined plane over such a heavily populated area and made a point of engaging in a lengthy conversation with pilots at the Cartierville airport that morning. By the time he was ready to go, Bill was fuming because they'd missed the morning light *and* the traffic. In true cinematic tradition, the director insisted on getting the shot, regardless of how long they had to wait or who was inconvenienced in the process.

When the shooting was more or less done for the flying film, the NFB assigned an experienced young picture editor to cut together the sequences into a whole film. Kathleen Shannon had been affiliated with Crawley Films and with the Film Board for seven years as a sound editor before she began editing pictures. Having worked with Christopher Chapman on a film about organic farming, she shared Bill's admiration for Chapman's film work. By all indications the Shannon/Mason collaboration began with promise; Kathleen saw raw footage, or the rushes, as it came in from Bill and Blake's escapades in the Ottawa valley skies, and she was excited by the prospect of working on the film. But as had happened every other time Bill had had to share in the creative processes of his films, creative friction began to build between the two of them. Shannon did a substantial amount of editing on the film—the prevailing understanding at the NFB was that it was not proper for the person who shot the film to edit it—much of it with Bill looking directly over her shoulder in the editing suite. She remembers the pivotal day:

> One day in the cutting room Bill and I realized that it was hopeless. He was *so* used to working alone and manipulating his own material, and he couldn't really *tell* me how to do it. He had to *do* it himself. Bill didn't seem to have confidence in the collaborative process. He didn't *see* what I saw in the material. He had preconceived ideas, and all the material wasn't in yet. I couldn't know what was missing. There was a moment when we both said, "This is impossible." We agreed that Bill would edit the film. Surprisingly perhaps, it was a cheerful moment. A long time later, another film editor said that I should have had a credit on the film for all the work I'd done, and I thought, "Yeah, maybe." Maybe I felt a moment of slight resentment. But at the time, it wasn't anything like a fight. It was really a kind of refreshing realization that "we can't possibly work together like this."

Not all reactions to Mason's doggedness were as charitable. As the only NFB film maker *not* working out of the offices in Montreal, he set himself apart creatively, but he also lacked the collegial infrastructure— the kind built around the lunch room and the water cooler—that would see him smoothly through such professional disagreements.

Colleagues at the Film Board knew Bill as an iconoclast, a bit of a square peg, a misfit—but a misfit who made great films. And in spite of the creative friction surrounding his work in film, his raw talent impressed people and, in the case of the head of English Production, Julian Biggs, earned him critically important support to carry on in his unique way. As Mason wrote:

> I'll never forget the time we were screening my edited work print of *Blake* with producer Doug Jackson and head of English Production, Julian Biggs. My film began but there was no academy leader on the head and there were lots of other small technical problems as well, but the film flowed beautifully. Jackson turned to Biggs and said, "Look, let's bring Mason in and train him through the entire film-making process." Julian replied, "No! Just leave him alone. He's doing something right so let's not spoil it."

As with all his films, Bill laboured with the commentary for the Blake film. He argued with the producers at the Film Board, and with Blake and others about how best to marry the music and imagery with the text of a script. Words were never his *forte*; he thought in pictures mostly, a visual thinker. When the words did come, they were most often wrapped up in the cryptic blank verse of cartoon captions. And with the Blake film he finally fought back the need to lecture, the urge to sermonize about the splendours of God's green earth, opting instead for a series of different anonymous voices with reflections on Blake and his cross-country fly-boy lifestyle. The comments were laid down on the soundtrack as if people were watching the film, thinking about Blake and just chatting. To any viewer who did not know the sound of his voice, his comments about Blake would be just a male part of the verbal pastiche; but anyone who recognized Bill's distinctive voice would have interpreted his comments about Blake as a longing Bill harboured in his soul that acknowledged the traditional importance of family and at the same time hungered for the carefree and adventuresome life of his freewheeling, unmarried, pilot friend Blake. The film opens with the following comments:

The impression that people get of him is a guy who has really got it made.

He has problems same as everyone else, except that Blake conceals his.

I think he really likes being alive and if he is depressed, maybe it's because he feels he is not doing enough. Like he feels maybe he is wasting his time working. Like people say: What do you do? Oh I just fly around, you know. I need money, I work. Nobody said: A man has got to work. A guy like that just moving into a scene and out of it, turns on people, you know, like you see him and you say: God he is free . . . he is free and . . . I should be like that.

Later in the film Bill comments: "I often envy this real sense of freedom that he has, that we would all like. But what I am not willing to do is give up what I have got in married life and my children." This was as close as Bill came to introspection about the life he came to live. The freedom he enjoyed as a film maker with a family devoted totally to his career he knew to be a compromise—not the life of the voyageur to which he had aspired as a boy—and substantially more restrained, but not without rewards, of course, than that of his friend Blake. And if one were ever to wonder if the chronic problems with his health ever got him down, one line from the commentary of *Blake*—"I think he really likes being alive and if he is depressed, maybe it's because he feels he is not doing enough"—could explain how and why that creative fire burning in his bones drove Bill to obsession with his work, leaving no time, no energy, for the creeping malaise of self-pity.

By the summer of 1968, as he was finishing *Rise and Fall* and completing the shooting for *Blake*, *Paddle to the Sea* was becoming a run-away success. In August of that year, T.V. Adams, Chief of the Liaison Division at the NFB, reported to a superior *Paddle's* distribution triumphs:

[*Paddle to the Sea*] has had one hundred and five television bookings (each airing over a single station being counted as a booking even if a number were simultaneous as a network release).

One hundred and thirty-nine prints were placed in free distribution by the Board and to March 31, 1968 we had 2,816 reported screenings to 213,857 people. Fifty-six additional prints were sold and of course we don't know how many people they have reached. Therefore, there is a total of 195 prints in the field in Canada. It is remarkable to sell 56 copies when 139 are available free in the field.

Abroad: It was sold theatrically to the Rank Organization for the U.K., Ireland, Gibraltar and Malta.

One hundred and forty-five copies in 16mm are being distributed by Canadian Embassy libraries abroad and other loan outlets, and a staggering 346 prints have been sold, mostly in the U.S.A. We have no statistics on the audience reached by this total of 491 prints abroad, but it must approach half a million per year, by my conservative calculation.

All of this exposure and popular success for *Paddle* led to many awards at film festivals around the world, but none more important than its nomination as best live-action short film by the American Academy of Motion Picture Arts and Sciences in Hollywood, for the 1968 Oscar awards ceremony. Ironically the film that eventually won that category was a revolutionary 17-minute film that had more than 100 minutes of actual running film in it, playing simultaneously in little inset windows within the main frame of the film proper. The competition for *Paddle to the Sea* was *A Place to Stand* by Bill's friend and mentor Christopher Chapman. Before Joyce and Bill even got to Hollywood, Mason was upset again about collaboration in the creative process because he had learned that, if his film won an Oscar, Julian Biggs, the producer, would be invited to the stage to pick up the award.

Nevertheless, Bill found the money to fly to California with Joyce. They stayed in Malibu with old friend Barrie Nelson, who lined up in the queue of star-filled stretch limousines with Bill and Joyce in the back seat of his old Volvo to deliver them at the main door of the theatre where the Academy Awards ceremony was held. Bill's rise as a film maker had been almost instantaneous, going from anonymity to sitting beside Natalie Wood and in front of Diahann Carroll at the Oscars in a very few years. He appears to have been unaffected by this early success, choosing to break protocol at the Oscars to yell out "Way to go, Chapman!" as Christopher went forward to receive his Oscar for *A Place to Stand*.

Back in the Meech Lake studio, awards piled up—a British Academy Award for *Rise and Fall*, and another Oscar nomination for *Blake* (which ran for months with the film *M.A.S.H.* in theatres across North America)—and still Bill pressed on with layer after layer of film projects. By the time *Blake* was released, he was well into yet another project, with Blake at his side.[1] This time they were chasing wolves, and creating the films that would constitute the pinnacle work of his film career. If a little shooting of chipmunks on the wooden model of *Paddle to the Sea* was fun, then a lot of shooting of wild wolves would be even better. The wolf films would see him dining with Her Majesty the Queen and parking his ramshackle red Chevy sedan with its plywood roof rack and canoe inside the gates of Rideau Hall and outside the prime minister's residence at 24 Sussex Drive.

12

COMPANY OF WOLVES

As Bill began his freelance career with the National Film Board, a strange phenomenon was evolving in Algonquin Park, late in the summer of 1963. University of Toronto biologist Douglas H. Pimlott and his graduate students were conducting unique wolf research, communicating with them at night by howling from darkened dirt roads and listening for eerie replies that drifted like smoke through the night air. Families holidaying at the Lake of Two Rivers campground and elsewhere in the park got wind of what was going on and questioned park naturalists incessantly. Visitors were so interested in this phenomenon, and naturalists so tired of explaining the wolf research program, that it was decided to try taking a few of them to a sure-hit howling place for a firsthand listen.

An announcement about the event was slipped into the back pages of the park newsletter, *The Raven*, on August 7, 1963. On August 17, the naturalists drove to the appointed meeting-place at the Two Rivers campground, off Highway 60, to see if anyone was willing to take them up on their offer. To their astonishment, 600 people in 180 vehicles jammed the roads of the campground, ready to go wolf howling. And so began the park tradition of a green park vehicle leading a several-miles-long snake of red tail lights through the darkened recesses of southern Algonquin. That first public wolf howl got only a faint reply from one lonely wolf, but, as the park staff got more organized, the results improved dramatically. On a good night, 1,000 people in 250 cars would park along a dirt forest-access road with impossible quiet. A naturalist would begin to howl, and another would join in and, as the wolves yipped and hooted in reply, the hair on the backs of a thousand necks would rise.

The wolf-howling program was an extraordinary marriage of science and intuition. Dr. Pimlott and his team had had no trouble locating wolves in the winter, when their kills could be spotted from the air on open lake ice or through leafless trees in the forest, but in the spring and summer, when the animals were denning, raising their young and free-range hunting at night, it was impossible to find wolves, let alone track or study them. Acting on a suggestion of his colleague Yorke Edwards, Pimlott enlisted the help of W.W.H. Gunn, a pioneer in the field of birdsong recording, and started playing the howls of captive wolves into the darkness to the wild wolves of Algonquin as they hunted on still summer nights. They located wolves immediately. It wasn't long before Pimlott and his creative graduate students learned that reasonable human imitations of howling were just as effective as recordings in communicating with the wolves. Before long, the researchers had located and mapped the home territories of two packs of wolves in the Highway 60 corridor through Algonquin Park and had made contact with several other groups. They knew that there was an element of predictability to the location of wolves in the summer— adults would park their young in protected sites and hunt alone until the cubs were old enough not to foil the hunt, and those young wolves would call back to even bad human impersonations of a wolf's wild cry. Reapplying the science of wolf howling to the purpose of park interpretation was a stroke of genius.

Why people took to this public wolf program with such enthusiasm is a mystery. In the early days of Algonquin Park, according to park literature, it was taken for granted that the destruction of wolves was a normal and desirable pursuit. George Bartlett, Algonquin Park superintendent from 1898 to 1922, regularly wrote articles for *Rod and Gun* magazine with such titles as "How Shall We Destroy the Wolf?" The only controversy in those days was whether the use of poison was legitimate. Up to and including the 1960s, and beyond, many jurisdictions in Canada offered a bounty to destroyers of wolves, five dollars a tail to rid the world of these marauding carnivores. At that time fairy-tale notions of "big, bad" wolves were amply buoyed by Jack London's images of yellow eyes and gleaming teeth in primordial darkness, instinctive canine killers licking the bloodied entrails of Klondikers and killing old Indians.

Curiously coincident with the upsurge of popularity of the public wolf howls in Algonquin was the publication of Farley Mowat's book *Never Cry Wolf* in 1963. Mowat's writing was much more sympathetic to the wolf's lot in life than most popular conceptions of the creature in literature, in the northern writings of Jack London, for example. Drawing more from the animal-writing tradition of Ernest Thompson Seton and Grey Owl, who both combined science with an imaginative sympathy for animal protagonists, Mowat ably countered London's wolf imagery, painting the wolf as a harmless and even altruistic dweller of the Canadian wild, indicting instead the evils of cities and their urban occupants. Although Mowat was hell-bent on changing the Canadian government's attitudes towards wolves following his success with publicly raising the plight of the Caribou Inuit—an article in *Maclean's* magazine at the time called him Canada's angriest not-so-young writer—*Never Cry Wolf*, according to one biographer, had "little direct effect on government regulations, probably because it seemed frivolous or fictional."[1] What Mowat's popular animal story may have done, however, was to galvanize latent sympathy for the wolf into public support for the Algonquin Park wolf-howl program and a series of other wolf initiatives in the 1960s in which Bill Mason would eventually be involved.

One of those other initiatives in governmental circles that represented a turn-about in thinking was a move by officials inside the Canadian Wildlife Service to supplement their established cull initiatives—wolf bounties and a long-standing poisoning program in various parts of the country—with more research and a film that would support and celebrate wolves in the Canadian wild. This change of heart was partly in recognition of the changing mythology surrounding the wolf. What was once a denizen of death and destruction was becoming a potent symbol of the deleterious effects of humans on the earth. Government documents show a desire to create a conservation film to convey three main points: (1) Wildlife is an important part of the Canadian tradition because of the effect wildlife has had on the exploration and settlement of Canada; (2) Wildlife is still very much a part of the current scene because of consumptive and non-consumptive uses made of the resource; and (3) Research and management are vital to wildlife's survival because of the changes that man is making to the environment.[2]

Logically, the CWS contacted the NFB, and together they turned for help with their conservation film, with wolves in mind as a possible subject, to Douglas Pimlott and, predictably, to Farley Mowat, who they thought might write a script for the film. In a letter postmarked Burgeo, Newfoundland, Mowat wrote back to Frank Spiller at the NFB:

> Situation is this: I agree with [the CWS] comments, and your own. Who needs another conservation film of the standard variety? I'd like to concentrate very strongly, almost overwhelmingly, on one really effective aspect of the problem, instead of drifting all over the damned shop, taking quick looks at a score of angles. Haven't yet thought of the most effective target. Might be caribou; might be seals—God knows, there are enough potential subjects.
>
> In other words, I'd like to have a crack at this, and think I could do something useful. BUT. I now find I have to leave here April 8 (with two incompleted books[3] on my hands) and fly to Spence Bay via Yellowknife, for at least two weeks. I will then go to Toronto where I will have to remain for at least six weeks—or about the end of June—putting these two books to bed and possibly another project. All this means that I couldn't concentrate on the conservation theme until about the end of June. I *might* be able to get to it earlier, but I couldn't be sure.

The CWS and NFB passed on Mowat's conditional offer of help with the wolf film and continued on through the summer and early fall of 1966 with preliminary investigations on where, how and by whom such a film could be produced. Possibility number one, the so-called Disney Option, was to retain William Bacon and Lloyd Beebe, animal-film makers with Walt Disney Corporation in Burbank, California; however, the costs for this service were high and open-ended, meaning if the filming took longer than anticipated the Canadian producers would be liable for ongoing per diem rates and expenses for the animals' feeding and care. Details of these negotiations indicate the Field Director and first camera being paid $18,000 per year, and other miscellaneous expenses such as veterinary costs of $750 and the rental of a black bear for two weeks for $150, one deer for two weeks for $50, and allowance for the purchase of two live beavers at $50 per head. This was well above the CWS budget figures, and, as it transpired, Bacon and Beebe were completing a cougar film and getting set to start a grizzly story as soon as the cat film was done. The second possibility was to work with Ontario Lands and Forests on Caribou Island in Lake Superior. The third and fourth options were to work with CWS personnel in Fort Smith, Northwest Territories, who already had wolves in captivity, or to complete the whole project using stock shots purchased from Walt Disney and other animal-film makers. It was quickly decided that the stock-shot option was weak, because of the disparate nature of the backgrounds and the differences in the featured wolves, leaving the option of Caribou Island and Fort Smith, which meant working with either Ontario Lands and Forests in Algonquin Park or with CWS personnel in Fort Smith. The high cost of building enclosures suitable for long-term post-film use, as stipulated by Ontario Lands and Forests, nixed this option—their original estimate for the job was $4,500, but, when this project was costed out in detail, the final figure rose to $30,000. Lands and Forests did offer to supply wolves to the NFB if they wished to build enclosures elsewhere for filming, but Fort Smith was the only viable plan of the original four. Bill Brind was assigned as producer by the NFB to bring the project forward, and all that remained was to find a suitable film maker to direct what was now called simply "the wolf film."

By this time, the fall of 1967, Bill was over his heart attack and his food-absorption problems—Joyce was giving him the monthly vitamin

B_{12} injections he would have for the rest of his life and had found ways to keep wheat gluten out of his diet. *Paddle to the Sea* had been in release for more than a year and was continuing to garner rave reviews and awards; its Oscar nomination was just around the corner. In among putting the final touches on *Rise and Fall of the Great Lakes* and shooting for *Blake*, Mason—in his delirious style—began a fifteen-week speed-reading course at Carleton University on Monday nights to help him in researching his films. Between editing sessions and meetings on his frequent trips to the NFB offices in Montreal, he found time to chat with Bill Brind about this wolf project that was getting under way. The awards won by *Wilderness Treasure* and *Paddle to the Sea* had been noticed, as had his fine cinematography on the voyageur film, and his abilities as an artist and animator. His reputation at the Film Board, however, was also that he couldn't work with other people or handle time and budget constraints. Nevertheless, Brind was able to convince his superiors at the NFB that the man for the "wolf film" project was Bill Mason, and drafted a contract which delineated the Board's desires "to secure the services of the Contractor as Director-Cameraman for a film tentatively entitled *The Wolf* (C76-67). This assignment beginning on or about October 1, 1967, with services to be rendered when required, will be for an accumulated period of 52 weeks, or until completion of assignment."[4] The contract went on to ensure Bill $350 per week, or $18,200 if computed on an annual basis, which was slightly more than the best-paid Disney animal-film makers, like Bacon and Beebe, made. Good money. Excellent money. However, Bill's reputation for having a cavalier attitude towards finances and accounting preceded him. Acting director of production, Frank Spiller, drafted a memo to Bill Brind as soon as Bill's services were secured, saying, "I have just initialled the contract with Bill Mason for the wolf film. In view of the large amount of time and money involved in this contract I think it very important that you get Bill Mason to keep an accurate and continuous record of the time he spends on the production."[5]

In a flurry of letters typed by clerks at the NFB, Bill wrote to every nature magazine he could think of, asking for articles on wolves. Even if he had ever learned how to research a topic in a library—which, in fact, he may not have done—the letter approach to background investigation for the wolf film was much more expedient, leaving time for other tasks, including the drafting of an outline for Darrell Eagles, at the CWS, and Bill Brind, his NFB producer. In that outline, Bill uses images that had been with him since childhood:

> The film will begin with a mood sequence depicting North America before the arrival of Man. We feel the presence of animals and occasionally catch fleeting glimpses of them. . . . This sequence would include shots of a wolf kill, the tracks of a small animal in the snow where they end abruptly and we see the signs of a struggle, wolves from a great distance.—We hear them howling.
>
> Shot of a deer. We move into close-up for the first time. We hear the twang of a bow, and an arrow thuds into a tree beside the deer. The deer bounds away into the forest. The thought is that at one time man did little to upset the balance of nature. . . . The Indian lived in harmony with nature—he was part of it.
>
> FADE OUT
>
> FADE IN
>
> A scenic shot looking over a lake; gradually we become aware of singing. We pan down and pick up a canoe as the voyageurs paddle by. This scene will represent the beginning change—the coming of the white man in search of furs, not to cover his own body, but to sell and trade.
>
> . . .
>
> The film ends with a mood sequence of canoeists observing wildlife as they go. A family on vacation, around a campfire, hears the howl of a wolf. Finally, we end on a long shot of the land from a high hill. Again we hear the cry of the wolf echoing across the land. The howl instead of instilling fear in the audience now represents life. For where there are wolves there are other animals; for the film has clearly shown that where there are no animals you cannot have wolves. The presence of wolves therefore represents a healthy living wilderness in ecological balance, and our lives are richer for it.

In the tumult of multiple projects, Bill followed up on earlier CWS and NFB wolf-film planning. With addresses from those files, he wrote to Douglas Pimlott and CWS biologist Ernie Kuyt in Fort Smith with questions about wolf dens, movements, locations, best season of approach and other very specific inquiries, and set out an eighteen-month shooting schedule for the project. This correspondence led to a preliminary visit to Fort Smith and to Prince George, B.C., early in the winter of 1968. The circumstances of these early trips, in which he had great difficulty finding wolves and got no suitable close-up footage, secured in his head the notion, planted by people at both the CWS and the NFB, that an enclosure was the way to go for detailed filming of these elusive animals.

The wolf-film shooting began in earnest with an extended trip accompanying Dr. Pimlott and his graduate students, who, by this time, had moved from Algonquin Park to a location outside the Fox III DEW Line station on the west side of Baffin Island. Before going, however, plans were laid to accept Ontario Lands and Forests' offer to supply wolves and to build an enclosure for filming right outside the rented house at Meech Lake. While Bill was away on Baffin Island, on June 25, 1968, Joyce took delivery of two eight-week-old wolf pups and began, with Paul, age seven, and Becky, age five, service as wolf feeders, handlers and pen cleaners in Dad's absence.

Life for the entire Mason family continued to be paced and scheduled around Bill's work, which in turn was frequently turned topsy by the caprice of circumstances, with wolves in the backyard and elusive wolves in the wild. Whether Bill was phoning in from the DEW Line station at Hall Beach to get Joyce to relay messages to this outfit or that, or coming and going on eccentric schedules, the family rolled with the disruptions, enjoying Bill when he was home and not engrossed in his filming, and learning to carry on their school lives and friendships, at times in spite of a possessed film maker. On the few occasions Joyce left Bill alone with the children while she went out to do the shopping or to run an errand, there was no guarantee that he would remember to feed them or, for that matter, to take them to where they needed to be or to pick them up when they needed to come home. Matters of house and family were always viewed, or so it seemed, as a subset of and support system for the filming. Some thought Bill got away with murder in terms of the attention he paid to Joyce and the kids.

For example, the family's first freezer, a useful item for people living some distance from a grocery store, came with the arrival of the wolves at Meech Lake, and long before it contained ice cream or frozen produce for the family, it was jammed with butcher scraps and roadkill for the wolves. Filming was a fact of family life. Paul and Becky grew up thinking that everyone lived as they did—with wolves in the backyard. Eyebrows did rise at project time, and especially at show-and-tell at school, when wolf stories would leak out, and never more so than the day the Mason kids were able to report that their dad had filmed wolves being *born* in their backyard, and that, after a while, they each got to hold one.

Partly out of his competitive nature—not wanting other film makers to know what he was up to—and partly out of pragmatism derived from his research into popular perceptions of the wolf, Bill was very careful about protecting his personal Meech Lake wolf pack and controlling what people knew about it. In a 1970 article in the *Ottawa Citizen*, under the slightly protective headline "Big, Bad, Wolf: Wright Family Filming in 'Secret,'" Mason recounted to reporter Burt Heward that he feared publicity would arouse animal lovers as well as wolf haters. And, interestingly, showing a level of political savvy and awareness for which he was rarely credited, Bill described the purpose of the film in terms that repeated almost verbatim the CWS written mandate for the film. Even as circumstances were altering the structure of the film as it was evolving through shooting, Mason did have the good sense to indicate to his sponsors at the NFB and the CWS through the newspaper that he was still on track with the main themes of the film. This article also provides a glimpse at the way in which Mason's mind was working: "From the film, he hopes to get a one-hour theatrical film, perhaps a shorter version for television, a separate film for scientists and students on wolf behaviour and half-minute film clips for use by television stations."[6]

On the occasion of the visit to research this article, Jean Alarie, *Citizen*–UPI photographer, took one of the first pictures of a big male wolf standing on his hind legs while a clean-shaven, distinctly boyish

Mason rubbed under his chin. Although the impression eventually conveyed in the films was that the animals were "wild"—they did in fact kill one of their number who went lame—the wolves got used to being handled, some more than others. As the *Citizen* photo clearly illustrated, the leader of the Meech Lake pack, and father of the two litters of pups that were eventually born in captivity, was more like a pet than a savage beast from the wild. Bill called him Charlie Brown— "Charlie for short"—an animal that outweighed him and looked down on him on occasions when he'd be invited to jump up and place his forepaws on the boss's shoulders, an animal for whom he held great affection. A darker female, Sparky, was more shy and withdrawn than Charlie but, with handling, became used to kibitzing with Mason and quite liked an occasional rub under the chin or on the belly. Sparky too was a favourite with the whole family.

With publicity surrounding Oscar nominations for *Paddle to the Sea* and *Blake*, a British Academy Award for *Rise and Fall of the Great Lakes*, and now news of a "secret" wolf project going on in the Gatineau Hills north of Ottawa, a certain mystique built slowly around Bill Mason, as a man, as a film maker, and as an environmentalist. Word got out as well, from the dozens of young people who came to play hockey, about this little guy who made films, who had a rink and a studio and nine wolves in his backyard at Meech Lake. People became interested about Mason, in spite of his efforts to keep to himself. The persistently curious in the neighbourhood would engineer a visit to play broomball or hockey, and people from farther afield sometimes found themselves phoning or knocking on the back door on unsolicited visits. Through it all, perhaps because Joyce was always there to take messages, Bill allowed himself to develop an aversion to the phone. He was never one for fancy machinery, but the phone was in a separate category. Speaking to the editor of an NFB newsletter around that time, Mason said:

> I absolutely despise the telephone. I hate it with a passion.
> When it rings it's usually for Joyce or the children. When it's
> for me it usually means it's something I have to do—write a
> letter, turn down an offer to speak—so it creates a problem

for me every time I pick it up. So I say to myself, "Who needs the publicity?" There's no way I'm going to say I'd be unhappy if I became known as a film-maker because publicity assures you of getting the jobs you want to do. But I'm not chasing it. If you get too much your life can become very involved and busy and sometimes I just like to play. I love it. I like to do nothing sometimes, or I want to paint. And I'm most happy when I'm at home working or out there in the bush making films.[7]

On one occasion, not long after Trudeaumania had swept the nation, there was a knock on the Masons' door at Meech Lake. Becky answered, and in the distracted Mom-there's-somebody-at-the-door kind of bellow that only a second-grader can muster, called Bill and Joyce to the door to meet an apologetic Pierre Trudeau, who'd been out walking from the prime minister's official residence overlooking the south end of the lake. He'd decided to stick his head in to see what all the howling was about. This chance meeting led to other visits that matured into a life-long friendship between Mason and Trudeau, based largely on their shared passion for canoes and wilderness. And after the Prime Minister married Margaret Sinclair in 1971, the two of them would come by. And in the come-one, come-all welcome that Bill extended to young people and other neighbours, he treated the Trudeaus as he would any other kindred spirits on the broomball court. One of the regulars, Bob Edwards, an Ottawa teacher, remembers upending some guy in a toque in the corner of the Meech Lake rink one Sunday afternoon and getting a spirited and colourful retort—all in good fun—only to realize afterwards that he'd just unceremoniously dumped the Prime Minister.

Between games, editing in the studio, shooting far afield, and running back and forth to Montreal, Bill continued filming inside the enclosure, requiring more and more ingenuity to motivate and cajole the animals into following the script. At one point, after a visit to Ernie Kuyt and his wolf enclosure in Fort Smith, he sent some exposed film to the Film Board for processing with a written explanation to his producer, Bill Brind, that sounds almost like an apology:

Dear Bill:

In regard to the footage I just sent in shot mostly in the enclosure. Don't be alarmed at the shortness of many of the
shots. The area was ridiculously confined and the wolf
would pass my snow backdrop in only about three or four
strides. I usually cut before the wire came in. These shots
would be valuable as quick cuts. . . .

Bill

Making the film he wanted to make, one that would please the sponsors and himself, meant more than filming wolves in the wild as well as
captive animals in enclosures. There was a human element to be added to
the wolf story. Blake James, who continued as Bill's able assistant
throughout the wolf filming as well, was the "star." Having played a
lighthouse-keeper in *Paddle to the Sea*, a time-travelling canoeist in *Rise
and Fall of the Great Lakes*, and himself—a wily First World War biplane
pilot—in *Blake*, James took on four different roles for the wolf film,
dressing differently for each incarnation: a trapper; a Skidoo hunter; a
wolf hunter, on foot; and an Indian, filmed from the back. The two men
spent long hours roaming about the country in the Land Rover, doing
one thing or another, like boys on a serious Saturday project.

At one point Bill decided that he needed to get shots of the pups
with water in the background, so he and Blake crated them up, loaded
them into the Land Rover with canoe on top, and took them north to
an island in 31 Mile Lake. The idea was that the young wolves would
not be able to get off the island. Bill could film them roaming with
water in the background and not have to worry about chain-link fenc-
ing in his shots. It would be possible to film more than four strides of
one animal before something man-made came into the frame. With the
jerry-built cages balanced on two two-by-fours across the gunwales of
the red Chestnut Pal, Bill and Blake transported the cubs to the island,
let them go, and spent the rest of the session trying unsuccessfully to
find them and, when the cubs gave up hiding, trying to catch them to
take them home again.

Bill and Blake pushed on with the film, flying Charlie, Sparky and two other wolves north to Fort Smith to see whether, having lived most of their lives in captivity, they could kill to eat. A portent of trouble came in the form of a phone call from a distraught baggage handler the night before Bill was to leave Ottawa, reporting that one of the wolves was eating its way out of its crate while waiting for shipment to Fort Smith. Not particularly bothered by this, Bill took himself down to the Ottawa Airport and found a union carpenter to make a new crate; as the man cobbled it together, he sat down and wrote to his friend Christopher Chapman. Wolves were on his mind, but there was something else bothering him. *Blake* had just been nominated for an Academy Award and Mason had realized it would be his nemesis, the producer, who would pick up the award because it was his name that was on the nomination:

> After *Paddle* I didn't bother to make an issue of this producer business because I didn't dream of getting nominated again. So with the news of the nomination of *Blake* I went straight to my Wolf Film producer and had a talk just in case. He agrees that I am the film maker and as such should accept and have my name on the award. . . . It's crazy to have the name of the producer who is really only representing the board.

Bill and Blake arrived in Fort Smith and found that the wolves too had arrived safely. They were met and hosted by CWS biologist Ernie Kuyt. Sitting in Kuyt's kitchen on this second trip, they picked a point on the map about 200 miles northeast of Fort Smith for the release of Mason's southern wolves. It never occurred to Bill—he hadn't done any of the reading or research about the ways in which predators are "wedded" to certain types of prey—that his wolves would be out of place north of the 60th parallel; it did not seem odd to him to expect wolves from Ontario, who might have known only white-tailed deer, to catch and kill a barren-ground caribou. Kuyt remembers thinking Bill's idea was a little unusual, but he went along. The problem Bill had foreseen, however, and one for which he needed Kuyt's help, had to do with the final step of his plan, which was to tranquillize and return with, at the very least, his good friend Charlie Brown.

Ernie Kuyt was as well versed as anyone in the gentle art of giving anaesthesia to large wild mammals, but it was not a particularly scientific process. No one seemed to know what dose of the available tranquillizer would be required to subdue the southern wolves sufficiently to get them back into their crates for shipment back home. As it happened, the local dogcatcher in Fort Smith had a large German shepherd who had been unclaimed for a long period, and it was due to be euthanized anyway. The dog was given over to Kuyt and Mason to experiment with dosages. Eventually they figured out what they thought to be the correct dosage per pound of animal body weight—just as the woman who owned the dog arrived back from holiday in time to see her pet struggling to get to its feet as it fought off the last of its drug-induced sleep. Happily, the dog survived the experiment. Shortly thereafter, Bill and Blake set off with their four southern wolves in a chartered Twin Otter with three weeks' supplies, a rifle and a licence to shoot a caribou to feed the wolves if necessary, a tranquillizer gun and a quantity of anaesthetic.

By the time the southern wolves were released from their crates, having been offered only water and dog kibble along the way, they had not eaten meat for four days. Blake thought they'd be ravenous and go for them as soon as the boxes were opened, but that was not the case. The two timid ones, who had not been handled very much, took off almost immediately to the edge of the lake. Sparky was wary, but good old Charlie Brown, in spite of the indignity and upset of travelling across the country in a confining wooden box, rubbed up against Bill long enough for him to cuff him playfully about the ears and send him off to catch a caribou. By the end of a week on the ice, the four wolves were still within sight of the camp, drifting in and out of the snowy woods nearby. But they had not caught anything to eat. The closest they had come to a caribou was when a group of curious animals had walked up behind the four of them in a light snowstorm, travelling upwind; the sudden realization that they were not alone on the ice startled the wolves and sent them fleeing—away from the caribou. Eventually, Blake had to shoot a caribou and cut it up to feed the hungry wolves.

Even as the four wolves started to wander farther afield, staying out of sight on the ridges beyond the shore of the lake, it became clear to Bill and Blake that their experiment had not worked—or it had, depending on one's perspective. To Bill, this experiment had proved that wolves were not natural killers. Because these wolves had lived most or, in some cases, all of their lives in captivity, he concluded that such animals must be taught to hunt and to kill to eat. Whether or not either man really believed that, they certainly had everything they needed in the way of film evidence to make such a claim in a theatre. It was time to pack up and go home.

Bill was never comfortable at the best of times with acknowledging the discomfort he felt about subjecting the wolves to pain and suffering on behalf of his film making. Later he would always claim that he did not "sacrifice" a single wolf for the sake of the film, but on the day they decided to round up the four wolves, call it sacrifice or accident, things went awry.

The tranquillizer dart was charged with anaesthetic, the light-duty 22-calibre shell that would inject the fluid implanted in the rubber plunger inside the dart, the heavier-duty shell to fire the dart loaded into the breech of the rifle, and all was set to go. With Bill in front, Blake behind with the gun, they headed out over the ice to where one wolf was standing. Even though Blake knew the trigger on the tranquillizer was twitchy, somehow, as they walked, he accidentally tripped the trigger and fired a dart that whistled past Bill's ear, narrowly missing implanting a dose of tranquillizer in his friend's head. They retrieved the dart, filled it again and set out anew. They approached and, at close range, Blake fired the dart. An animal dropped immediately, too soon for the drug to have taken effect. Something was wrong. Bill listened for a heartbeat and then started trying to administer mouth-to-mouth resuscitation. To no avail—the wolf was dead.

Still kneeling over the dead animal, Bill and Blake shivered simultaneously as a long plaintive howl drifted in from far away, on the opposite shore of the lake. Said Blake, thinking back on these events: "It was the most mournful howl. It was like they knew an animal had died. It was very, very heart-breaking. It was the most eerie feeling in a way, but also it made you very, very conscious for that moment of what they say about the spiritual aspect of all life and the relationships in that sphere."

The two film makers never spoke about this again, although they did return the body to the Ontario Department of Lands and Forests to complete the department's long-standing records. Looking back, Blake was unsure whether Bill was unaffected by the loss or so deeply affected that he couldn't show his feelings. The films he made on wolves suggest that the latter was the case. As time went on, Bill's work on the wolf took on an emotional edge that had not been there in the beginning.

Bill had read *Never Cry Wolf* during his two years with wolves at Meech Lake, and certainly after the ill-fated final trip to Fort Smith, he came to the same conclusion about the killing instinct of wolves. In a simplistic and anthropocentric way, sharing the view of many naturalists and writers before and since—among them, R.D. Lawrence and Farley Mowat—Bill was sure that wolves were not natural-born killers. His preoccupation in the wolf film became identical to Mowat's passion in his wolf book—namely, to set the record straight. That sentiment eventually was channelled into the title he chose: *Death of a Legend*. But it was never enough for Bill to work a problem through intellectually; he had to try it out for himself, he had to test his theories his way. With the wolf films, as with everything else to which he turned his creative force, he met the world with his emotions. This smouldering zeal started to get him into trouble, not only with his superiors at the Film Board, but with his sponsors at the CWS.

Having spent time with trapper and wolf hunter Fred Riddle east of Great Slave Lake, a man who had been hired by the Canadian government to implement a poisoning program for wolves in earlier years, Bill began to damn the government for its wolf policies. The CWS would obviously appear hypocritical in sponsoring his film, which told the world how beautiful and symbolically important the wolf is, when the service was simultaneously killing it with strychnine.

After much dispute, a grubby cutting copy of a final assembly of the film was viewed with draft narration on June 17, 1970. In the days leading up to this important screening, Bill had driven the commentator, Stanley Jackson, nearly mad with last-minute additions and changes to the script. No one was more pleased than Jackson at the first response from the screening. The secretary noted: "There was general agreement that there was nothing much wrong with the commentary; that just a few points needed 'touching up.'" But as one reads on in the minutes of that meeting, Bill's burning passion to make his point about wolves is evident in the choices he'd made (text from the film script appears in quotation marks):

3. Over the caribou shot. "The healthy ones couldn't care less about the wolf in their midst." . . .
   —It isn't the health of the prey that counts, it's whether or not he is being chased.
   —Get away from the "health" kick. It's the availability of the easiest prey that counts. . . .

4. Question of whether we have used too much anti-wolf material. Will not the effect on some be to reinforce the anti-wolf legend? . . .

5. "Wolves don't kill other wolves." That flat statement is not true. . . .

8. All the human killing is in the Middle Ages. Bill Mason said that he had included material right up to the present, but it was too much. . . .

11. Sequence of Okanagan helicopter taking off. Make sure that the animal is described as a moose, lest people think it's a domestic cow. . . .

13. "Wolves are nothing if not intelligent." —rather a negative way of putting it —rather damning with faint praise.
    . . .

14. Problem of using Fred Riddle.
    —does he have to be named?
    —danger of the Wildlife Service appearing hypocritical.
    —he was merely carrying out the policies of the service at that time.[8]

Knowing that Bill was not happy with this final cut of the film, and having a sense that he would go ahead and recut the film and tinker with the script on his own, NFB executives Frank Spiller and Bill Brind, who were set to go on holiday for six weeks later that month, took Bill off the NFB payroll and forbade him doing any more work on the project until they returned. By that time, Barrie Howells had been assigned to the project and, although he and Bill saw eye to eye on very little, he did feel moved, as many of Bill's producers had before him, to lobby on his behalf. In a supportive memo, he writes:

> On the 22nd of June I learned that Frank Spiller and your-self have decided that while you are on holidays for six weeks Bill Mason was to stop working on the Wolf film.
>
> Neither Bill Mason as Director or myself as producer, were consulted in this decision. Bill and I were in the cut-ting-room working on the film when you met with Frank and we could easily have been at the meeting.
>
> I believe the Board is being highly unfair to Bill Mason in making this sudden decision. Bill has turned down other work (for Chris Chapman for example) which he could have done in July but refused because he would be working on the "Wolf" film. You state in your note that he will not be paid beyond the week ending 21st June—even though the decision was made on Friday 19th June and you surely must realize that it will take a few days to store trims and outs, re-turn NFB equipment and ship away remaining wolves. I have therefore told Jane Daly to pay Bill Mason for the week of 22nd June.
>
> If you had checked with Bill Mason or myself you would have learned that Bill Mason will be away the whole month of August and is not available until September. This means you have postponed working on this film eleven weeks. What excuse do you plan to give the sponsor for nearly 3 months delay?[9]

By the late fall of 1970, the situation had gone from bad to worse. Bill wouldn't back down—he would tell the story his way. By December, the NFB was worried that Bill was so far from the original three objectives that the CWS would not accept the film in its finished form. Although Barrie Howells supported him and tried to work with him to see the film to completion, he, as producer, was answerable to the sponsor. In an act of desperation, the Film Board tried to bring Mason to heel by strengthening Howells's position. NFB liaison officer Evelyne Horne wrote to Darrell Eagles, Director of Information Services, Department of Fisheries and Forestry:

> Barrie has only recently been involved in this film, and was never in a position to learn the requirements of the project directly from the Department. Except for the most recent screening, everything he has heard about it has come second-hand and to a large extent, I am afraid, it has been coloured by strong personal opinions or at least by another person's interpretation of the requirement. Bill Mason, as you know, has become so emotionally involved that his objectivity at this point must be questioned. It is extremely difficult for Barrie to exercise the strong control that is required of a Producer. What he needs is a brief, factual review of the requirement to put him in the position of personally knowing what the sponsor wants. I am convinced that you are the person who can do it best.
>
> It is for this reason that I am asking you to see Barrie Howells for no more than half an hour. (He says that fifteen minutes would be enough!) He would meet at your convenience. You might have lunch; you might even talk to him on the 'phone.

Bill and Barrie finally resolved their differences, but a viewing of the film suggests that Bill won in the end. Five or six years after the first communications between the NFB and the CWS, and four years after Bill Mason signed onto the project, the "wolf film" was finally released as *Death of a Legend*. Although everyone involved in the project, not least Bill himself, was fed up, a prompt and enthusiastic public response to the film did much to soothe raw nerves. In the first autumn of its release, it garnered an Etrog for Best Colour Cinematography at the Canadian Film Awards, an Award for Exceptional Merit at the International Festival of Short Films in Philadelphia, and a Gold Medal at the

International Festival of Films on Tourism and Folklore in Brussels, Belgium. There was a special screening of *Death of a Legend* and a shorter NFB film, *The Sea*, at the National Arts Centre in Ottawa that fall, sponsored by the Honourable Jack David, Minister of the Environment, and preceded by a formal dinner hosted by the American ambassador and Mrs. Schmidt. Bill and Joyce, who had all but been written off as members of the lunatic fringe by their parents since adopting the wolves, were marginally reinstated in at least Bill Sr. and Sadie's eyes by the unavoidable notoriety of the film and the gold-leaf eagles on their personal invitation to dinner at the American Embassy. Bill and Joyce opted to cruise up to the guarded door of the embassy in the heap of the day, complete with body perforations, terminal rust spots and a 4- by 8-foot sheet of plywood bolted to the roof for canoes. Officials at the door took one look at the car and suggested they might be in the wrong place, until Bill produced his invitation and convinced them not only that was he invited but that, in fact, he was the guest of honour.

Death of a Legend had a profound effect on the way people thought about wolves. It was aired across the CBC television network on September 28, 1971, to large audiences and critical acclaim. A measure of its impact is contained in a 1988 history of wolf howling in Algonquin Park.

The Algonquin Park wolf-howling program had been suspended for several years in the mid-1960s following the eradication of the entire wolf population in the Highway 60 corridor "to determine the age and sex structure of the study population." Revisiting this Draconian final step in the wolf research program, chief park naturalist Dan Strickland writes: "less than a decade later, even this sort of destruction of wolves had become unthinkable. For in that period the public image of the wolf had been transformed from a mysterious, fearsome beast to the very symbol of the wild country people come to enjoy in Algonquin." Strickland acknowledges the significance of the wolf howling in this shift in public perception, but notes that "many other factors" were also at play. Significant among those factors were Farley Mowat's *Never Cry Wolf* and Bill Mason's *Death of a Legend*.

Bill's film making had moved beyond simple stories about the beauties of nature to a strong message about environmental responsibility.

These wolf films established him permanently as a leading voice in the growing environmental movement in Canada and internationally. But what is also interesting about this point in Bill's career is just *how far* he had come. The main source of wildlife films at the time had been the massive and deep-pocketed Walt Disney Corporation in California, with its professional trainers, handlers and large film crews. In his inimitable way, Bill had side-stepped the "Disney option" and, with his family to help handle the wolves, his friend Blake James to play all the on-screen parts, and himself as principal—on both sides of the camera—the little guy from Winnipeg had become a force and a presence in the international film community. Industry people who didn't know Bill assumed he made his films the same way Walt Disney did. People who knew him, especially his colleagues inside the NFB, knew that he had made a feature film with a budget that wouldn't have covered the catering on a California animal shoot and, although they may have been uncertain of his operating style, parked up in his forest studio at Meech Lake, and envious of his meteoric success, they held Bill in high esteem as a colleague and fellow Canadian film maker.

13

WATERSHED

BY THE TIME *DEATH OF A LEGEND* was gaining a hold on the Canadian public consciousness and winning awards around the world, Bill was on the career treadmill and losing control. Life at that point became a blur of film projects, public appearances, and meals at Rideau Hall and 24 Sussex Drive with such notables as Prime Minister Trudeau, former prime minister John Diefenbaker and other heads of state, including Her Majesty the Queen and Prince Phillip. He canoed when he could with old friend Blake and some of his hockey cronies and, as a way of escaping the unavoidable call of the Meech Lake studio on the days when he was at home, he started paddling more regularly with Joyce and the children. Joyce started to put her foot down to limit activity in the revolving-door restaurant, arena and Mason film fun house that took its toll on Bill (to say nothing of keeping up with food, drink and dirty dishes for the endless but enthusiastic lines of passers-through). More than ever, Bill loathed the phone. The next three years would become the crux of his career; they would also have an impact on him physically, psychologically and spiritually; tough decisions would have to be made.

At the heart of the emerging dilemma was success—rapid, unassailable, international success. On the one hand, Bill thrived on exercising his creative impulses in film, gallivanting around the countryside in aeroplanes and canoes, alone or in the company of wolves. And, to a point, he hungered for the adulation that came his way when people liked what they saw. He knew that success would lead to more film projects; and that was good. But, on the other hand, new and bigger film projects meant more producers and other creators whose filmic impulses might run contrary to his—people who might, in the end, finish up with their name on an award that was rightfully his. That simply wasn't fair. He'd made that point several times to various people, including a new boss at the NFB. But nobody seemed to understand. Success meant there were people all over the world who wanted him to do things that took him away from the process of film making, and it was the film making that kept him in touch with the wilderness, kept him in touch with his God. His canoes were collecting dust.

Bill's creative fire burned not so much to satisfy a hungry ego— although on the surface, people often interpreted what he did in this way—as to exercise his faith. And what he could see happening, as life in the early 1970s spun out of control, was a widening gap between himself and the wilderness, between himself and the divine on earth, between himself and the God of all Creation. In it simplest and most pure incarnation, this connection was made with the canoe and consummated by doing something creative with what he found there. And the simplest and most honest way to create was with brush or palette knife and paper. But since picking up a camera, first his Rolleiflex for slides and then a succession of ever-more-sophisticated ciné cameras, he had done precious little painting. He talked about his art a lot, and in that process painting had been reduced to a metaphor for understanding and rationalizing what he did through film. The highest praise he heaped on his friend and film mentor Christopher was that Chapman "painted with a camera." Although he only rarely attributed this characteristic to himself, lest he sound boastful, the camera was a way of painting pictures for a huge audience. Bill acknowledged that fact several years later:

> Given the choice I much prefer the painting medium but
> film is for me the most powerful means available today for

communicating with people. I attempt in my own feeble way to suggest the how and why. We look at the evidence written in the face of a mountain and then guess at how it got there. I think that some understanding of how things came to be leads to a deeper appreciation of the world around us and I hope results in a greater concern for how we care for it.[1]

But still he yearned, throughout his film making, to paint. After his death, daughter Becky would say that her dad "painted in his head," which was her way of acknowledging the paucity of actual canvases. In the midst of everything in 1971, and in spite of the fact that there was not a lot of money in the family accounts, Joyce supported a seemingly whimsical notion on Bill's part to attend an exhibition of work by Joseph Mallord William Turner, the Romantic British landscape painter, at the Tate Gallery in London, England. Better than anyone, Joyce had a sense of how success was eating into Bill's soul. Turner, like Tom Thomson, was a hero of Bill's and, if he couldn't get things together sufficiently to paint himself, he could do the next best thing and put himself in the presence of the master's work.

Still, Bill honoured his commitment to the NFB and the CWS and completed a second, shorter film about wolves. *Wolf Pack* was only twenty minutes, compared to the hour's length of *Death of a Legend*, and attempted, with measured success, to illustrate the yearly cycle of a pack of wild wolves. Jurors at the American Film Festival had mixed reactions when it was submitted for judging. One juror compared it to another competing film about wolves, *Following the Tundra Wolf*, saying that *Wolf Pack* contained essentially the same information but that it was "a little too long" and "especially wordy at the end." Another agreed it was "not as inclusive as many other films on wolves." Another liked the photography but thought the story line "oversimplified." And a fifth juror shared that view, adding "the blend of music and narration leaves much to be desired; too anthropomorphic; over-simplified; fits into the category of nature writing."[2]

Work on the making of *Wolf Pack* was suspended when the film was all but completed because of a notion about a full-length feature film on wolves that had been niggling away in the back of Bill's mind. During filming on Baffin Island, in northern British Columbia and at Fort Smith, when weeks passed without wolf activity of any kind, Bill used his self-timer, as he had done so often with his stills camera in the early years in Whiteshell, to film himself in the process. Over the years he had compiled many such sequences that told the story of one man in the wilderness, making a film about wolves. Unfortunately it was a story that was of absolutely no interest to the CWS or the National Film Board. Sometime during the long hours alone, waiting for wild wolves to enter his viewfinder, Bill had come to the conclusion that there was another film to be made in the wolf series, only this one would not be an instructional device, a short for television, library and classroom use; rather, it would be a theatrical feature that would play in movie houses across the country. By now, however, things had soured sufficiently with producers and sponsors of the wolf project that they would have nothing to do with the idea. Mason had lost it. A feature film from out-takes? Impossible.

Bill, however, was sure the idea would work. He knew, and certainly he had been reminded of this point repeatedly by higher-ups at the NFB, that a film about himself was not something that should be created with public funds. But that was exactly what he liked about the idea. Through public speaking about his experiences with wolves, he had learned that people were fascinated by the process through which the films were made. A trip to see *Endless Summer* in Ottawa on a Tuesday night convinced him that first-person narrative in a feature film could work. But the more he pushed, the more entrenched government brass became in their resistance to the idea.

Dejected but unbowed by this frustration, Bill backed away from the feature idea, cut the film to an hour in the Meech Lake cabin studio, and showed it to Murray Creed of CBC Television's fledgling program *The Nature of Things*. Creed loved the film but did not have sufficient funds in his budget that year to complete the project. As it happened, the NFB Distribution Branch had contracted with the CBC for thirteen films that year and was still looking for material. The hour-long assembly about Mason making the other two wolf films was sold to the CBC as part of that package. And in the meantime, Bill accepted contracts to make *In Search of the Bowhead Whale* with the NFB and an American co-sponsor, and another film, *Face of the Earth*, about the formation of the earth's crust.

At that juncture, Ralph Ellis of Keg Productions in Toronto, a man who had worked for many years in distribution for the NFB before branching out into his own film-production and -distribution company, called Bill to ask if he could cut together a thirty-minute film on wolves for the Audubon film series he was assembling. Bill told him about the one-hour film he had just completed and about his dashed hopes for a feature film. In an unpublished manuscript, he recalls his meeting with Ellis:

> I'll never forget that screening. He positively drooled. He was climbing the walls. He said, "I've got to have that film. It's a feature." He asked, "Can you edit it to an hour and a half?" I rolled my eyes heavenward and explained that I could. He went directly to Sydney Newman and talked him into buying it back from CBC. I began reediting it back up to 90 minutes. But instead of putting the old stuff back I dug up and edited whole new sequences from outs that I had previously discarded. . . . I completed the film to my satisfaction. I was extremely pleased with Larry Crosley's score and the sound and effects by John Knight and Ken Page. Michel Descombes put it all together at the rerecording. A superb and sensitive job. The blow-up [from 16mm to 35mm to allow the film to run on movie-house projectors] was beyond my wildest dreams.[3]

What happened next was also beyond his wildest dreams. Amid much publicity hoopla, the wolf feature was test-released in Edmonton. Bill was so out of his element with the publicity that at one point Ellis, the perennial joker, had him convinced that he would be dressing up in a rented wolf suit for the premiere. That isn't what happened, of course; Ellis flew in a tame wolf and, at the pre-release press conference, a now white-bearded Bill in buckskin jacket, with live wolf under his arm, was photographed by the press before a dramatic poster showing one of his drawings of Charlie Brown with yellow eye against a silhouetted yellow moon. Local papers ran a colouring contest for kids (of a simplified version of the poster image) to win a pass for the whole family to see the film. Ads ran in the Edmonton papers announcing an "Edmonton World Premiere" for *Cry of the Wild* at the Jasper, Klondike and Plaza Two theatres, proclaiming in large print under the title that "All of Edmonton Is Talking about 'Big Charlie' THE WOLF." The film didn't do spectacularly as a result of all this hype, but it did perform well enough for Ralph Ellis to cement a deal with a U.S. distributor, American National Enterprises.

American National Enterprises, a so-called four-wall distribution company (a term describing its practice of entering a city and renting theatres to show its films as opposed to working through the theatre-owning film-distribution companies like Odeon and Famous Players) was very interested in *Cry of the Wild* because of Pacific National Enterprises' recent runaway four-wall success with *Vanishing Wilderness*, a nature film that made an estimated $16 million in its first year of North American release. Upon signing the deal with Keg Productions, ANE decided to open the film in New York City, first saturating the local television markets with spit-teeth-and-bristle clips of Charlie, and talking it up in a big way with the local press. The film opened on January 2, 1974, in thirty-five New York City theatres and expanded to eighty film houses two days later. The results were staggeringly successful. In the first week, the film made $965,000, outgrossing *Papillon*, *The Sting*, *Serpico*, *Magnum Force*, *American Graffiti*, *The Way We Were*, *The Godfather*, *The Paper Chase*—every major film except *The Exorcist*.[4] Distribution expanded westward across the United States and north into Quebec, and before everything went wrong with the deal between Keg and ANE, the "impossible" feature film had made $8 million and become Canada's most successful feature-length documentary to date.[5]

The agreement between Keg and ANE provided for a quarter of the net revenue from *Cry of the Wild* to be returned to Keg. And through the agreement with Keg, the NFB had royalty provisions for theatrical revenues outside the United States and television revenue within the United States and a special clause promising the NFB 85 per cent of all net revenue received by Keg from ANE.[6] There is no doubt that some of these agencies made a great deal of money from *Cry of the Wild*. But, early on, ANE tried to renegotiate the deal, writing to the NFB with the following concerns:

> As you know, we entered into a contract with Keg Productions, Ltd., of Toronto, and the National Film Board for distribution rights to the movie *Cry of the Wild* filmed by Mr. Bill Mason. Mr. Pedersen and Mr. R.V. Coalson, president of this company, are disturbed that there are apparently many identical sequences from *Cry of the Wild* in *Death of a Legend*. . . . We also have indications as well that *Death of a Legend* was shown recently on Los Angeles television. . . . TV exposure of even a similar film, even if there were no identical sequences, can do harm to the success of the theatrical distribution of *Cry of the Wild*.

ANE, contending that their distribution costs were higher than expected, and revenues lower than projected (as a result of the television exposure of *Death of a Legend*, they claimed), ended up in messy legal wrangling with Ralph Ellis and Keg Productions. The irony of all this was that Bill Mason, who made the film while under contract, received not a penny of these revenues. He noted:

> People ask me whether I am angry or bitter that I didn't make a bundle. My answer is, no way. I received an adequate salary while I was working on [*Cry of the Wild*]. The film has a message I wanted to get across to as many people as I could, and it's been seen by millions. American National distributed it with a pizzazz that no other distributor could have begun to equal. The film has been sold all over the world to both theatrical distribution and TV. My failure to negotiate a royalty for myself is nobody's problem but my own.[7]

What bothered Mason much more than the money were two aspects of the industry that underlined his love/hate relationship with the NFB and the Canadian film establishment. He was irritated in the extreme that more Canadian publications didn't pick up on his work the way the American media had, and didn't credit his work when they did discuss it. For example, in the April 1975 issue of *Maclean's* magazine, John Hofsess wrote an article about Ralph Ellis entitled "In the footsteps of Walt Disney" about the theatrical release of *Cry of the Wild*. The article gave the impression that *Cry of the Wild* was developed, produced and marketed by Ralph Ellis of Keg Productions. NFB Director of Information and Promotion, David Novek, responded in a letter to the editor, saying, "*Cry of the Wild* owes its success to Bill Mason who is one of the outstanding but unsung film makers in Canada. His other NFB films, *Paddle to the Sea*, *Rise and Fall of the Great Lakes*, *Blake*, *Death of a Legend*, and *In Search of the Bowhead Whale*, rank among the most popular ever produced by the Film Board and have won some 20 awards." But that didn't salve the wound. In his own letter to the same editor, Mason's bitterness shows through:

> I was surprised to see something in print relating to *Cry of the Wild* in a Canadian publication. For me that's a noteworthy event. To my knowledge there has been only one write up that could pass for a review in a Canadian newspaper. There have been 16 reviews in American newspapers that I am aware of, all favourable to extremely enthusiastic. However I would like to take exception to your comments on *Death of a Legend*, the film you referred to as "unremarkable, destined to have a brief play on television and disappear". As a reviewer you are entitled to your opinions . . . but if you had checked with the National Film Board you would find that *Death of a Legend* has become one of the Board's best selling, most used hour length films. In regard to *Cry of the Wild* where did you get the idea that it is an expanded version of *Death of a Legend*? In the entire film there is only one duplicate shot. Just because the film is made by the same person and on the same subject doesn't make it a version. In fact I have just completed yet another film about wolves called *Wolf Pack* which is also a version of neither. Your article also erred seriously in attributing

the production to Keg Productions. *Cry of the Wild* was produced by the National Film Board of Canada and was made possible by the Canadian Wildlife Service. And I ought to know because I researched, scripted, directed, photographed, edited and narrated the film. . . . Ralph Ellis deserves all the credit for recognizing the possibilities of *Cry of the Wild* as a feature film and for putting some money where his mouth was, as the saying goes.[8]

Later that same month, Hofsess published an article entitled "Headless Horsemen," in *Cinema Canada* and raised Mason's ire a second time. In typical style, Bill wrote:

> Your article Headless Horsemen was fantastic. . . . But darn it, you did it again. You credited Ralph Ellis with the making of *Cry of the Wild*. This really is very frustrating. I get just as angry when I see the film credited to the NFB as though in some way the building churned it out. The film was made by me. . . .[9]

Bill also had a few words to say about journalists who continually criticized the NFB. An arts writer for *Maclean's* damned the NFB with faint praise after the Film Board had won fourteen out of twenty awards in the non–feature-film category at the Canadian Film Awards. Mason was incensed, and shot this reply to Canada's national magazine:

> If you can't kick it ignore it. If it's Canadian and you can't kick it, ignore it. . . . There are things wrong with the NFB that are common to all government agencies that well deserve criticism. Kick it where it deserves it. Many of us who work for the NFB kick in the right places all the time. But to completely ignore the accomplishments of the NFB in the producing of films that are highly regarded around the world is definitely not responsible journalism. You are following in the great Canadian tradition "if it's Canadian and it does something right, ignore it."[10]

For Bill, there was a much more pressing problem: hassling over rights and revenues kept him firmly in the secular world and separated him from his spiritual sense of self. Awareness of this rift was particularly acute in the wake of *Cry of the Wild*'s bittersweet success. Thinking back on this pivotal time in his life, Mason wrote "Some Private Thoughts," which surfaced after his death:

> What is the most exciting and the most frightening experience that I have had during my twelve years of filming I am often asked. It is one and the same. The moment I signed my contract to make the wolf film. . . . I had never seen a wild wolf in its natural habitat. And I was terrified at the possibility of blowing a big budget and coming back with nothing. . . .
>
> Filming at 40 below is never easy but I like it. I like the feeling of experiencing the natural world where nothing has been changed by man. Experiencing nature as God made it. Not that the changes wrought by man are always bad. On the contrary the works of man can also be very exciting. But there is a lot to learn from the natural world if we learn to listen. The big problem is hearing what nature has to say through the loudness of what we are and have created in the natural world. . . .
>
> My films are to the best of my ability an attempt to bridge the gap between ourselves and things natural. I am dealing with things closely related to the spirit. The spirit of man, the spirit of nature which is for me God. The God who created it and breathed life into it. I am convinced that our problems in relation to nature and also in human terms are because of our alienation from God the Creator. An alienation caused by us. Not God. It is not His fault that we prefer to leave Him out of our lives. To disassociate Him from nature. To assume that the world around us is the result of nothing more than a process of natural selection. I just don't buy that. The world around us speaks to me of an incredible mind. A mind beyond our comprehension. A mind

that designed it and put it into operation and then gave us
the various senses and a mind capable of wonder and awe.
We are born to ask questions—why and how.[11]

With now dozens of awards for his films and in the glow of international success with *Cry of the Wild*, Mason was at the peak of his career. He was in the studio with Eric Weissburg, Nexus and the Canadian Brass recording the soundtrack for *Face of the Earth*. He was affiliated with scientists and world whale authorities, flying to New York City and Alaska on his commissioned film *In Search of the Bowhead Whale*. They were dining with Her Majesty at 24 Sussex Drive: Joyce sat flanked by Prince Phillip and David Lewis. Bill was across the table from John Diefenbaker and beside a lovely woman in an evening dress, who couldn't stand to toast the Queen because the leg of Mason's chair was on her dress, pinning her in a sitting position. There was a big wolf conference in Washington, where Bill was keynote speaker. He agreed to go with Joyce and their landlords, Dave and Moiya Wright, for a winter vacation in Antigua. The 1974 awards banquet for the Mason rink broomball league was held around the table in the prime minister's residence, with Margaret and Pierre Trudeau. And in October of that year, Bill was elected to the Royal Canadian Academy.

No one had any idea about the private turmoil underneath all the glitter and success. The Royal Canadian Academy elected him to the status of academician for his competence and success in the art of film making. To the members of the RCA who applauded his investiture, Bill Mason was the epitome of what a Canadian film maker should be—independent, talented, headstrong, committed, a rugged-looking wilderness type, resourceful, and slightly irascible on matters of conscience—a film maker's film maker. But Bill, in his heart of hearts, had never considered himself to be anything other than an artist—a painter, to be precise. This film business was just a means to an end, a way of sharing his love for the natural world with a larger audience, a way of showing the world the majesty and power of God's work on earth. In the midst of all the pomp at the November annual RCA dinner in Toronto that year, Bill approached one of his old buddies from the Winnipeg School of Art, Tony Tascona, an earlier inductee in the RCA for his fine art, print making and painting. After slaps on the back and a few laughs about the old days, Tascona was dumbstruck to learn from Bill that he had decided to stop film making and paint full-time. Recalling that moment, Tascona later said:

> I couldn't believe what I was hearing! You just can't do that. Billy was a damn fine film maker and a superb commercial artist and illustrator, but he was no painter. You just can't do that. I thought he was crazy, telling me that. I don't think he ever studied art. He went to art school with the rest of us but he only took out of it what he needed. I spoke to Billy about structure; he understood it from the film point of view, the film maker's perspective, but remember when you work in that format it's a two-dimensional plane. In painting you have to make it into a three-dimensional plane or a four-dimensional plane, if possible, and at least create an illusion. Well, Billy wasn't into illusion—Billy was into *fact*. You know? He got in among the goddamn wolves. He had to get into the canoe and actually paddle it; he had to portage with it. He had to do all the physicality things. Illusion was not part of his life. I had no idea why he ever thought he should be a painter.

For Bill Mason the great adventure was always pushing ahead to the next challenge, realizing the next impossible dream. The key to achieving the turn-about to painting would be similar to the shift he had made in the filming of *Cry of the Wild*, the walk from behind the camera to in front of it. Fortunately for Bill, he did find some middle ground. Deep inside, he knew Tascona was at least in part correct—he hadn't painted much, but that didn't mean he couldn't try, and succeed. The next best thing to actually becoming a painter was to create a character, just like Tom Thomson, who would roam the wilderness in a canoe, painting as he went. It may be at this moment that the canoeing films had their genesis in Bill's imagination. The plan was that *eventually* he could become that character in real life, and paddle off into the sunset.

What would drive such a talented film maker to apparently abandon his craft at the height of his success? Producer Bill Brind wrote of Mason in the late 1970s:

> Bill is perhaps the most complete film maker I have ever met. Who else directs, edits, shoots, researches, writes and reads his own commentaries? He is truly a great talent and a splendid fellow. And in a strange way I think that only Canada could have produced such a man. Anyone who thinks we don't have an identity should spend time with Mason—he couldn't possibly be anything other than a Canadian.[12]

But this Canadian was in need of a new professional and creative challenge. Bill was searching for a deeper understanding of wilderness, for clues about humanity's role in the natural world, and to satisfy a spiritual hunger he could no longer ignore. He always looked for challenges, pushed himself creatively, and, at this point in his career, having been so successful in film, it was time to move on. It was as simple as that.

Though it may appear that at the peak of his career Bill planned to stop filming and start painting, in *his* mind he was simply continuing along his chosen path as an artist. Art, in whatever medium, was Bill's way to go beyond physical wilderness of Canada into the rich landscape of his imagination. In his *paysage intérieur*, rapids and waterfalls had metaphorical more than functional significance; canoes were vehicles of spiritual quest, and creativity was the one ability that separated people from all of the other creatures. With film one could only go so far in this terrain, and with *Cry of the Wild* he'd gone about as far as he could. But with painting, the possibilities for exploring inside were limitless.

Back even to the days of the solitary drawing and painting in his studio at 209 Oakwood, drawing for the annual art competition at Kelvin High School, painting frozen hockey players, rendering Wild West scenes for his dad, or experimenting with his oils and pencils on trips in the Whiteshell, Bill had confirmed time and time again his gifts as an artist. He was not a big man, a football player, a word man, or a man who was good with numbers—he was an artist. He needed to create, to exercise his God-given talent. This ability had led him to success, first in commercial art, and then in film, but he had to progress. Not to create was to stagnate artistically, and to do that was to squander his talent—and that just might be a sin.

In this sense, it was perfectly natural and an obvious move for Bill to keep creating, to celebrate the canoe, and to set his sights on painting. Just like the character he would create in the canoeing films he was about to make, in his mind's eye he was that Tom Thomson–like character who quit his job every spring to paddle and portage beyond the threshold of wilderness and paint. As a boy alone in his room or sitting in the canoes at Grand Beach—in fact, throughout his conscious life— he had been a canoeist. Over the years, however, the character had developed and matured from the collegial paddler—the voyageur—to the solitary canoeist searching with his palette and canvas to celebrate the divine on earth. Painting made perfect sense. Even though he didn't actually do much for most of his adult life, he affirmed the plan repeatedly with what he said, especially retrospectively:

> I look around me at the colours, the textures, the designs. It's like being in an art gallery. God is the artist. And he's given us the ability to enjoy all this, to wonder, and in our own small ways to express our creativity and that's why I like being here.[13]
>
> When I go to the wilderness—to me that is like entering the painting that God has made, because evidence of who God is and what kind of a person he is, is all around me. The power in a waterfall, the storm, the lightning, the wind blowing in the trees, the waves on a lake. And to see that power . . . you realize what that power is when you paddle against huge waves on a lake—or you fire through rapids and your canoe is just taken and tossed like a leaf against a cliff.[14]

With that challenge firmly entrenched in his mind, Mason was ever the pragmatist. *Saying* he wanted to paint was an excellent way to crystallize the ideal. Making the canoeing films would allow him a creative outlet for his exploration of this general theme. One day he *would* paint, but he was over the watershed. He still had to make a living. Film had been good to him that way. The canoe films would allow him to do that en route to his ultimate dream.

14

MR. CANOEHEAD

WHILE BILL PONDERED HIS LOVE/HATE relationship with the National Film Board, and schemed to find ways to realize the dream of painting full-time while still maintaining an income, he accepted an offer from the NFB to make a series of instructional films about canoeing. Until this point in his life, work as a film maker had pre-empted painting and serious canoeing, which in turn had left him feeling disconnected from nature. But this project was the perfect compromise. He could film *and* canoe simultaneously. It would be like old times at Manitoba Pioneer Camp and Whiteshell Provincial Park. Bill accepted the canoe-film contract, shortly after his induction into the Royal Canadian Academy in the fall of 1974, and told everyone that this series would be *it* with respect to his career in film. However, he had no idea how this work would increase his popularity to icon status in the mythology of the Canadian wild. The plan in the back of his mind was to get out of film permanently; unfortunately, the farther along he moved with the canoe-film project, the more distant became the possibility of retiring to the life of a wilderness painter.

The wolf films, especially *Cry of the Wild*, positioned Bill firmly in the middle of the burgeoning environmentalism of the late 1960s and early 1970s. Unknown to Bill, when he embarked on the canoe project, he was riding a wave of concern that had been building slowly for nearly a century and that was now just beginning to crest. Parks, forest reserves, bird and wildlife sanctuaries had been created in Canada since the latter decades of the nineteenth century, and people had vague notions of the need for protecting natural areas, largely for self-serving recreational purposes, actions that were informed by European writers such as Jean-Jacques Rousseau, William Wordsworth, Lord Byron and, of course, Canada's great conserving impostor, Archie Belaney. Likewise the works of American conservationists and writers like John James Audubon, James Fenimore Cooper, Ralph Waldo Emerson and Henry David Thoreau, John Muir and Gifford Pinchot influenced thinking in Canada about notions of nature and wilderness. In 1962, just as Mason was getting settled at Meech Lake, Rachel Carson published *Silent Spring*, a book that convinced people for the first time that this vaguely romantic notion of conservation and environmental degradation had real and practical consequences.

During the 1960s, as Bill worked towards the wolf films, concerns about pollution and awareness of exponential population growth piqued public concern for the environment. Specialized groups such as the Society for the Promotion of Environmental Conservation (in Western Canada), Pollution Probe (in Ontario) and the Ecology Action Centre (in the Maritimes) were formed to focus growing public awareness about air and water pollution, hazardous wastes and the careless use of pesticides. It was as if at some point in the 1960s people suddenly realized that *Silent Spring* was not science fiction, and jumped to take action against the effects of our own consumption.

In Ontario particularly, as Bill filmed wolves in the spring of 1968, his new friend and colleague, the wolf biologist Douglas Pimlott, along with Abbott Conway, Walter Gray and Patrick Hardy, founded the Algonquin Wildlands League, thereby marking out the territory for the entrenchment of the modern era of wilderness preservation over logging and the future of Ontario's provincial parks. The Wildlands League reiterated for Bill the environmental concerns he had heard from his friend Christopher Chapman in Quetico a decade earlier. At the time Mason himself had only passive interest in the progress of wilderness conservation, instead—almost unwittingly—focusing on the here and now in his wolf films with a strong sense of righting a wrong with respect to the wolf's reputation as a savage killer, and only a vague and diffuse notion of the wolf as a symbol for diminishing wilderness. That larger view would come later. Although from that point on in his life, his actions with respect to the environment, especially his associations with conservation organizations like the Algonquin Wildlands League, made Mason appear to be an active environmentalist, his real motivation to celebrate the wolf and to be concerned about the wilderness had to do with his allegiance to another environmental organization—namely, the Church.

By 1972, environmentalism was becoming a political reality: the United Nations Conference on the Human Environment was held in Stockholm; the first Earth Day was convened across North America; and the Club of Rome published its seminal report *Limits to Growth,* on the predicament of mankind, that featured the powerful allegory of the pond—the day the pond is half-covered with lily-pads is only one day away from its being totally covered—to illustrate the principle of exponential growth. Part of the reason why people responded so enthusiastically to the wolf films, especially *Cry of the Wild,* was that here was a fellow who not only embodied their concern for humanity's effect on the earth, but did so in a caring, humble, humorous and artistic manner. Almost inadvertently, Mason became a purveyor of hope, someone doing something good for the environment who passed on the same message people had been hearing everywhere else, but did so without hitting people over the head with it, without immersing them in gloom and doom. In his light style, Mason made the points gently, through spectacular visual images and accessible narrative. He put a face on people's dreams for a better world.

The same phenomenon happened with canoeing at more or less the same time. With the uncomplicated good fortune of Forrest Gump or the baffling serendipity of Peter Sellers's enigmatic character Chance Gardener in the film *Being There,* as Bill turned to an activity he loved and naïvely prepared to make instructional canoeing films for the NFB, canoeing was riding a wave of unprecedented popularity that had been building invisibly since the turn of the century, noticeably since the

Second World War, and that was beginning to crest in the early 1970s. No one else was making films about canoeing. Canoeing associations were hopelessly mired in their own bureaucracy, and the countless canoeing camps, clubs and other organizations across Canada and the United States were hungry for anything to supplement their blossoming programs. Almost inadvertently, Mason fed this need and in doing so gained almost instant recognition and adulation for his efforts.

In order to understand the context in which Bill created his canoeing films, one must loop back to the evolution of recreational canoes following the Second World War. The war had forced the Grumman aircraft company to perfect aluminum fabrication techniques that were transferred almost instantaneously to canoes in 1945. And the Aircraft Division of Canadian Vickers in east-end Montreal, which had turned the science of wood lamination into an artform through the wartime production of Mosquito bombers and other wooden aircraft, did the same. Vickers was sold to the U.S. Electric Boat Company, and it was only a matter of time before that technology too would find its way into the Plycraft Canoe Company, which produced canoes that were sold to eager consumers across the country via catalogue marketing, eager consumers like a young Bill Mason who, in 1954, was tired of renting canoes and finally had enough money of his own to purchase a brand-new Plycraft from the Hudson's Bay Company catalogue.

But what also happened in the wake of the Second World War was a gradual but inexorable increase in the number and popularity of children's summer camps across the country, many of which concentrated not so much on the styles and techniques of flatwater racing, as Mason had done at Manitoba Pioneer, but on canoe-tripping, branching out into wilderness to build character in the youth of the day. By the late 1950s and early 1960s an accomplished canoeist named Omer Stringer was legendary for the way that he had inspired summer staff and campers in Algonquin Park to master the art of paddling and to go forth into the wilderness with their newfound skills. And other camps, such as Keewaydin, Temagami, Wanapitei, Kandalore, Kapitachouane and Widjiwagan, were adding their force to the growth of wilderness canoeing by pioneering a great variety of routes through Northern Ontario and Quebec.

In the realm of private recreational canoeing, there was steady growth too. Lighter, stronger boats and improved rail and road transportation allowed people who hadn't grown up in the wilderness tradition to at least try a short canoeing trip. Many of these aficionados were male hunters and fishers, but women were involved as well, as they had been all along. There is no doubt, however, that it was the Ottawa Voyageurs, led by the irrepressible Eric Morse and his wife Pamela, who pointed the way north from the mid-1950s onward, proving again and again that it was not only possible to travel the remote routes of the original voyageurs and gentleman adventurers, but that one could live to tell the tale.

By the late 1960s the growth in wilderness canoeing, in concert with increased concern for the environment, appeared to reach some kind of critical mass, causing an explosion of interest. Eric Morse published his epic article "Summer Travel in the Canadian Barrens" in the May 1967 issue of the *Canadian Geographical Journal*, describing his adventures on all of the major watersheds of the Northwest Territories and the evolution of the U-Paddle one-way canoe rental service he had engineered with the Hudson's Bay Company. The how-to flavour of this article played down the monumental significance of Morse's accomplishments as a paddler and his vast contribution to wilderness paddling. The text of the story was matter-of-fact, just like Morse himself, and realistically set out the risks, hazards and rewards of northern canoe travel, so much so that the article was almost immediately reprinted as a travel brochure by the Northwest Territories Tourist Office in Ottawa, which began as follows:

> For anyone wanting a *different* holiday the Barren Lands beckon: rugged scenery, unbelievable colour, tremendous sweep, big game, fabulous fishing—all spiced with just enough risk to border on adventure, in one of the few large areas of uninhabited virgin wilderness still left in the world.[1]

In the following year, 1968, Morse published his first book, *Fur Trade Routes of Canada/Then and Now*, with a foreword by the Rt. Hon. Pierre E. Trudeau. *Fur Trade Routes* piqued the enthusiasm of anyone even vaguely interested in voyageurs and/or canoeing in any form or style, and became the impetus for many people, individually and through camps and clubs, to follow the voyageurs using Morse's guide as example and inspiration. One of the most potent spin-offs of Morse's example was the establishment of the Wild River Survey by Trudeau and the reigning Liberal government which, from 1971 to 1974, systematically surveyed the recreational paddling potential of almost every major navigable waterway in the country. When these reports started to appear, and certainly when the subsequent series of river guidebooks was published, they fell into the hands of eager paddlers. Not least of those who took vicarious pleasure in reading this literature was Trudeau's Meech Lake neighbour Bill Mason, who did what he could to exercise his paddling interest with junkets on the lake and in nearby creeks in the spring, but who was otherwise far too occupied making films about whales and wolves to dally with long canoe trips.

Another person who read Eric Morse's work and the Wild River Survey guides, and who *was* in a position to act, was Ottawan Wally Schaber. In the early 1970s, Schaber applied what he was reading and what he had learned at summer camp to commercial wilderness canoe trips expedited out of his mother's west-end garage. It was only a matter of time, or so it seemed, before Schaber would hook up with Mason. They took their first trip together in 1974, beginning a friendship and professional canoeing collaboration that would ground everything Bill would later do and say about canoeing. Schaber's business, Black Feather Wilderness Adventures, was just one of an abundance of such outfits that got started across the country. Canoeing was a phenomenon. Thinking back on this time, renowned paddler and canoe collector Kirk Wipper said, "It was as if the canoe had just been invented!" And with the wave came ever more people who were hungry for instruction, for inspiration and for images to help them live out the great Canadian canoeing dream, hungry for the teachings of an accessible, informative, entertaining and committed public leader like Bill Mason.

So it was that Bill moved onto the early stages of his canoeing films, buoyed by a hundred-year-old tradition of wilderness canoeing that was taking off again in the early 1970s, partially as a way for people to reconnect with the environment, partially as an expression of the growing conservation movement, and partially also because canoeing was such a non-consumptive, healthy, restorative thing to do. Bill himself saw the canoeing assignment as a vehicle that would convey him out of filming, towards his painting, back to nature, and back into league with his God, the God of Creation.

Curious though it may seem, the first business move Bill made on acceptance of the canoe film project was to join the National Film Board as a salaried staff member. Strange that a person intent on getting out of film would parley himself into a more permanent association with a film organization. But there were pragmatics to be considered: a full-time salary would give the family a regular source of income, but, more important, work as an NFB staffer entitled him to pension benefits that might one day support his painting. By this time Bill had an extremely impressive portfolio of films and awards to his credit, and despite the fact that he had run amok with many people at the Film Board (he would say near the end of his career that he made a "clean sweep," meaning he never finished one film while still on completely cordial terms with his producers), there were still people at the NFB who thought it an excellent strategic move to bring Mason's talents in-house.

The prime motivation for joining the Film Board was to stabilize the family income. Years of freelancing had been good years professionally for Mason, but in many ways they had been lean years financially for the family. With the steady stream of people coming through the house for meals of various kinds, along with the intensive fiscal demands of Bill's travel and work in the Meech Lake studio, there was often little or no financial reserve to cushion the family should Bill fall ill again or should they be faced with some other large, unexpected expense. Joyce did the family finances, in addition to taking the lion's share of responsibility for raising the children, and had turned stretching a little money to go a long way into an artform. But enough was enough. They had watched *Cry of the Wild* become one of the highest-, if not *the* highest-grossing feature film produced by the NFB, and they had watched the awards pile up, but in the face of all that, it was frustrating that their bank balance did not reflect this success.

Mason turned to his old friend Wilber Sutherland—the man from Inter-Varsity who had given him his first film assignment to make *Wilderness Treasure* for Manitoba Pioneer Camp. By now Sutherland had left Inter-Varsity and headed Imago, a private foundation whose purpose was to help Christian creators in the arts. Mason explained the situation to Sutherland, who in turn retained James F. Kennedy, a lawyer with the firm of Osler, Hoskin and Harcourt in Toronto, to negotiate Mason's full-time contract with the NFB. One of the many strategic moves made by Kennedy was to ask the Masons for breakdowns of expenses reaching back eight years; it had occurred to him that one of the reasons they had less money than they should have had was because Bill had not claimed for legitimate costs for repair of NFB equipment in his care. A letter written by Kennedy to the NFB director of administration indicates the thoroughness with which he attacked the task of formalizing Mason's full-time relationship with the Film Board:

Dear Marc:

Bill Mason has forwarded to me a breakdown of his outlays for camera equipment and repairs during the years 1967 to 1974 inclusive which totalled the remarkable amount of $10,092.75 on account of capital expenditures and $1,019.22 on account of repairs and expenses, or a total of $11,111.97. These figures include expenditures made in 1971 in respect of studio facilities on his property totalling $3,293.11, but do not include any expenditures in respect of canoes and other camping equipment. During the same period, Bill received total revenue from the Film Board (exclusive of his regular contract payments) totalling $3,735, or a short-fall of approximately $7,400. Bill has a detailed breakdown of these figures and what they relate to, and I have suggested that he meet with you when he is next in Montreal to go over them further. . . . I am sure you will agree that at the very least they indicate that some adjustment should be made by the Film Board to Bill to cover this

200

short-fall. I had no idea when we spoke about this earlier that the amount was as substantial as it is.[2]

James Kennedy was successful in completing these negotiations, and in the months leading up to Bill's forty-sixth birthday in 1975, he became a full-time member of the National Film Board, joining the ranks with Eugene Boyko (*Helicopter Canada*), Derek Lamb (*I Know an Old Lady*), Colin Low (*Universe*), Norman McLaren (*Fiddle-de-dee, Neighbours*), Claude Jutra (*A Chairy Tale*), Grant Munro (*One Little Indian, My Financial Career*) and Gerald Potterton (*The Railrodder, The Ride*). As a freelancer, Mason had been nominally affiliated with an organizational unit within the NFB known as Studio C. By the time he entered full-time employment with the NFB, his pattern of working alone and away from the Board offices in Montreal was well established. In that sense, it didn't matter to which studio he would be assigned as a staffer; because of his distaste for Montreal and for ensemble film work, no matter what unit housed his efforts, Mason would turn up only as a name on staff lists and a budget line. He began his full-time work inside Studio C and, before long, was invited to join a new unit, Studio D.

By this time, Kathleen Shannon, the film editor and former Crawley Films employee who had bailed out from editing *Blake*, had become executive producer of a new production team within the Film Board, Studio D, the so-called Women's Unit. In spite of the tiff about the editing of *Blake*, she and Bill had parted friends, and Shannon remained a fan of Mason's films. Thinking back on Bill's early work, she laughs and remembers showing *Paddle to the Sea* at her son's fourth birthday party. The film was such a hit that her son requested a showing at every birthday party until he was well into his teens. While her son was growing, Shannon had become a film maker in her own right at the Film Board, but when given the opportunity she jumped at it in the early 1970s to "see what we [women film makers] would do when not directly supervised by men."[3]

At first, when Bill happened to be in Montreal to participate, his affiliation with Kathleen Shannon and Studio D worked reasonably well. Studio D was the best of a bunch of bad options. Even though he was now an NFB staffer, he was well set up at Meech Lake and used to working alone and being in control: he harboured no intentions of becoming part of the "family" in Studio D or any other group in the NFB head offices in Montreal. From the other side of the fence, Shannon remembers the tension that came from the blending of men and women under the original mandate for the Women's Unit. The men didn't often come to meetings and, when they did, were by and large uncomfortable with the "groupness" that the women tried to foster. Shannon learned that "the men in the studio took an enormous amount of energy." Nevertheless, under Kathleen Shannon's leadership, Studio D gave each of its members an administrative home inside the NFB and allowed all of them, including Bill, to go about the business of making films. The irony of this unlikely match between Bill and Studio D was that this was the creative environment in which courageous and radical films such as *If You Love This Planet* and *Not a Love Story* were made. Like much of Bill's work, Studio D films were different from anything the Board had ever done, and yet the way that Bill achieved *his* difference, in his solitary, iconoclastic way, never meshed with the collegial, collaborative style of Kathleen Shannon and the women of Studio D.

When it came down to actually making the film, Bill didn't need much to proceed: a budget, a camera, an editing table, a supportive family. And now, with canoes as his subject, he was away. Unlike previous films, in which the first step was to sit down and ponder where and how to begin, he had been making some kind of canoeing film in his head since his days in the tethered boats at Nelson's Livery at Grand Beach. There was no question in his mind that he would continue his starring canoeist role that had begun in *Quetico* with Christopher Chapman. So, as with every film previously, he enlisted the support of his buddy Blake James, to serve as cameraman for the project. James participated in preliminary, exploratory shooting in the Ottawa area, but before the canoe films were really under way, Blake had drifted on to other projects.

This left Mason with two personnel problems before the canoe filming could begin: he needed a camera person, and, because he intended to produce instructions for tandem as well as solo paddling, he needed a canoe partner too. For a partner, he promoted son Paul, now in his early teens, who had had cameo performances in all his dad's films up to this point. For a cameraman, he enlisted the support of Ken Buck, a young high-school English teacher who had begun his association with Bill during the wolf filming.

Like Joyce and so many other people, Ken Buck's attraction to Mason began with a viewing of his slide show. Fifteen years Bill's junior, Buck had grown up in Ottawa and started to date a woman, Susan Hayashi, who knew of the Masons because she had been a nanny for Budge and Judy Crawley. Ken and Sue would visit Sue's sister, who lived near Meech Lake, and hear stories about the crazy guy who portaged his canoe up and down hills while recuperating from a heart attack. One Christmas, when Ken and Sue were visiting, Susan's sister invited Mason over to show his slides. They sat through "God Revealed," the show including the best of Bill's large-format slides projected in time to a tape of Blake James plunking away on the guitar. The stories were captivating. Says Buck, thinking back, "I just couldn't believe the images we were seeing on the screen that night! It was just amazing. And after that, it seems like every time I did anything, it was always kind of in context with him."

Ken and Susan later married; when they moved to Meech Lake in 1969, they began a close association with the Masons. Ken likes to say that his first job in film was with a shovel, digging a trench to bury the fence so that the wolves couldn't dig under it and escape. But as time and his association with Bill progressed, and trust between them developed, Buck was given more and more responsibility as a filming assistant. He played hockey with Mason, and between games, drinking hot chocolate in the Mason house, he marvelled at the tire ads and other commercial art that would be on Bill's drawing board. Gradually, he started to become a cameraman and film artist in his own right. There was a chemistry between the two men, and it grew until it eventually eclipsed Bill's long professional association with Blake James.

Buck, naturally, was excited and energized by the idea of being cameraman on the canoeing films, but with a spouse and young family by this time, and a full-time job teaching high school in Ottawa, he was reluctant to drop secure permanent employment for contract work. The logical route was to request a leave of absence for a couple of years to pursue his friendship and his growing passion for film. Buck's employer was slow to respond to the leave request. The NFB was anxious to sign someone and demanded an answer. Finally, letting his heart dictate his action, Buck took a chance, and before his school board's leave decision was made, he resigned his teaching position and signed with the NFB.

For a paddling partner, Bill of course thought of Blake, but he was on to other things. Joyce was a possibility, but she was happier supporting Bill by keeping the home fires burning. Becky might have been good, but she was only ten and more interested in her art than in canoeing with her dad. The situation with Paul was quite different. Throughout his life there had never been doubt about whether he would participate in his father's projects. In the Mason household, that was a fact of life. Provided you played Dad's game, be it hockey, broomball, canoeing or filming, you fitted right in. Bill had no interest in driving his children to play at other kids' houses or in supporting them in football or other extracurricular activities at school. Inside the family cocoon, you could join in on whatever was going on, but Dad would be at the centre. Partly because it was the path of least resistance, partly because a grand adventure was in the offing, thirteen-year-old Paul agreed to be his dad's partner and to spend as long as it would take, summers, evenings and weekends, as a member of the canoe film crew.

And so began the *Path of the Paddle* filming: Bill, Ken Buck, teenage Paul, a few camping supplies, camera and film, and a red Chestnut strapped to the top of a battered Chevy sedan with plywood roof rack bolted to the roof. Everyone had learned on early family canoeing trips with the Bucks and the Masons that Bill was not to be trusted with packing or with food. On one occasion, on Georgian Bay, they ran out of food when windbound on an island, thanks to Bill's planning. After that, Joyce quietly collected and packed all of the food that not only kept the three of them alive in the wild, but that catered to Bill's various allergies, requirements and food preferences, some of which had plagued him since birth, and some of which had made themselves known only since the troublesome post–heart attack summer and fall of 1965, when the food-absorption difficulties had nearly killed him.

Becky, Joyce and Paul in 1970 with two wolf pups from the litter born in captivity in the
Meech Lake enclosure. Much later, the Mason children realized that not everyone
had a family of wolves living in their backyard.

Bill with his favourite wolf, Charlie, the big male and star of *Death of a Legend*,
Wolf Pack, and *Cry of the Wild*.

Blake James played a number of different roles in the wolf films. As a trapper for *Death of a Legend*, he stands in the woods outside the Mason house at Meech Lake.

To get footage of wolves in the wild, Bill travelled alone on Baffin Island, in northern B.C., and here in the taiga north of Fort Smith, NWT. Uncharacteristically, he is shown here with a Black's pup tent instead of his beloved Baker, which was too heavy for solo travel on snowshoes.

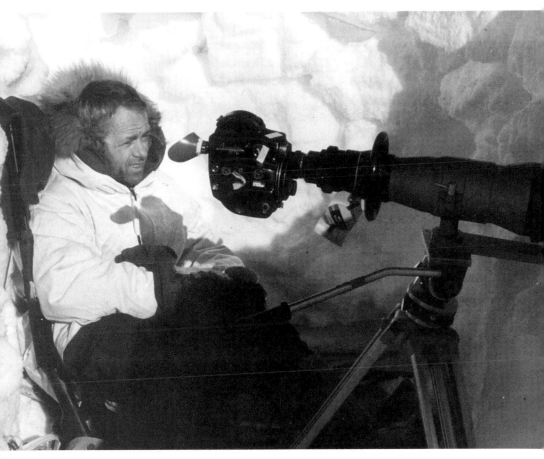

Shooting alone in the wild, Bill used igloos as blinds for his filming, but he was never able to depict himself inside such a structure. Needing shots of this for *Cry of the Wild*, he built a snow structure outside his house at Meech Lake where this still and supplementary cine footage were shot.

Bill checking rushes for the Path of the Paddle films with his manual Moviola viewer in the tiny propane-heated studio in the woods at Meech Lake.

Fixing the fleet at Meech Lake, Paul and Bill putter for a photograph taken for the book *Path of the Paddle*. Bill would chastise friends with more than one car but saw no contradiction in owning a couple of dozen canoes, among them two birchbark and several historic boats, including a horizontally planked cedar rib Peterborough canoe (*foreground, second from right*) rescued from service as a planter.

The man in the red canoe, paddling his beloved Chestnut Prospector at Old Woman Bay on Lake Superior. For many of his canoeing shots, Bill preferred to paddle the less cumbersome Chestnut Pal which, though also sixteen feet in length, was a smaller and lighter boat.

Old Nahanni Bill ready for action.

Mason signed his abundant letters, homemade cards and his fans' books with a characteristic cartoon caricature of himself, often holding what he felt was the all-purpose, all-Canadian tool.

Bringing Paul and Ken into a team had its struggles, but it was easier than working with other colleagues. With Blake James, for example, there had always been creative tension in the filming, especially during the shooting of *Blake*, when Bill would fidget on the ramp at the Carp airport, just west of Ottawa, as James would fly for hours over the ordered fields of the Pontiac, catching updrafts at the edge of the rugged Gatineau hills, filming clouds and trees with a 35mm movie camera fixed to the fuselage behind the open cockpit, shooting anything his creative heart desired, deliciously out of touch with his director, Mason. But with Paul, his son, and with Ken Buck, his protégé, Bill was firmly in control of the whole operation. Ken and Paul carried on through take after take, demonstrating the patience of Job and the apparent life-expectancy of Methuselah.

They revisited all of Bill's canoeing haunts near Ottawa—the Barron, Petawawa, Madawaska and other rivers flowing east, down from Algonquin Park. From April to November, in all types of weather, they filmed strokes and manoeuvres, shot the rapids, portaged the falls, jumped off cliffs; kicked back and drifted through acres of sweet pine pollen hiding the fish and masking reflections of cedar and hemlock and filtered blue light. On the north shore of Lake Superior, they shot in the sun, and they shot in the mist cliffside at Gargantua, Agawa and Old Woman Bay, sitting out for long stretches in the flap-fronted Baker tent when the west winds made paddling impossible. On these days Bill would get restless and turn to his sketchbook or pace on the beach, and occasionally, when the light was right and he was feeling up to it, he'd get in the canoe with his patented sea anchor (an aluminum cooking pot tied to the stern with a bridle and line) and tempt fate in the waves.

A typical filming run on the Petawawa River (which Paul reckons they descended thirty-five times in the making of the Path of the Paddle series), would begin on Lac Traverse, just below Poplar Rapids, within sight of the big dish antenna of the Algonquin Radio Observatory, having come by Mason jalopy through the east gate of Algonquin Park and up the long dirt road past Achray to the interior. Bill, Paul, Ken and often one of Paul's friends, would load up two canoes, paddle down the lake, shoot Big Thompson Rapid and drift down with the current to the campsite on the north side of the river just above Little Thompson Rapid. Over the course of a couple of years of filming, they stayed at this campsite for three or four days on as many as five different trips. Bill would always be the first up and would get a fire going, provided, of course, that it was not a day to move downriver to the calm water and island stretch below Little Thompson, predawn, to get shots of boats in the mist, in which case *everybody* would be up-and-at-'em first thing.[4] For shoots in Big Thompson Rapid, Bill and Paul would portage up to just below the big island before the old logging dam at the head of Big Thompson, and, depending on the kind of footage they were hoping to get, Ken would set up either high on the rocks on the north side of the river or down low, at river level. Again and again, Bill and Paul would front-ferry across the river just upstream from a rocky ledge, turn into a welcoming downstream V between an elephant-sized rock and the north shore, proceed downriver in a back-ferry position to miss the ledge sticking out from river left, shoot through the deep-water V and then pull in to the end of the portage.[5] Filming had to be done in full sunshine to ensure continuity in the editing; hence, any time the sun would go behind a cloud, Ken would instinctively turn off the camera, and Bill and Paul would pull into the nearest eddy and wait until the shadow passed. During these long idle moments in the canoe, Paul sat patiently, while Bill's creative eye panned the rich textures of bark, rock and water, dappled with Petawawa pinks, purples, greens and riparian blues, dreaming of future paintings or of Tom Thomson sitting, perhaps in this very spot, bringing *his* visions to life with brush and sketch canvas.

Through his friendship with Wally Schaber, Bill's eyes were opened to other rivers on the Quebec side of the Ottawa—the Dumoine, Fildegrande, Coulonge, Noire, Picanoc and Rouge. These rivers were much like the Algonquin rivers they'd paddled on the south side of the Ottawa valley, but the drops were steeper, the rapids longer and the locations more remote. And again through Schaber, who with his company Black Feather Wilderness Adventures was guiding canoe trips across the country, Bill and Paul were eventually able to leave the whitewater rivers of the Ottawa valley and the Great Lakes watershed and try out the whitewater canyons of the Nahanni River in the Northwest Territories for the first time in 1977.

As with everything else he had done, and in spite of any strictly instructional purpose for the canoeing films anticipated by the higher-ups at the NFB, Bill simply couldn't help touching the spiritual in how the films were scripted, shot and edited. Just as he had done with his slide show and in his earlier films, he felt compelled to reach beyond the technical to show people the more aesthetic aspects of what he had found in nature in these wilderness river valleys, wishing to develop in viewers an attitude of regard for the natural world. As such, the canoeing project was merely an extension of his slide show and *Wilderness Treasure*. The more time Bill spent on the rivers filming, the more he realized the responsibility he had to inculcate safety principles in his viewers too. Mason described this imperative as it dawned:

> During the course of shooting we witnessed a tragedy that resulted in the changing of our priorities. We were camped below a set of rapids on the Petawawa River. A body drifted out and upon reaching the drowned man Ken began artificial respiration, we got him into the canoe and paddled him back to our campsite. He never revived.
>
> At about that time the interest in canoeing and running rapids was growing at an ever-increasing rate. The skill levels of people we met was very low. One weekend we saw five canoes swept into rapids because the paddlers had insufficient skills to make a safe landing above the rapids. We had already rescued four canoeists from the icy cold water below the rapids. I decided to concentrate on how to canoe.[6]

Calvin Rutstrum's *Way of the Wilderness* by now was second nature for Mason, and it, combined with Ronald Perry's *The Canoe and You* and *Canoe Trip Camping*, published in the early 1950s, along with some interesting musings about river canoeing in a 1968 book by Robert McNair, gave Bill a technical grounding for the canoeing technique he and Paul would portray in the films. Since branching out into the whitewater rivers of Whiteshell from his base at Manitoba Pioneer Camp, since wrecking his beloved Plycraft canoe, Bill had more or less made up his canoeing style as he'd gone along.

Never one to be too concerned about dogma and never one to be swayed much by reading, he'd glanced at what the Red Cross and other canoeing-related organizations at the time had to say about style and technique, but when it came to the canoeing films, while the focus was clearly technical at one level, at another Bill conveyed the message that there was no point in simply learning the techniques and manoeuvres if one did not then use that knowledge and skill to access and appreciate God's green earth. And likewise, with the focus on getting out into nature and onto the rivers, the underlying assumption was always that learning to paddle flatwater was not enough. To paddle a river and get the most from the experience, one needed to know about paddling in current, negotiating whitewater, and, as a result, his films progressed from basic strokes done on flatwater, to application of those strokes in moving water, and finally to using those strokes to paddle down rapids. This progression and subtext in his canoeing films (and later in his canoeing books) set Bill's apart from other instructional materials for paddlers.

The main source of actual teaching methods and terminology in Bill's paddling films, and later in his books, was his friend Wally Schaber, who, with guides and associates in Black Feather, was out every weekend, from the early 1970s onward, teaching people by the hundreds to river canoe. Bill had notions about what worked for him, and what didn't, in different current conditions on the water, but aside from the instructing he'd done way back at Manitoba Pioneer Camp, he had never confronted the practical problems of teaching canoe skills. Schaber and his Black Feather associates, by contrast, had invaluable knowledge and experience in actually having tried to teach novice canoers.

Aside from the odd canoe-tripper like Eric Morse, who would take a loaded canoe through the most modest of whitewater ripples, the only people who were paddling whitewater in the early 1970s were the kayakers. Recreational paddlers stuck to flatwater and were hesitant to risk life and limb in whitewater. There was much to be learned from the kayakers. Says Schaber:

> We both were working on trying to develop a style of teaching that was just barely evolving but just bursting onto the

scene—converting kayak techniques to canoeing techniques, front-ferries, back-ferries. We had nothing to do with inventing them—just figuring out how to *verbalize* them so that raw beginners could learn.

There was no right and wrong with Bill: there was just "this worked for me; it might work for you. If it's not working, maybe you could move your weight forward so your steering is lighter, and that might work better." We found ways to help individuals find their own technique. For most other guys, like the CRCA [Canadian Recreational Canoeing Association], there were standards. It was: "Here's how it's done; you will be measured against doing it *that* way" kind of thing.

Bill's contribution was mostly publicizing the joy and the enthusiasm of canoeing, and the fact that there are techniques to reduce the danger, if there is any danger, and the canoe is a vehicle to get someplace. The joy was in *getting there*. Bill's contribution to technique is mostly getting more people involved *in* wilderness recreation so that they would become spokespersons for preserving wilderness.

Using pieces of paper from a 3- by 5-inch scratch pad, which would be mounted to create a story board, Bill sketched out the main elements and movements in each planned shot in the film, using arrows to show canoe movements and boxes and arrows to illustrate camera pans and zooms, in or out. By now he understood the importance of abundant camera angles and perspectives to give as much latitude as possible in the editing stages of the film. Often when Ken and Paul would set up at a rapid, providing the light was right (if it wasn't they would wait—days, even weeks, if necessary), they would set up and shoot the same whitewater sequence a dozen times before meeting the requirements of Mason's plan. That, of course, did not include extra takes to redo shots gone wrong, or takes to meet new creative whims that came along in the process of filming all the planned sequences. Nor did this often gruelling schedule account for the nights of shooting late around the campfire and getting in position, predawn, to film what became the signature of silhouettes in the black and gold of misty Magnetawan mornings.[7]

With Mason in charge, there was no point in even suggesting that they eat and sleep anywhere other than in the Baker tent on location, wherever that happened to be. Scrimping on crew costs by avoiding the unnecessary expenses of hotel nights and restaurant meals, Bill was able to buy more film stock and get better coverage. He always contrasted this bare-bones approach with the large-crew siege-style canoe-film making—days on the water, nights in hotels—which had disgusted him during the making of *The Voyageurs* back in 1963 with the NFB. He took pride in the fact that, when he was in charge, things were done differently. As a director, he was convinced that getting the unexpected shots of storms and sunsets meant spending every available second in the field. Ken and Paul, having grown up with only Bill for reference, did not know any other way, and hardly ever complained. In fact, there may have been no other way to make films with the longevity and popularity of the Path of the Paddle films. Long after he'd been acting as cameraman for Mason, Buck saw *The Seasons*, *Quetico* and some of Christopher Chapman's other early films and remarked in astonishment, "That's my shooting!" Not surprisingly, perhaps, the tutelage Bill had given Ken Buck over the years was similar in style to that he had learned from Chapman.

With producer Bill Brind dealing with "terminological inexactitudes" on his behalf at the NFB—translating shoebox receipts into believable numbers etched with suitably supportive bureaucratese in government ledgers—and with the compliance and indulgence of his partner and his cameraman, Bill was free to do whatever he wanted. During the shooting phases of the canoe film project, he was spending more time in the wilderness and getting a little closer to the spiritual life, but the problem of his desire to paint lingered.

However, at some point, Bill decided that there was much more in the canoeing project than four simple instructional films. There was, he was sure, an instructional film about family canoe camping, and another, perhaps a feature like *Cry of the Wild*, that would tell a more biographical story, about his relationship with canoes and the natural world. It was the desire to make these additional films that encouraged the scrimping on food and accommodation to buy more film stock.

And so the canoe shooting continued: flatwater sequences on

Meech Lake, Old Woman Bay and many points between; whitewater segments amid ghosts of loggers and voyageurs at famous rapids on the rivers of southern Ontario and western Quebec. Bill, Paul and Ken came and went on their river filming forays in relative obscurity, and except for immediate friends of the family at Meech Lake, the odd person they met on the trail while shooting and, of course, the people in Wally Schaber's Black Feather orbit, no one associated Bill with canoes and/or canoeing. Bill was the person who made wolf films. Still, shot after shot, day after day, trip after trip, month after month, editing session after editing session, the Path of the Paddle films took shape. Bill and Paul's canoeing skills increased dramatically. They learned techniques, tried out methods and terms suggested by Schaber and the Black Feather instructors, honed manoeuvres, and then filmed them until the action was perfect and the filmic variables—light, wind, background, clothing, angles, equipment—were tuned to Bill's exact specifications. When Paul grew out of the plaid shirt Blake James had worn in *Rise and Fall of the Great Lakes*, they cast around all the general stores from Whitney to Eganville and Bissett Creek to find another similar enough in pattern and colour to ensure continuity over the duration of shooting.

There was always room for adaptation and modification of equipment and technique, but never room for compromise. Sometimes other people would accompany Bill, Paul and Ken on filming trips. More than once the family lost friends because of Bill's inflexibility when it came to getting the shot. If he was set up at Rollway Rapids on the Petawawa and it was Sunday afternoon and the light was not right, they would wait, even if visitors had to be at work next morning, for days if necessary. If they wished to leave the group and walk out, that was fine, but should they decide to stay, the priorities were set by Bill. Film came first.

As the canoeing films came to completion, instructional canoeing elsewhere in the country was ironically in a state of near paralysis. Fellow native Manitoban and camp director Kirk Wipper, working with Canadian Camping Association and Canadian Recreational Canoeing Association colleagues, established a set of "Standard Tests of Achievement in Canoeing" to encourage canoeing instruction across the country. A series of national canoe instructor schools were designed and run in the late 1960s and early 1970s in several locations. This initial solidarity within the canoeing fraternity splintered almost immediately into various regional and provincial camps, who—despite good intentions—bickered mercilessly over the minutiae of paddling nomenclature, strokes, techniques and teaching progressions. Bill spoke to Wipper and Claude Cousineau of Ottawa, the other principal mover in the national canoe school movement, but at a time when any one of the provincial canoeing associations or the CRCA itself might have been catapulted into public prominence by joining with Bill, no such deal was ever struck. Bill went his own way in the end.

With canoeing organizations tied up in the certification debate, and more people every day wanting to learn how to canoe and to get out into the wilderness, by 1977, when the four films in the Path of the Paddle series were released—*Solo Basic, Solo Whitewater, Doubles Basic* and *Doubles Whitewater*—they fully answered people's need for instruction in canoeing, and camps, outfitters and canoe schools snapped them up. More than that, they fed a much deeper desire to affiliate with the natural world through this unlikely little grey-haired prophet in his red Chestnut canoe.

Unfortunately for Bill, the central drive of his existence remained unrequited. The runaway success of the paddling films, just like that of his previous films, came between him and his desire to paint. The camera was a creative tool, but painting was somehow more honest than filming in bringing his talent to bear on what he saw in nature. To a large extent, however, the painting he did with Paul and Ken as he thought about canoeing films beyond the instructional series was not so much painting for painting's sake (although it would be convincingly presented that way in later films) as it was scripted action for a film in Mason's mind's eye. Thanks to the skilful negotiations of James Kennedy in setting up Mason's full-time contract with the NFB, however, Bill was granted a leave of absence immediately following the release of the canoeing films, ostensibly to paint.

During that leave he did paint, more than he had in years. His trip on the Nahanni River was an especially inspiring subject that got him going at the easel when he returned. Working from photographs, he fussed and fumed to create paintings of Virginia Falls and Pulpit Rock on the Nahanni. And when those were done, he would do them again, layering on paint and scraping it off to get the quality of texture and light he saw in his head. After that he got out slides of some of his favourite spots on Superior—Cascade Falls, Denison Falls, Old Woman Bay, particular shorelines—and rendered these onto paper and canvas. When his arm got tired he would walk to the bookshelf in the studio and pull down *Canadian Landscape Painting, 1670–1930*, working the book with his dirty fingers; the pages still fall open to Tom Thomson's *Sunset, The Pointers* and *Jack Pine*; F.H. Varley's *Squally Weather, Georgian Bay*, A.Y. Jackson's *The Red Maple, Night, Pine Island* and *Northern Lake* ; and Arthur Lismer's *A September Gale, Georgian Bay (study)*. Over cups of hot tea, he studied book renderings of J.M.W. Turner's skies and seascapes in works like *The Mew Stone at the Entrance of Plymouth Sound, Tintagel Castle, Cornwall, Mouth of the River Humber* and *Folkestone*. Bill enjoyed the early twentieth-century Canadian painters but, more than that, he loved the look and the feel of the Turner paintings filled with what Turner's contemporary William Constable disparagingly referred to as "tinted steam," and did his best to achieve the same effect in his work.

Bill worked primarily with oil on paper, using brushes initially and later experimenting with his own technique involving laying on different colours of paint with a palette knife and then scraping off surface hues to achieve the desired effect. His paintings were mostly small, many 3 by 5 inches or even $2^{1}/_{2}$ inches square. He spent hours sketching and replicating Turner images. He painted from photographs, and in large part produced fairly realistic renderings of his favourite wilderness places. Many of the paintings have the feel of a man looking over the gunwale of his canoe into the reflections of wilderness and a restless sky, and in this sense the painting was every bit as much drawn from Bill's experience in the wild as were the canoeing films. And, as with his films, when he got it right Bill's paintings resonated with the essence of wilderness, especially to the eye of fellow paddlers who had been to Bill's locations.

But Bill had trouble sitting still, at least with a brush in his hand. And this, in fact, stands as a fascinating contradiction. He could sit for hours, even days, in a canoe or a tent, waiting for a shot, or for better weather. He could spend interminable time at the editing table with such intense concentration that Paul and Becky stopped trying to get his attention because so often they had been unable to break through. Many days, the only way Joyce could get Bill to stop to eat or sleep or come to the phone was to shut off the power to his studio. With painting, by contrast, he had unbelievable difficulty in finding the time and the frame of mind to concentrate. Nevertheless, he did complete several dozen small works, which he set aside as other projects took his attention. Additionally, from September 1978 to September 1979, he finished and released the family camping film *Song of the Paddle*; wrote a book based on the canoe films; finalized arrangements for the publication of *When the Wolves Sang*, an illustrated children's book for Greey de Pencier publishers, and became possessed by the notion of a feature film, assembled just like *Cry of the Wild*, featuring the best out-takes from the canoe shooting.

Looking back on this unusually frenetic year in Bill's life, and his prodigious creative output, it was as if he were driven by some mysterious force to live every day as if it was his last. He said no to no one. Besides tending to his painting, films and books, answering fan letters, giving speeches to environmental clubs and canoeing organizations across the country, during the leave he returned to Manitoba at the request of his old pal Don Campbell, who was now making films for the Manitoba Department of Education, to star in an instructional film about a returning artist's view of the geography of his home province. He stayed with the Campbells, travelled all over the province, shooting with Don, and did his best to sketch before the camera and produce finished monochromes for shooting in the evenings. Thinking back, that reunion is a bittersweet memory for Campbell. "Billy was pale and distracted. He wasn't himself. He didn't seem right. I remember wondering if he was sick or something down deep in his bones."

15

GOD ON WATER

THE PATH OF THE PADDLE FILMS, and subsequently the book by the same name, in addition to the family canoe camping film, *Song of the Paddle*, were immediately popular with an expanding market of canoeists and environmentalists. They made Bill a much-sought-after speaker and organizational affiliate.[1] The sense of down-to-earth authenticity, practical competence, woods wisdom and rough-spun charm that came out of his films and books was reinforced by his presentations in person. Mason would turn up dressed nicely but with the free-wheeling air of the original Gatineau Hillbilly and would "golly, gee, shucks" his way through film reels made up of spliced-together highlights from all his films. People hung on his every word, wrote to him, called him, visited the house at Meech Lake. He never once turned a person away. It pleased him no end to think that his word was getting out. But while the canoeing films gave the impression of great confidence and of a man on track with himself and his career—many of his newer converts at this time had no idea that he had been anything other than a canoeist all his life—in fact, he was wandering and the schedule was taking its toll on him physically and spiritually.

A Plasticine animation, or "claymation," film project called *Dragon*

Castle he had begun with Paul and Becky using a Christmas present of every available colour of the modelling medium, finally got into line for completion. Paul and Becky had played with this throughout the canoeing filming era, making the figures, setting up scenes on a backdrop in the Meech Lake house, and shooting them with film ends from the canoeing project. It was nominally their project, but Dad was never too far in the background. And as Bill struggled to find focus following the release of the canoeing films, there was time to help out with script and final editing, and money to commission music to support the narration.[2]

In 1980 Bill's dad, now in retirement in Kelowna, B.C., took ill. Bill went out west, stayed a few days until his father's condition stabilized, and then returned home. In a week's time, Bill Sr. took another turn for the worse. In spite of stressed family finances, money was found for a second return ticket to Vancouver, and Bill was able to be with his dad during the final days. Relations between the Meech Lake Masons and both sets of parents had not been all that close since Bill and Joyce had left Winnipeg in 1959. Everyone agreed that Bill Sr. had never looked and sounded happier than the day he retired, and son Bill was able to take some stock in that, but beyond the connection to hockey in the early days in Riverview there was never a strong bond of friendship between father and son. If he was affected, deeply or otherwise, by the death of his father, it did not show, at least not publicly. In a letter to his mother written soon after his father's death, one gets some indication that Bill has accepted his father's death and is moving on with his life:

Dear Mom,

. . . You are certainly coping very well in your new life but I can imagine how difficult it is too. I find it amazing how Dad will pop into my head when I am doing something. For some reason he comes to mind and I stop and think of him. The times I think of the most are canoeing at Grand Beach. I guess memories fade in time but I think of him a lot.

After Bill's busy leave from the NFB, he was obliged, as a full-time NFB staffer, to accept other projects as they were assigned. In this period he assisted in the production of two safety films—*Coming Back Alive* and *Where the Buoys Are*—and accepted responsibility to direct a film about Pukaskwa National Park and another film with Dr. Joe MacInnis called *The Land That Devours Ships*. He took to these with enthusiasm, but never with the passion with which he'd attacked his earlier, more focused projects. As it happened, Joe MacInnis, co-producer on *The Land That Devours Ships,* stirred up international controversy when he raised the wheel of the *Breadalbane,* one of the ships lost in the search for John Franklin, without the permission of the Canadian government. In an unpublished, and very ironic, response to an article about MacInnis, Bill expressed his general discontent with the Canadian government on behalf of his associate:

> Oh Canada, what a shame that Dr. Joseph MacInnis has gone and stuck us with the wheel of the *Breadalbane,* a supply ship involved in the search for Sir John Franklin. Imagine those Americans spending all that money to have it shipped all the way to Washington in a special truck for a press conference and a grand celebration at the *National Geographic.* Imagine them getting all excited about the recovery of a ship's wheel from under 6 feet of sea ice at a depth of only 350 feet of water. Those guys are so dumb down there I'll bet they'd fall all over themselves accepting it if it was offered to them. I wouldn't be surprised if they would even preserve it and stick it in a museum down there.
>
> Not us boy. We know when we've been had. The only thing MacInnis gets from us is a curt reprimand for finding the ship without a permit. The search for Sir John Franklin in the 1850s is just about the most fascinating period of our arctic history. If he had been American he would have had songs composed about him and a television series extolling his explorations and the fate of him and his men. It is very suspicious to me that Parks Canada personnel regard the ship's wheel from the *Breadalbane* as something dumped on them by MacInnis.

. . . No single agency, including Parks Canada or the *National Geographic,* could mount such an expedition. Your article said the expedition cost millions. Actually it didn't cost that. It was worth about a million but much of the cost was in the form of donations and volunteer labour. In Canada, MacInnis is a dilettante adventurer, in the U.S. he is regarded as a hero.

What irritated Bill about how his friend Joe MacInnis was treated by the government was that it reminded him of how he was being treated by the NFB in this late stage of his career. This letter was written shortly after he'd been to Buckingham Palace with MacInnis to shoot an introduction for the film by Prince Charles (a trip on which MacInnis remembers walking through a courtyard outside the palace and hearing Mason remark, "Gee, wouldn't this be a great spot for a hockey rink!"). He had achieved unprecedented numbers of awards, unheard-of gross receipts for his films, and never-before-seen popularity for his projects with the NFB, including the "impossible feature" *Cry of the Wild,* but still he could not convince anyone that there was a feature film still lurking in the out-takes from the canoeing films. Instead, he was being assigned to make industrial safety films which brought little joy to anyone, least of all Mason.

Ambivalence about the NFB and about life in general was obvious to the family, but the only place outside the home where Mason's discontent and anxiety registered was in letters to Christopher Chapman. A long letter in response to Chapman's congratulations to Mason for winning a British Academy Award for *Path of the Paddle: Doubles Basic* acknowledges his confusion:

Now that I've joined the NFB I feel a bit like a traitor because I sure sympathize with the complaints of private industry. I sort of feel like I'm copping out. The way I figure it the board <u>should</u> turn out very good films. The opportunity is here. The best part about the place is the fantastic distribution set-up. The films really do get seen. . . .

I don't know what my plans are yet. Probably considerable time painting along Superior, my favourite place. But I don't know yet. I'm almost afraid to begin painting, in case nothing happens. I've been away from it for so long. I want to read every book ever written on Turner. It will be a great pleasure to read something not relating to film. . . .

[Signed with just the outline of a canoe, no name]

This letter to Chapman provides what may be the key to understanding why Bill had such difficulty acting on his desire to paint—as he writes: "I'm almost afraid to begin painting, in case nothing happens." Bill was driven to *communicate* his faith, as he had done with his films and books. He had a sense of mission guiding him that was predicated on public acceptance of his work. Now, more than ever, having been wildly successful in commercial film and publishing, he *had* to succeed with the painting. Failure would be very difficult to swallow.

Life was slipping out of balance. And yet, frustrated and confused though he may have been, a phenomenon his young friend and musical protégé Alan Whatmough called the "Elvisization" of Bill Mason occurred. Bill had tapped into something elemental with his canoeing films. People all over North America hung on his every film, his every word, and he became a celebrity. In Salt Lake City, Utah, a group of dedicated fans, whose interest in Mason soared when American National Enterprises had four-walled *Cry of the Wild* in that city, founded a film festival in his honour. Terry Tempest Williams, assistant curator of education at the Utah Museum of Natural History, wrote to the director of production at the NFB:

> I can't remember when an artist has been so warmly received by such a diverse audience. He seems to touch chords in all of us, regardless of background. We have been altered in a very beautiful way as a result of his visit. . . . We salute the NFB of Canada for supporting film makers such as Bill Mason. We all glean the rewards of artistic endeavour. The genius of film crosses national boundaries and binds souls.[3]

Success breeds success. Farley Mowat turned up one day at the

Meech Lake house with a person Joyce described as "some agent" to speak with Mason about participating in a project called *The World of the North*, "a look at the Arctic world through the eyes of best-selling and controversial Canadian author Farley Mowat." Mason was to be one of three film makers on the project working out of the NFB with producer Andy Thomson and two other award-winning directors. Though this project never made it beyond the printed-prospectus stage, it indicates the phenomenal way in which Mason's popularity as a film maker was spreading. It is not clear why Mason did not participate in this project; after playing second fiddle to Joe MacInnis in the *Breadalbane* film, it is unlikely that Bill was even remotely interested in relinquishing control again, even if it was to such a luminary as Farley Mowat and his cronies.

Bill addressed canoeing groups all over North America. In places where he used to canoe in anonymity, he would be mobbed by people at the end of portages who would ask him to sign their paddles or PFDs. There were people who would often produce a dog-eared copy of *Path of the Paddle* from a waterproofed pack.[4] Others wrote long and detailed letters about the minutiae of canoe design or technique, or asked for advice in decisions they were making about equipment purchases. For example, one fan wrote a long letter that begins with musings about canoes and a trip he took on the Petawawa River and concludes with a favour to ask:

> I am a very strong believer in slower than current technique for recreational canoeists in white water. I enjoy doing some of the things in an open canoe that are so much fun in a white water kayak when the circumstances permit. On a trip I firmly believe in the back-ferry as the basis for safe canoeing. The trip I described above was with a person I had introduced to back-ferries last summer when we went down the White River to Superior. In Algonquin, we worked on becoming a team and I must say that the run we had down Rollaway was one of the most satisfying I can recall. . . .
>
> Personally, I feel that the concepts of proper weight transfer and the use of back-ferries is the foundation for safe and

enjoyable recreational tripping and white water canoeing. I succeeded in convincing some of the participants on the French River trip of the merits of the back-ferry quite easily, but the ones who have more influence in the club remain skeptical. The course instructor has an ORCA [Ontario Recreational Canoeing Association] level III certification and I have none. I think perhaps that when back-ferries are used properly, they make running rapids look too easy. The observer on shore does not appreciate the control being exercised. [Mason, along with Wally Schaber and instructors at Black Feather, pioneered and popularized the back-ferry, slower-than-current paddling to which the letter refers.] . . .

In *Path of the Paddle*, you make several references to the importance of back-ferries but I would appreciate it if you could put down several paragraphs that clearly outline your opinion on the importance of back-ferries, weight transfer and faster-than-current maneuvering. . . .

Yours in canoeing[5]

All of this adulation confirmed Bill's belief that Calvin Rutstrum's wood and canvas equipment and his homespun canoe camping techniques and paddling moves were the *only* way to approach wilderness safely and respectfully. There were critics, especially in canoeing organizations, who were developing their own views on equipment and technique, but their voices were never loud enough for Bill to hear. However, when Aqua-Field Publications of Point Pleasant, New Jersey, commissioned and then rejected his text for a canoeing guide sponsored by the Old Town Canoe Company, he discovered that not everyone agreed with his views. A senior editor wrote the rejection:

Dear Bill:

I'm sorry to inform you that our sponsor has rejected the use of your manuscript in the OLD TOWN CANOEING GUIDE. As you know, in your own conversation with Pete Sonderegger, Old Town has strong objection to the use of a wooden canoe for whitewater. Even with heavy editing I could not illustrate the piece with your photographs. I know you objected to using photos from another writer.

Pete Sonderegger feels there are more modern teaching methods that cannot be overlooked and the manuscript would take too long to rewrite.

I am personally sorry for the inconvenience to you. There seems to be a basic difference in ideology between you and Pete Sonderegger on the subject of canoeing.

Pete will be happy to discuss it with you if you have any questions. Once again, for myself and Aqua-Field, I am very sorry for the inconvenience.[6]

Mason was taken aback by this perfunctory rebuff, but his reply demonstrated that he had few illusions about who he was and what he was doing:

Dear Mary,

I was surprised that my article was rejected because "there are more modern teaching methods." I would have thought the rejection would be for the quality of the writing. If there are better ways of writing about how to canoe I would like to know about them. It wouldn't be the first time I had to change direction.

A couple of years ago I was invited to do a workshop at the Strathcona Outdoor Education Lodge on Vancouver Island. It turned out that I learned a lot more than they did. They had a sixty year old guy[7] who showed me a very aggressive technique using bow pry eddy turns. He never used cross bow draws. I learned how to do it and discovered that the bow pry turn is more than twice as effective as a bow draw turn. When I returned east I had trouble convincing paddlers to unload the cross bow draw for the pry. Now I've got a trail of converts to the bow pry turn. So if you know of a better method for teaching basic strokes I would greatly appreciate any information or literature you could let me have illustrating this.

I am aware of a recent article by Mike Gault that describes the basic forward stroke very well. By calling the stroke the hook (also shallow c) he is adding to the already confusing array of terms but I like his logic. Calvin Rutstrum is the original proponent of this stroke and it is my favourite stroke. I didn't explain it in my article because I wanted to be basic and cover a lot of ground. . . .[8]

Mason's response to rejection from Aqua-Field Publications may have missed the editor's main concern—using wooden canoes for whitewater—but it provided a rare public glimpse of Mason's resolve and discipline. Behind the accessible and easy-going public persona and the wilderness-man myth first created in *Cry of the Wild* was a person who needed to show the world that his work was better. He asked for feedback and for comment on his work in a benign and benevolent sort of way, but underneath he was competitive and determined to set the record straight.

He again encountered resistance when shopping around the *Path of the Paddle* book manuscript. In a letter from Wendy Wolf of Pantheon Books in New York City, Mason picked up a whiff of rejection (ultimately the company rejected the book outright because of the high cost involved in reproducing hundreds of black and white photographs). Ms. Wolf hinted that there might not be a need for another canoeing book in an already crowded marketplace of such books. Bill was moved to respond with vigour. In an eleven-page missive (Bill was prone to writing very lengthy, chatty letters), he tries to show systematically why his book would eclipse all the others:

Dear Wendy Wolf:

Thank you for your letter expressing interest in my canoe book. I would be very pleased to give you my impressions of the canoe books now on the market. I believe I have read all of them or at least the more important ones. In fact I weighed the pros and cons of yet another book on canoeing for a long time before proceeding. Some of the books on the market now are excellent but most are mediocre with very amateurish artwork, layout and design. Then there are those with good to excellent text but poor artwork and design.

Because I have worked as a designer, illustrator and photographer I knew I would have no trouble surpassing all these books in these areas. Writing was my major problem. I believe I have overcome most of the problems by writing it as I would say it. I have also relied on a lot of feed back from other writers and canoe experts. I have just completed my fourth rewrite and am fully aware it will require a final reworking by an editor to correct some of the grammatical errors and clumsy sentence construction.

. . . I cannot imagine how anyone could set out to go me one better in the area of photography. As you can see it is almost like a movie in book form. Each stroke has six photographs to illustrate the path of the paddle. . . .

Besides the nuts and bolts material on how to canoe, I decided it would increase my potential audience by including personal accounts of my experiences over many years of canoeing. I am intending to reach the reader who is only nominally interested in canoeing as well as the fanatic. The colour photos and large black and white scenics are also meant to accomplish this. . . .

Right now we are riding a crest of tremendous interest in canoeing. And I believe this is only the beginning. The National Film Board have informed me that my four canoe films *Path of the Paddle* are the most used and best selling films of the year. There's nothing even coming close. Judging by the mail that is coming in from across the country we've got a lot of sure sales out there for the book. . . . The fact the films preceded the book is of great value.

He goes on to point out the unique nature of his book:

. . . No one had depicted white water dynamics with realistic diagrams, photographs of the obstacle and then the obstacle being negotiated by canoe. . . . After describing manoeuvres and the various dangers I often illustrate the situation with a personal experience. This is what Rugge and Davidson [authors of *The Complete Wilderness Paddler*, New York: Alfred A Knopf, 1978] did superbly but I have carried it one step further with detailed diagrams and in many cases actual photographs taken at the time. . . . One of the original concepts I am bringing to the art of canoeing is the unweighting of the upstream end. Riding deep in the upstream end of the canoe is the most common cause of problems in running white water and making safe landings in a current. Yet no other book has ever dealt with this. And very few instructors are aware of this problem. The description of how the man drowned really lays the clincher on it. . . . The description of the danger of being pinned by a canoe is more complete than other books. . . . I think an overall perusal of the canoe books on the market today would reveal an overall sameness with the exception of about three of them. I have designed mine to make it stand out as unique in design, photos and style of writing. I regret the grammatical flaws in the writing but assume these can be corrected. I only hope that there is a spark or flavour to the writing that people will enjoy.[9]

After a frustrating attempt to publish with Macmillan in Toronto, Bill finally found a publisher for *Path of the Paddle: An Illustrated Guide to the Art of Canoeing*. Garry Lovatt, publisher of Van Nostrand Reinhold, recognized its uniqueness immediately. From the beginning it sold steadily (total sales of the first edition topped 100,000 copies) and added measurably to the mystique, success and growing popularity of the canoeing films and their enigmatic maker with his floppy canvas hat, Baker tent and red Chestnut canoe. It didn't hurt that Bill's Meech Lake friend and neighbour, Pierre Trudeau, appeared in one of the instructional photographs, and provided a glowing foreword:

I have paddled with him, traded outrageous stories with him about past canoeing expeditions, and listened for hours as he shared his rich experience of nature, of wildlife, and of rushing waters. . . . [Bill Mason] is, as you will soon learn from the following pages, a genial fanatic on the subject of canoeing. He is a man so enthralled with the sheer joy of guiding a canoe through challenging rapids in the early spring, so awestruck by the beauty of nature as seen over the bow of a canoe silently traversing a mirror-smooth lake in the early morning, that he cannot understand why every man and woman on earth does not share his passion.[10]

In the year *Path of the Paddle* was published, Mason spent a month in South America doing preliminary filming on a project with his friend Wilber Sutherland of Imago. Through a convoluted series of Christian mission connections, Sutherland had agreed to consider producing a series of films on the plight of the native peoples of Amazonia.[11] With no real chance for a personal encounter with the native peoples of the Amazon region, Bill shot very little film on the trip, although customs documentation from the jaunt shows him travelling with a Beaulieu movie camera, a Nikon FE 35mm single-lens-reflex still camera, and lenses that would fit both units: Nikon 24mm, 50mm, 100mm and 300mm.[12] In spite of his friend Wilber's impressive Christian contacts in Brazil and Colombia, and his official status at the conference in Peru, he was detached and distracted throughout the month-long trip. Sutherland remembers him on benches and at dining tables, inside and out, fiddling with a $1\frac{1}{2}$ by 3-inch sketchpad, drawing cartoons for an animated film about the environment that was running in his head.

That same year, in addition to this activity, he was speaking all over North America and getting requests to join organizations. Paul and Becky's claymation film *Dragon Castle* was launched at an animation festival in Ottawa. The safety film *Coming Back Alive* was released. His children's book *Where the Wolves Sang* was published by Greey de Pencier. And to boot, his friend Barrie Nelson arrived to work on animation for the film *Heavy Metal*—came for two weeks, stayed for five months. It was a disquieting time of turmoil and great discontent.

In the months leading up to his first and only art show in 1980, Bill had an epiphany of sorts with his painting. When he did paint, he was always bothered about the small size of the works he produced. Alone in his studio, surrounded by his miniature oils, he grabbed a still camera with a macro lens and began examining the detail of his palette-knife technique. What he saw through the lens of his camera was much closer to what he wanted to accomplish than anything that could be seen with the unaided eye. In no time, he was hooting and hollering, jumping about, imploring Joyce to come up and share in his unbelievable discovery. "Wow! Would you look at the depth and detail in that! Can you believe it? *Look* at that!"

Unlike the paint, the camera was something he knew well, something that he could control. At first, the through-the-lens revelation spurred him on to paint more, but it was only a matter of time before he loaded film in the camera and began photographing the paintings and blowing up the resulting images to wall-size prints. In many respects, in doing this Bill was following the path of Group of Seven forbears who painted sketches in the field and went to larger canvases in the studio afterwards, only in his case the enlargement was photographic. In that sense Bill was a decade ahead of his time with his artistic techniques, and again thwarting his espoused desire to "paint" full time.

Nevertheless, with the support of his friends Wally Schaber and Wilber Sutherland, Bill mounted a show of his art that was exhibited in Ottawa at Trailhead, Schaber's outdoor store, and in Toronto at the Enoch Turner Schoolhouse, with which Wilber had a connection. In a curious, almost apologetic, explanatory note at the beginning of the catalogue for the exhibit, Joe MacInnis wrote:

> Since his first encounter with Lake Superior, alone in a canoe, Bill Mason has been searching for a painting technique that would allow him to record his deepest feelings for that wild and lonely land. . . . Bill has found that technique, but it has proven to be as unpredictable and unmanageable as Superior itself. . . .
>
> So far, it is only in his small paintings that Bill has been able to capture the feeling he wants. . . .

It was Bill who decided to photograph and enlarge his paintings. It would allow a new intimacy and permit the details of his unusual technique to be studied at a distance. In addition, it held the excitement of a fusion of a new medium with an old one, and, fortunately for us, allows his work to be enjoyed by a larger audience.

On the facing page Bill himself provided his context for the exhibit:

How we see the natural world and the depth of our relationship with the land depends to a great extent on how we travel and how long we stay there . . . to achieve a relationship with the land one must travel on foot or by canoe. Even those of us who do are so often in such a hurry that we see and feel very little. Too often it is the destination that matters and not the journey itself. . . .

Creativity is one of God's greatest gifts and in fact is one of the things that differentiates us from the rest of the animal kingdom. As an artist the urge to create almost consumes me.

It has taken me almost a lifetime to learn to look and to listen to what God has to say through His creation. The more I am able to do this the greater the pleasure I derive from what I create.

As in nature, how much you enjoy my paintings depends on how close you let yourself come to them. Ideally, they should be viewed through a magnifying glass but this is impractical in a show. For this reason I have resorted to the photographic medium. The enlargements make it possible to enjoy the paintings more fully but without revealing how the paint got there. . . . I prefer not to reveal the method at this time except to say that it is oil on paper and is a very bold technique, not a slow, painstaking one as the size of the paintings would suggest. It is a very elusive technique and my success ratio is extremely low.[13]

The body of work offered for view and sale included 111 images in all, 56 originals and 55 framed photographic reproductions. Some who came to the event were surprised by the pious tone in Bill's program remarks but were quickly intrigued by the array of tiny originals and larger-than-life blow-ups of portions of the real paintings hanging side by side. Most of the originals were priced in the $700–$1,000 range. Framed 11-by 14-inch prints were priced around $150, and the catalogue offered unframed prints and wall murals in sizes up to 48 by 120 inches for varying prices up to $1,000. The imagery was exclusively variations of rocks, water and trees—no people or canoes. Originals were painted with oil on paper except *Pine Island Storm*, which was watercolour and ink, and *Virginia Falls–Nahanni River* and *Denison Falls–University River*, done in charcoal. The visual impression was particularly moving for canoeists who knew Bill, and especially those familiar with locations depicted.

The show received no serious reviews—no notice, good or bad. The art community was conspicuously silent about his work. What they might have said, one can only guess. Bill was coming out of the dusty old romantic landscape-painting tradition; he used far too much green paint; the art was not within the temper of the times; religious overtones were out of fashion in an increasingly secular world. Bill was a realist but not a super-realist like Ken Danby or Robert Bateman and just didn't fit into the art world of the late 1970s and early 1980s.

For the first time in his life, after instant and enthusiastic response to everything he'd touched, Bill was surprised and devastated by the cool response to his art. Nothing in the way of comment was published in either city. Those in the know who did see the work characterized it privately as "pretty standard illustrative stuff." Bill hoped for more. Everyone agreed that with time, he had the potential to become a good painter, as long as he kept working at it. His art-school crony Tony Tascona was still incredulous about Bill's intention to leave film and turn to painting when he received an invitation to the art show:

> Billy could do an illustration, a very interesting painting of landscape of trees, of stone, of rocks. Everything he did in his paintings had to be honest. . . . [But] in art, you can't do that. If you're doing a painting there should be some of *you*

in there—some of the mystery, some of the unexplainable, however that comes out in your work. I don't think that ever happened in one of Billy's paintings.

But Tascona was quick to recognize Bill's talent:

He was a damn good film maker; no, an excellent film maker, and a superb commercial artist and illustrator. Maybe Tom Thomson and Harold Town crossed the line from commercial artist to fine artist, but it was not an easy thing to do, by any means. Why did Billy get out the camera and start photographing his paintings? Fear. Fear! . . . That was a tough decision to make. It should have been the toughest decision he ever had to make in his life. The camera he could control. The paint he could not. It takes years.

Bill picked himself up, remembering some of his own home-spun wisdom: "too often it is the destination that matters and not the journey." As destination, the first art show was a failure. But when he contextualized the show as part of the great journey, he understood that he had achieved measurable success. It was an affirmation to continue what he'd been doing for his whole life. What he needed was another route, another journey involving his art and his beliefs, one that would take him out of the spotlight and back to the land from which he was becoming increasingly disconnected. This was a route that took him back into the thick of film making one last time.

After the art show, Bill struggled to get all of this sorted out. In an article for a conservation magazine, he wrote:

Painting, for me, is the ultimate form of expression. But strangely I have never used painting to express my concerns, only to portray my feelings for the land, and feeling is a culmination of all my experiences. This might be because I cannot film and paint at the same time. When I am filming, I am storing up experiences and impressions of places I have been. Then later my real feelings for a place, a mood, or a moment come out through my brush. Painting, for me, is incredibly hard work. . . . Most attempts fail, but when a painting takes off and leads to a finished work, the feeling is very good. It is very exciting. I don't experience these difficulties in drawing. As a draftsman, I know exactly where I am going and I work on a drawing or a charcoal until I am satisfied. They are very representational and enjoyable to do, but I never experience the feeling of exhilaration I get from a painting that works. Compared with the complexity of film, I love the simplicity of drawing and painting. All you need is paper and charcoal or canvas and paint. There are no mechanical contrivances, no technicians between you and your finished work of art. I have only myself to please, but of course I am delighted when others share my joy in something I have created. The good thing about being a painter is that no time spent outdoors goes to waste. Even when I sit and do nothing, I am storing up images. And since all the days, weeks, months, and seasons are far too short, I can't afford to waste any time. I would much rather paint than make films, but I have found in film a much more powerful way of expressing my concerns to a much wider audience.[14]

This final sentence acknowledges that, as much as he would like to paint, a brush would *never* be as effective as the camera for getting out his message. Finally, he resolved the contradiction of why he didn't paint more: "I would much rather paint," he said, "but I have found in film a much more powerful way of expressing my concerns to a much wider audience." He needed the audience. He needed to get back to film.

Unfortunately, the canoe feature was a non-starter at the NFB. He had burned too many bridges on earlier projects. When it came to rational discussion of the proposed script, there were only a few people left still inclined to listen. Bill found it nearly impossible to bottle his anger that, even after all his success and all his awards, he would have to begin at first principles in the genesis of a new project, no matter how far-fetched it might seem. Even though he'd more or less given up on the canoe feature several years earlier, and told Christopher Chapman so in a letter, circumstances now demanded that the feature be completed.

The solution was clear: if he was ever to get to finish the canoeing feature and finally—finally—concentrate on his art, he would have to leave the NFB. Following the completion of his films about Pukaskwa National Park and *The Land That Devours Ships*, taking advantage of an early retirement scheme available in 1983, after 8 years and 244 days of pensionable service Bill Mason retired from the National Film Board with a pension of $440.73 per month, severance pay of $3,962.66 and an early-retirement incentive payment of $41,351.20.[15]

The money gave him room to breathe and allowed the family to move down the lake into a house of their own after twenty-six years of renting at the Wrights. Ironically, the lot they purchased overlooking Meech Lake was adjacent to Mel Alexander's property. And the log house they purchased at auction (almost by accident, with a comically low sealed bid) from a woodworking class at a high school in Aylmer, which was moved and set on a foundation dug into the steep bank looking out on the Wilson House, a government conference centre where the Meech Lake Accord was signed, was within sight, during the winter, of the original log cabin in which Bill and Joyce had started their life together more than a quarter of a century before. Unknown to Bill or Joyce or the children, it would take another eighteen months of hard work and turmoil in the full second-floor studio of the new house before *Waterwalker*, the canoe feature, would finally be completed. Under the skylight that streamed with the fullness of Gatineau sunshine, this angst-ridden year and a half would harbour the darkest moments of Bill's professional life.

16

IMPOSSIBLE FEATURE

A "SIXTH" CANOEING FILM is mentioned in NFB memoranda in the late 1970s, soon after the release of the four Path of the Paddle films and *Song of the Paddle*. By the time an idea gets into print, however, it has usually been the subject of conversation for some time, and it is not a stretch to imagine Bill and cameraman Ken Buck in the early days of the canoeing films, sitting on the smooth tanned rock at the mouth of Old Woman Bay watching the sun set on Superior, musing over tea about the possibility of making a feature film. Roots of the idea may even go back past the days of *Blake, Rise and Fall of the Great Lakes, Paddle to the Sea* and *Wilderness Treasure*, and perhaps even the "God Revealed" slide show days in the early 1950s, or the Grand Beach times of his youth. Bill's imaginative image of himself had alternately been that of the voyageur, the adventurer, the one man in the red canoe, and now, the painter-canoeist.

The possibility that a feature film could be made with out-takes from years of shooting was proved true by Bill's experience with *Cry of the Wild*. He had scrimped on restaurant meals and accommodation costs while in the field on that film, bought extra film stock with the money he saved, shot every scene this way and that, and come up with footage that, while it adequately covered the needs of the NFB script at hand, left an abundance of excellent material to craft a feature film. Having teased *Cry of the Wild* from the wolf-project footage, he was too creative and competitive not to set an even greater challenge for himself on the canoeing footage.

But there was more to it than that. Bill had been raised in a home that questioned the legitimacy and authenticity of film as a vocation, particularly as a vehicle for Christian teaching. And while it was true that the Christian message in Bill's films had been steadily eclipsed by the secularity of the trees and the animals and the stories, Bill had never lost his faith. At mid-life, however, it was time to reach out to others with his real message. If he could not do this entirely through his films, or through his painting, then perhaps the way to convey the joy and fulfilment he had found in the works of God in the wilderness was to create a film about a *painter* canoeing in the wild. In this sense his first film would be the pilot for his last film. *Wilderness Treasure* was a creative touchstone that travelled with him throughout his career in the secular world. Only the fullness of time had allowed him to recognize this unrequited evangelical dream. The calling to "return to his painting" was a reminder to himself that at some stage he had to return to his Christian roots. Bringing film making and painting together—painting the metaphor, film the medium—would allow him to make a final public statement of his views about faith and the wilderness before moving on into the next phase of his life.

Along the way, as Bill ticked items off his canoeing shot list, it became clear that much of what he and Ken were shooting with Paul (and with Joyce and Becky when *Song of the Paddle* was made) would never be used within the tight editing and discipline of half-hour instructional films. One of Mason's great strengths as an artist in film was his ability to remember the details of individual shots; in his mind he catalogued instructional sequences in one place, and somewhere else in the library of his mind and imagination he stored an accumulation of all the other canoe-related scenes that coalesced, over time, into sequences for a sixth canoeing film, the feature.

When the Path of the Paddle series and *Song of the Paddle* were completed, and as Bill struggled with fame, his long-time producer Bill

Brind moved on to other projects, leaving Mason with his old friend and nemesis Studio D executive producer Kathleen Shannon nominally in charge of the project. From time to time the idea of a feature film from the canoeing out-takes had come up in planning meetings at the Film Board, and time and again everyone had shunned the idea, except Shannon, who valued Mason's innate capabilities as a visual storyteller. His first-person approach was much more resonant with the expectations and operating principles of the Women's Unit than it was with any other studios at the NFB. Like all the men in the unit, however, Mason took an abundance of time and energy to "manage," meaning he left much of the budgetary detail and reporting to his producers without providing much supporting detail or paperwork. Still, Shannon valued his work and encouraged him to continue with the canoe-feature idea. Bill, as well, knew the Film Board was the only place where he could do what it was he had learned to do in film, and that Studio D was a fertile niche under that roof. But, for the longest time, the project lacked focus.

In the period of struggle following his decision to leave film and the release of the first five canoeing films, Bill had drafted a long memo to his supervisor, explaining, among other things, his view of the situation. It is apparent, even in 1978, fully seven years before *Waterwalker* would be released, that to do what he had in mind he was going to have to work outside the Film Board. He wrote:

> It would be a feature film in the style of "Cry of the Wild" and would be made partly from what's left over from the five canoe films. For various reasons I am suggesting that the film should be made as a private venture. I would endeavour to buy from the Board approximately 2,200 feet of original left-over footage for a price to be negotiated. I realize this sort of thing is unheard of but so is the cutting of feature films from outs. It's a unique situation that will necessitate discussion for and against such a venture. I think the standard reasons that are presented for not selling original film should not apply in this situation. I won't go into them here because I am not fully aware of what they might be. I just feel that reasons such as "we can't do it because of

setting precedents for private industry" etc. etc. should not apply. I don't see a situation in the future where people will be lining up to buy original outs to cut features from. . . .

As I mentioned, I also intend to deal very much with the spiritual element in the film. In fact it would be the main reason for making the film. I have never imposed my deep personal views on any of my films at the Board and would like to do so in the proposed film. The kind of investment money I am seeking and can get would be in sympathy with my motives and intentions. In other words, I might limit my possibilities for potential box office success but that's okay with me. This is one film I really want to get into and deal with the nature and condition of man and God's provision for the redemption of both man and nature.

Another reason for desiring to do the film independently, is that I would like to at least have the prospect of a royalty situation. I am aware of the Board's problem in talking royalties so I am suggesting a way out.[1]

Bill may have been one of the most successful film makers in the history of the NFB, with a portfolio of completed films and an even more impressive pedigree of film awards, but neither of these points seemed to have any effect on the intransigence of the Film Board with regard to entering into any kind of deal in which their footage would be sold off, even if it was to one of their own. At the core of the problem was Bill's choice to operate on his own, outside the physical premises of the NFB. He was an outsider, an abrasive if charming one, at that—creative and talented, but giving little back to the Film Board other than his films. Had he been more politically aware and more astute inside the NFB, a deal to purchase his own footage to make a private film might have been more successful.

The one person at the Film Board with whom the idea of incorporating spirituality did appeal was Kathleen Shannon; unfortunately, by the time the canoe feature had gone around a couple of dozen times, she, and most of the other women in Studio D, were sick to death of the way in which Mason clung so tenaciously to his Christianity, and especially to the idea of a male God. Studio D valued a more inclusive spirituality, and at times hung on as tightly to their notions of faith as Bill did to his parochial Christian views. Nevertheless, Shannon continued to support Bill by finding money for some additional shooting on Lake Superior during the summer of 1981, but the problems between them swelled. Shannon backed Bill in continuing with the first-person narrative, but, as it was evolving, with Bill including more and more footage and talk about his painting, trying harder and harder without result to say something about his faith that didn't sound like a sermon, the film floundered. The more Bill tinkered with the film, the worse it got.

Finally, after another crack at the commentary, another assembly, yet another screening, the problems persisted. Spirited internal memos were circulated, including the following two:

Bill and Kathleen:

I am very disappointed that the male god idea has not been removed since the last screening. Nature is for all of us, including women. The Great Spirit is genderless. After all the beauty, love and serenity the film portrays it's a downright insult to narrate it with all this allusion to men and males. But what is worse—it's as if nothing women say has any impact or credibility. I am SICK + TIRED of being EXCLUDED from the HUMAN RACE.

P.S. Whoever is the camera person must be highly commended!!

Dear Kathleen,

I hope I didn't over react to the sexism in the film. I found myself trembling with rage. Why over this film when we experience it all the time? I guess I felt my space of worship invaded. Must they bring their male God idols into mother nature's sanctuary? While the film was long and told me to be silent and listen it screamed at me continuously about mankind, and him.

What a contrast with Elizabeth Dobson Gray's experience of women's spiritual connections with nature.[2]

Bill replied to Shannon, his executive producer, knowing he and the film were in deep trouble:

Kathleen,

The screening was so so. The problems are with me. After three screenings I am the one who is having difficulty living with it. The commentary is the greatest problem but I think that we have set ourselves an impossible task. People see what they see. They simply cannot imagine how it will be improved. It is too much to ask of them.

The third problem is my structured flaws in the film. My solution of putting the quiet scenes, scenics, painting, children at the end, in order to avoid the feeling of the white-water taking over, is a disaster. The film thuds to a halt. I tried to remove this stuff and move it up but the commentary bridges across the cuts.

I have little enthusiasm for launching the test as is. So we've got a problem, or many problems.

And after a day or two's thought, he wrote again to Shannon:

Kathleen,

A very interesting proposal has been put to me today as I discussed the film with various people who were there. It comes as a complete and total surprise but the more I think about it, the more I think it might have some merit.

It was suggested that the narrator be a woman, playing the role of Joyce telling it as she sees it. Her understanding of why the canoe and outdoors has been such an important part of my life and how I have attempted to share it with them and others. How she responds to this, and how the

children respond. A few more recent shots canoeing together would suffice, as well as a few outs from "Song of the
Paddle." I am not convinced but I am very interested in getting your reaction.

She can say things I cannot. She could explain my interest in
the native voices better than me. I could say a few things possibly but very few to juxtapose against her to illustrate a point.

You know, it's worth thinking about.

Bill was more in touch with the Native peoples of his childhood
imagination than he was with the sensitivities of his colleagues in Studio
D. But what he knew about Indians, he knew mostly from movies and
stories like *Paddle to the Sea*. In all his outings as a film maker, he had
never actively sought to find out if the movie image in any way matched
the contemporary reality of First Nations life. And so, when he had
trouble articulating what it was he wanted to say in the canoe feature
commentary, he turned to *Touch the Earth: A Self-Portrait of Indian
Existence*, a collection of texts variously attributed to North American
Indians. The book spoke of the genderless Great Spirit and of the healing
and instructive power of nature. These Native voices said what he could
not about the bonds linking land, body, mind and spirit.

Assistance in interpreting these Native voices in the context of his
commentary came from his old friend Alan Whatmough. Having also
grown up in a Plymouth Brethren family, Whatmough connected with
Bill spiritually; like Mason, he was not a regular church-goer, but he
was an active searcher for truth in the Christian frame. When Mason
turned to Whatmough to help him out of the jam with the canoe-feature
commentary, Whatmough responded with the frank and honest critique
that only a friend of long standing can deliver. Knowing Bill's new and
burning hopes for the Native voices he hoped to include in the soundtrack of the film, Whatmough sat him down, turned on the tape recorder
and fed him lines and questions about why this was important. What Bill
answered back in those circumstances sounded much more off-the-cuff,
less rehearsed and preachy. Whatmough also contributed to the effort
by reminding Bill of the disciple Peter's faith, and from this exchange—
finally—came a title for the sixth canoeing film, *Waterwalker*.

Evolution in the ending of the script illustrates the scope of narration changes brought about by Whatmough's persistence and provides a small glimpse of the trouble Bill had in trying to convey his message in *Waterwalker*.

Early version:

BESIDE CAMPFIRE

The only compassion we show for the land is expressed in setting aside of land as parks. But even parks are rarely for the benefit of the plants and animals. Parks are usually created for recreational purposes. Rarely do we set aside a piece of land for the sake of the plants and animals that live there. The idea that other forms of life have a right to exist other than to serve our needs is not dominant in our culture but it is there if you look for it.

Emerson said, "All I have seen has taught me to trust the creator for all that I cannot see."

I have given you a glimpse of what he was talking about. But it is a journey you should take for yourself, and you can take it wherever a tree grows or a stream runs.

Later version:

There is a beautiful piece in Job that says, "Ask the animals and they will teach you: or the birds of the air, and they will tell you, or speak to the earth, and it will teach you, and the fish of the sea will declare to you. Who among all these does not know the hand of the Lord has done this? In his hand is the life of every creature and the breath of all mankind." Knowing this makes a difference in how I perceive myself in relation to the world around me.

Night shot of river
Reading in bed

Lies back in bag, looks at candle

You have accompanied me for a while to share my love of wild places. But it is a journey you should take for yourself. And you can take this journey in your own way wherever a tree grows or a river runs.

Blow out candle
Montage of fall and winter
End

Still later version:

WIPE-OUT

Well . . . you know what they say . . . you can't win them all. I guess I've had my fair share of wipe-outs, but very few when I'm travelling alone. The greatest danger is from the canoe itself. Full of water, it can weigh a ton, so getting pinned between the canoe and a rock is almost certain death. I stay well clear of the canoe until we reach deep water.

We call it wilderness, the Native people called it home. I wish I could be but I can't. I am only a visitor here.

The native peoples talk constantly about the Creator. The way they see nature touches me very deeply.

INDIAN QUOTE 58:

"Civilized people depend too much on manmade printed pages. I turn to the Great Spirit's book which is the whole of his creation. You can read a big part of that book if you study nature. The Great Spirit has provided you and me with an opportunity to study in nature's university, the forest, the rivers, the mountains, and the animals which include us."

Final version:

Repair canoe

I know what you're thinking . . . You're wondering where on earth I found a set of rapids like that . . . well . . . I cheated . . . that's all the best stuff over the past few years. So there you are . . . film can be deceiving but when it comes to the beauty of the world out here . . . the camera has not lied.

I have shared with you many of my favourite places and I have shared them because I think the only hope for what's left of the natural world is to rediscover that love and compassion for it that the native peoples talk about. And I think that's possible because God created us with the ability to do the impossible.

When Jesus called Peter to walk to him across the water . . . Peter was doing just fine . . . until all of a sudden he remembered that people aren't supposed to be able to do that . . . and he began to sink. . . . I think we've just forgotten how to walk on water!

Unfortunately, Bill's excitement about this new narrative, the new title, and the Native voices was badly overshadowed by structural problems with *Waterwalker*, and especially by the growing rift between himself and the rest of Studio D, particularly Kathleen Shannon.

Time would show that Shannon was unmoved by Mason's efforts to mend his ways—the gesture was of far too little consequence and much too late. By the time Whatmough was on the scene, sharing the views of female colleagues in Studio D, Shannon had left the project, asking that her name be removed from the credits. Unlike their amicable parting on *Blake*, when Shannon was editor subordinate to Mason, the director, the parting during *Waterwalker*, on which Shannon was the senior collaborator, was less friendly, but nevertheless professional. Speaking about this long after the fact, Shannon recalls:

I would share my perceptions with Bill, and I would think we'd agreed on what was to be done next, and he'd come

242

back with something totally different. And, at one point, we were talking about what seemed to be at the heart of our difficulties, and he said, "The way I like to work is this—I like to take a film, sit down with my friends, and I show it to them, and they *tear* it apart." That was the way he told me he liked to work. And I realized he needed something to— he needed opposition to bounce off of. That was *not* my way of working at all, providing opposition for someone to bounce off of. What a waste of energy!

I don't know whether to ascribe these differences to Bill's Christianity and my feminism, or to the difference in two different approaches to film making. *I don't know.* He used the word "stewardship" quite a bit when he talked about nature, but "stewardship" to him meant a great chain of being with God at the top, and then men, and then women and children and animals and animate nature, inanimate na- ture at the bottom. My approach to nature is much more of a feminist spirituality, one where I see humans as part of the web of life. I don't think Bill could conceive of himself as a cell in the body of the universe. I feel it was kind of a rigid skin Bill wore. It didn't allow for real questions; it didn't allow for really thinking things through. Bill insisted that the term "men" meant "men and women." And so I would ask him, "Bill? Would you say that half of all men menstruate?" And he would say, "Hmmmm. You've got a point there," and then go on to something else. There was never much room for discussion. There was never a moment in our con- versations when one would say, "Oh, *that's* what you mean! Oh, I see!" It never came. It was kind of a coat of religious armour he wore that was impenetrable to other points of view. I don't think I ever saw the final film.

Shannon's final substantive creative contribution to *Waterwalker*, and the point at which she gave up in spirit on Bill and the *Waterwalker* project, occurred during a dinner meeting with Bill and Wilber Sutherland while she was in Vancouver helping to promote the Studio D Oscar-winning documentary *Not a Love Story*. Wilber remembers the dinner conversation as clearly now as the night it took place:

> We had a lovely meal in a French restaurant and started to talk about the impasse we'd reached with *Waterwalker*. Bill was so discouraged. So discouraged. And Kathleen said, "Look: how long is it since you've been out for a canoe trip without a camera, by yourself?" Bill said, "Oh, I don't know. A long time. Three years ago, maybe more." And she said, "You're stale. You're not tapping the roots. You're letting them dry up. Your roots are *out there*." She looked him right in the eye and said, "I want you to go back to Ottawa, and I want you to take two weeks off and just go canoeing. I don't want you to take anybody else. I want you to go off." And Bill says, "I can't! I can't do that! We've already put so much money into this thing. We all know we haven't got the money to do that kind of thing. I can't do that." And she says, "Well, why can't you?" And he made all kinds of protest noises, groans, moans and the like. And then I got into the act because I thoroughly supported what Kathleen was saying. And I said to him that in a very real sense he had to renew his spiritual vision in the wilderness. But he wouldn't buy what we were saying. He was *so* obstinate about it. And Kathleen leaned over to him and said, "You're not the producer; *I am*. You go off. I have to worry about the money; it's none of your business." And he demurred again, and then she reached across to him and said in a quiet voice, "You know, Bill Mason, I have more faith than you do." Mason just sat there and went sort of "Humph."

Bill eventually did go on a short solo trip on the White River, but it was too little too late. His mind was too cluttered to even contemplate remaking the connections with nature that had nurtured him as a younger man. In a note written to Christopher Chapman on this trip, he sounds lonely—bored even—nothing like the resourceful, independent character in the films, so comfortable with his own company. In his characteristic scrawl with the trademark cartoon at the end depicting him shivering in a sleeping bag, he wrote:

> Hi gang:
>
> Just thought I'd drop a note to say hello.
> HELLO.
> The reason I'm saying hello is because there's no one else to talk to. I'm on a solo trip down the White River and I'm wind bound at the mouth on Superior. Man I aint going nowhere until it quietens down.
> I'm on a sketching trip and it's great with no camera. I love it . . . The sunken-ship film *The Land That Devours Ships* will be on T.V. sometime around the middle of November on C.B.C.
> We had a festival screening of *Waterwalker* and the reaction was just fantastic. We are really excited that this turkey really is gonna fly. Hope everyone there is cool. We are, especially me, right now huddled in my sleeping bag.

But in his heart, all was definitely not well. *Waterwalker* was a mess. Having never been challenged in this way in his life, Bill knew there was truth in Kathleen's reaction to his work and in her prescribed cure. Maybe she *was* right. The indulgence surrounding an only child, and an asthma-stricken and small child at that, had followed him into his marriage and adult professional life as well. Whether because of size or disposition, or because of his need to isolate himself to control his surroundings, or because of the way in which Joyce and the children had put him first, Mason had been able to avoid confrontation and go his own way. He had been a lucky man. At first he was a little bemused by the resistance, thinking he could retain control and carry on in his iconoclastic way. Maybe he would try a short trip to see if she was right. Where once he had been deemed charmingly rebellious and creative, he was now dubbed parochial, pig-headed and narrow-minded. Even the last-ditch effort to break the canoe-feature commentary impasse by using the "Native voices" to which he refers in the memo to Kathleen Shannon after the fateful screening failed, at least in the eyes of many NFB colleagues who viewed the early versions, to save the film.

It was about that point in the evolution of the film in early 1983, still hanging onto the dream of getting out of film and painting full-time, that Bill understood that to break the stalemate and finish the sixth canoeing film he would have to leave the Film Board and try to finish it privately. And it was at that point, just as he had done under the pines at Manitoba Pioneer Camp twenty-five years before, with *Wilderness Treasure*, that Wilber Sutherland, a third character in the *Waterwalker* supporting cast to have grown up in a Plymouth Brethren household, arrived on the scene to help steer *Waterwalker* to completion. While Mason negotiated his early retirement from the Board, Sutherland dickered with the Film Board and secured a deal in which Imago and the Board undertook co-production of *Waterwalker*. Had it not been for Sutherland coming on the scene at precisely that moment, coming to the rescue of Bill and his precious last film, *Waterwalker* would have faded into obscurity.

Wilber had always been in the background, ready to help Bill. In discussions surrounding Bill's turning from film to painting and his efforts to reconcile the two in his final film, Wilber had come to appreciate the depth and complexity of the struggle he was having with *Waterwalker*. Abiding belief in Bill's creative abilities, and mutual love for each other and for their God, took Sutherland through the negotiations with the NFB and into the somewhat frightening position of having to make good Imago's end of the bargain by raising $305,000. In early 1984, Imago entered into a unitholders' agreement whereby its 55.3 per cent interest in *Waterwalker* was divided into 61 units, which were to be sold at $5,000 per unit. Sutherland managed to sell 60 of these units and retained one unit as an investment. With that, the table was finally set for the completion of Bill's final film.

By the time the ink on the Imago deal was dry, the whole Mason family was so fed up with posing in summer clothes in November to pick up summer scenes for the film, and shooting all manner of scenes in and around Ottawa to ensure continuity between this sequence and that, that they implored Bill to do what he said he was going to do and get to his painting seriously. The only way he could force himself to stop this compulsive shooting, most of which involved him in front of the camera in plaid shirt, floppy hat and cut-offs, was to shave off his signature white beard. The only problem with this dramatic and effective move was that one of the stipulations which needed to be met in order for Imago to ensure advantageous tax status for its unitholders on the *Waterwalker* project was that so-called principal footage for the film needed to be shot during the same year in which the money was given. For better or for worse (many people were shocked at how jarring the segment was in the finished film) the extra principal footage that was shot during the summer of 1984 to honour this investment obligation was of helmet-topped, rubber-clad, day-glow paddlers hooting and hollering in a wild whitewater canoe hot-dogging segment shot on the Ottawa River and its tributaries. People who look closely at the finished film see a false beard that flops up and down as the diminutive Mason rides the haystacks in the bow of his friend Wally Schaber's canoe. By this time, all that mattered was that the film got done.

Mason, the creative dreamer, was hopelessly mired in the unresolved complexities of *Waterwalker*, some of which he saw, some of which he felt, and some of which were completely beyond his conscious comprehension. The project had gone on too long. By contrast, Sutherland, although an intellectual by disposition and training, was also a pragmatist. He knew, perhaps better than anyone, with the possible exception of Alan Whatmough and maybe Bill himself and Joyce, how much of a struggle the commentary had been. From his position as a skilled and practised film producer and supporter of the Christian arts, Sutherland could see that no matter what Bill came up with in the way of commentary, the plot line of the film was still unconventional and thin—charitably described as subtle, but more likely weak or non-existent. He knew he needed a very strong musical line to hold the film together and make the visuals flow. Throughout that part of the process at the NFB, Bill lobbied hard for the work of his friend and long-time collaborator Larry Crosley, who had done the music for most of his earlier films. Kathleen Shannon favoured a female folk musician, like Ann Mortifee, but by now Shannon was completely out of the picture. On a hunch that contemporary popular music might fit the bill, and urged on by Alan Whatmough, Sutherland got in touch with singer Bruce Cockburn, who liked the idea of working on a Bill Mason film, and eventually teamed up with musician Hugh Marsh to compose and record the musical score for *Waterwalker*.

As an Ottawa boy, Cockburn had chummed around with one of Budge and Judy Crawley's sons and had met Bill either through that connection or through a visit on Hockey Film Night at the Masons during a short stint as a youth leader at St. Paul's Church in Ottawa. Cockburn later recalled that first meeting with some regret, saying:

> I think it was back when he was doing the wolf movie *Cry of the Wild*. It was way way back. I was introduced to him, and I sort of thought he was a bit of a crackpot. I didn't pay much attention, you know, because I had my *own* attitude at the time. Later, when I saw the movie, I regretted that I'd been hasty with him because the movie was absolutely beautiful. Here's a guy who doesn't just make a movie about wolves, he goes off and lives with them. And gets intimate with them. And it's not your basic *Animal Kingdom* or Walt Disney nature movie. It doesn't pull punches. There's heart in it. You feel his love of his subject through the film, which is something you may find in dramatic films but not very often in documentaries. The film was full of passion.

Trust on Bill's part for this musical decision made by Wilber allowed him to enter into the creative process—at least in so far as it was possible for a strong-willed creator like him to do so—with Cockburn and Marsh, even though music was one of the few aspects of film making about which Bill knew next to nothing. Cockburn and Marsh set up in a little studio in Toronto, designed for recording advertising jingles, and began improvising to the *Waterwalker* visuals. Bill watched in awe. Intuitively he knew the feel he was hoping to give his audience and, musically, given the subject of wilderness, he knew that emotion could be achieved, and had been achieved in earlier films (and in his slide show) with simple voyageur songs and basic guitar chords. Sutherland knew that *Waterwalker* needed more than this and laboured to convey the point to Bill. Cockburn remembers Bill having a very clear idea about what he wanted, but failing almost every time in efforts to describe how this might be achieved. Cockburn described the collaborative process:

> He was very particular, even though he didn't know any-
> thing about music at all. He would communicate clearly
> what he felt about things, and he was not shy about doing
> that. But he could be persuaded too. I found him very en-
> joyable to work with. I've worked with other film makers at
> different times; some of them are plain pig-headed. Mason
> *did* have to go through the process of weeding and refining
> and so we worked on the music for a long time. But invari-
> ably when we'd play a musical idea, he'd get excited. I
> mean, mostly, he just got excited, even though most of the
> ideas we came up with were generally beyond his compre-
> hension and outside his understanding of music. . . .
>
> There was one area where he didn't agree with what we
> wanted to do musically, and I remember having to persuade
> him on one occasion that this was a good way to go. And I
> seem to remember there being something that he didn't re-
> ally like. But we worked it out. I mean, generally, there was
> some discussion over how much music should be in it, and
> he wanted *lots* of music, and it was generally felt—I felt, and
> Wilber maybe felt too—at a certain point it starts to seem
> absurd to have so much music in a movie. There was some
> concern that if you had to have that much music to carry the
> movie, then there was something wrong with the movie.
> But in the end I don't think that was a problem.

The final mix-down of the *Waterwalker* soundtrack, done in Dolby stereo to play in the big theatres, was completed in the spring of 1985. That summer, while Wilber was arranging the promotion and launch of the film for late October, Mason joined Alan Whatmough, Cockburn, Wally Schaber and two other canoeists on the Hood River, the third north of the 60th parallel he had paddled in his life, generating stories that would later be told in *Wild Waters,* a book about Canadian rivers to which Bill had contributed, and in his second how-to canoe camping book, entitled *Song of the Paddle.* One story from that trip, never told by Bill, that conveys Bill's child-like exuberance for life in spite of all the hassles with *Waterwalker,* was remembered by Bruce Cockburn in thinking back on that Barren Lands trip. Soon after they landed to begin the trip, Mason galloped up the steep side of an esker, a long sandy hill laid down by a river flowing beneath a receding glacier. Standing on top of the esker, in command of an endless view across the rolling tundra of the Hood River valley, Bill tipped back his head and let out a long, mournful howl, to be greeted only by whispers of arctic silence. The shoulders dropped, and crestfallen with disappointment at not raising a chorus of arctic wolves, he kicked stiff-legged down the esker, hands pocketed.

Predictably, on return from the North, Bill was all for tinkering more with the final cut of *Waterwalker.* In truth, while he had been away, Wilber had had second thoughts about the film too, and in concert with his co-producer at the NFB had found a way to cut out some of the scenes of Bill painting in the field—he feared people might think them indulgent—without messing up the soundtrack. Not surprisingly, the changes Bill had in mind were totally different from the ones Wilber conceived. The bickering continued.

The hope was that *Waterwalker* would get picked up by a large film distributor, as had *Cry of the Wild,* and play in theatres across Canada and the United States. Unfortunately, that never happened. The film had its world premiere in the Rideau Theatre in Ottawa to a warm reception from the canoeing community. Other people weren't so sure. Reviews were decidedly mixed. The positive ones tended to damn the work with faint praise. Wilber was able to have the film shown in a couple of other locations in Ontario, but he did not have the money to four-wall *Waterwalker* with the kind of media and publicity saturation American National Enterprises had given *Cry of the Wild.* The film got limited television exposure, and almost as soon as it was given theatrical release it was transferred to video and offered for sale. One of the most symbolic viewings of *Waterwalker* happened just prior to its world premiere in Ottawa, when Christopher Chapman visited the Masons in their new house high on the side of Meech Lake. Wanting to give his friend and film mentor the best possible chance of appreciating the stereo sound-track, Mason chose to set the projector on the balcony outside the studio loft and project through a window onto a screen inside. Something happened to the take-up reel on the projector and, while Bill held his breath, waiting to hear what his mentor had to say about his cinematic swan song, the film quietly spilled off the balcony and onto the ground below.

After all their years of friendship, Chapman knew Bill had somehow missed the mark with *Waterwalker* and yet had not the heart to tell him so in so many words. Years later, Chapman is more able to articulate the mixed emotions he felt that night during his first and only viewing of *Waterwalker*:

> While he had *enormous* success in so many things, in *Waterwalker* he was still trying to achieve what he had tried to achieve in all his films to some extent, to explain his life and his love for the canoe and for his God. *Waterwalker* shows that it can't be done, or at least couldn't be done in the time available to Bill. If he'd lived longer, he would have achieved many, many more things, but I don't think—as an artist, I don't think he would ever have been happy, really happy.

Whatever the intrinsic weaknesses or strengths of *Waterwalker* as a film about canoeing, wilderness and an environment ethic, it was Bill's last film. Getting the film onto the big screen took a monumental toll: tapes of television interviews to promote *Waterwalker* do not hide his exhaustion and residual anger, in spite of efforts to put a brave face on the situation. When people who knew Bill as a canoeist saw the film, some were intrigued, others confused, especially by the footage depicting Bill and his paintings. Some even called *Waterwalker* indulgent in that regard, cynics speculating that the film was nothing more than a thinly veiled ploy to advertise and promote a career shift. Even his friend and *Cry of the Wild* co-producer Ralph Ellis at Keg Productions in Toronto had trouble with the film, saying:

> I felt that what Bill was attempting to do was something that was not really possible. I challenge *anyone* to do something—

whether it's Albert Einstein to talk about his $E=MC^2$, or if it's Picasso talking about how he did this or that—I think you get into a very tricky area when you want to articulate something like your own personal kind of inner spiritual beliefs. It was a valued attempt. But to me it came out as a little bit self-indulgent.

One reviewer, who clearly harboured great passion for Mason's earlier films, was dismayed by his final film, saying it was like Henry David Thoreau returning to Walden Pond in his maturity to write his swan-song and not knowing what to make of it all. He went on:

> Aside from the fact that Mason has diminished himself to the role of a tour guide and dispenser of rather conventional religious and environmental wisdom, his loss of faith has caused him to resort to some gimmicks of his own. Half-way through *Waterwalker*, with the narrative dying from lack of action and a glut of pretty pictures, Mason inserts a breath-taking montage of whitewater canoeing in the guise of a dream conjured up to relieve his feelings of solitariness. It's a cynical device and amounts to a virtual declaration of the death of the Romantic idea. And it happens again at the film's wild climax. Here Mason negotiates a long series of whitewater rapids. When it's over, he confesses that the sequence is a compilation of all the best footage. "So there you are," he declares, entirely too flippantly, "film can be deceiving."[3]

Whatever the truth in this review, Bill had definitely *not* lost faith. His feelings may have overcome his artistic sense—as often happens to directors—but his following—secular and Christian—was as robust as ever. *Waterwalker* presents the story of a man who felt the need, as many people do in middle age, for a more overt expression of his faith. He wanted to *be* what he believed in, he wanted his *life* to express his faith. The film met that desire; it was a personal celebration of belief. Bill was interviewed about *Waterwalker* for a profile about his life and work in the *United Church Observer*, and appeared to have everything in perspective. He acknowledges that, in the midst of all the activity associated with *Waterwalker*, there was little time to paint. Writer Tim Bentley concludes the piece by quoting Bill: "I wonder," he asks with a twinkle, "if I'll get to paint in heaven?"[4] In retrospect, this simple comment was a strange portent of what was about to happen.

Once the "impossible feature" was behind him, Bill finally turned full-time to his art, and this brought him closer to his daughter. Much like her father, Becky was plagued with allergies and was sick at various times throughout her life. Unlike her brother, she wasn't much for hockey. But, on top of the allergies, she had a learning disability and could never produce art that pleased her father. As a child, when she had to stay home from school and Joyce had to go into town to buy groceries, she would trundle out to the studio and, as long as she occupied herself gainfully with pen and paper—Bill couldn't bear to have someone in the studio just sitting, watching—the two would coexist in the same space. One day, sitting under her father's editing table while he was at work, he saw her idle and asked her to do something. "I'm sick," protested Becky, to which Mason replied, "Well, you should be doing something when you're sick." With that, he handed her a model and told her to draw it. But her ship—partly because she preferred to render it that way, and partly because of her learning disability—was unlike any ship Bill had ever seen. Becky continues:

> This was the first artistic clash we had. I think I was six or seven. I wanted to draw a ship that was sort of abstract, chaotic, going all into the water. He wanted a nicely drawn *ship*! He didn't understand. I tried to explain to him that, just because it didn't look like the ship he might draw, it was a ship in my eyes. He used to get so caught up in making things exactly like they are in reality.

Becky knows that it was after her dad retired from the NFB that he started working again with the palette knife he'd first used to paint animation backgrounds, and remembers fondly the new appreciation he developed for her less representational style of art as his own technique loosened up, away from the detailed technical renderings he would achieve with a brush:

> It was like night and day. He picked up the palette knife and was *so* excited. He would come to me and show me what he was doing. We both—we'd come to each other whenever we discovered a new technique, or when something emerged from a painting. We'd rush over to each other in the studio and say, "Look! Look! Look!"

Like Becky, Paul had followed in his father's footsteps and gone to art school; his work was much more conventional commercial art and illustration, with a special emphasis on and affection for cartooning. Unlike Becky's, however, Paul's art appears not to have overlapped much at all with Bill's, except in so far as his cartooning was an adaptation and outgrowth of the work that had been in the house since he was born. Bill enjoyed Paul's work but appears not to have been threatened or moved by it in any particular way.

Becky's art, on the other hand, at least until Mason began experimenting with the palette knife, triggered a creative dissonance in her father that at times he couldn't bear. He was sure she needed to go through the basics, meaning learning how to draw straight ships, before she could relax into abstraction. Although Bill had sympathy for his daughter's learning disability, he could not make the connection between it and her art. He steadfastly believed that if she persevered and tried harder she would be able to draw accurately. Thinking about that after his death, Becky said:

> You tend to get stubborn when somebody tells you that your work is not valid, when you present him with something that you feel in your inner core is okay. It's you, and it's your soul coming out on the paper. It was interesting. It was hard. You don't *need* your father to tell you that you're going on the right track, but it's really nice to hear once in a while, because I respected him artistically so much. I thought he had the

most *incredible* artistic eye. He did everything *very* well, so it was important to get his approval. But actually, all through my life I found he was looking *down* a little bit on my art, saying, "Well, it's nice, *but*—it's crooked." Or, "It's not quite all defined—like it's in the mist. It should be in the bright sun." Or something like that.

Through most of 1987, as Mason soldiered on, developing his own technique from photographs of his recent canoe trips, Becky was incapacitated with a mysterious, broadly based set of environmental allergies that sapped her strength and, at times, nearly defeated her will to live. Bill was petulant about that at times, too, even though he had his own history of severe allergies. But this strife eventually brought father and daughter together. In the moments when they spoke of their painting in the upstairs studio—Bill in his representational style, with oils and a knife on small canvases; Becky in her impressionistic style, with watercolours on large surfaces with a brush—there were nights when they would talk into the early-morning hours about art, drinking tea, laughing, arguing in voices that drifted down the central staircase where Paul and Joyce would be sleeping. Becky remembers these times with great affection.

Better than anyone, Becky knew how protective and secretive her father was about the palette-knife technique he was developing. She watched with interest from the edge of her watercolour easel, and she was pleased to speak with her father about technique and her impressions of his work but, beyond that, his medium and the technique were of little consequence to her. One day, after Bill had started to gain confidence in his new way with the knife, he took Becky aside and made it clear that he wished to pass on the Mason technique. In spite of her cheerful protests about not being all that interested, professionally, as an artist, he took her through his method step by step, from laying out stripes of different colours of paint, one on top of the other, in a vertical ribbon of paint, to slicing down through all the layers, smearing these across a small portion of canvas, and then, using the tip and the edge of the knife, scraping away layers until the right colour, form and texture were achieved.

To this day, Becky is the only person who knows exactly how Bill's later paintings were done. All he would say in public was what he wrote in the text accompanying his 1980 show about not wishing to reveal his technique at the time.

Becky was one person who could read the brochure for her dad's only show and see it as something other than an apology for the small number, diminutive size and experimental nature of her dad's paintings. Working in the same house with him through the trials and tribulations of his painting career, she knew that Bill's love for the subject-matter was authentic and that his search for a way to celebrate God's work on earth was genuine. And, perhaps better than anyone, she had a sense of how fearful a move it was for her celebrity father to even entertain the thought of hanging his reputation on painting. She knew that most of the painting he had been doing throughout his career had been done in his head, while looking through the lens of a camera. With the secret of the Mason palette-knife technique, she also held the truth about his angst over becoming a painter and the way in which *Waterwalker* had been instrumental for him in sorting out this dilemma.

Why Bill did not become a Sunday painter and continue to make films, or at least rest easy and derive satisfaction from his astounding achievements in the cinematic world is understandable. Having grown up in an imagined world of his own, full of romanticized cowboys, Indians and two-dimensional voyageurs, perhaps it was only a matter of time before he started to believe he *was*, in real life, the myth of himself that he'd painstakingly crafted in the film-making process. This seemingly self-destructive and obsessive desire to paint was the most graphic evidence of all that somehow, late in his film-making career, Mason the myth and Mason the man had merged into one and the same character within a driven film maker's vivid imagination. And yet, he had reconfigured himself professionally once before—twice, if you count his move from film maker to author. For a man who loved a challenge, it was entirely consistent for him to persist with the notion that he could change one more time.

The use of the knife, as opposed to the brush, was certainly in keeping with his straight-ahead, hands-on approach to life. Jean-Paul Riopelle and other Canadian painters who used a palette knife exclusively in their work produced art that was bold and textured and abstract. Bill, with his film maker's eye, was undoubtedly attracted to the "feelings" and multi-dimensional quality of such painterly technique. To get the right feel in his films, he had had to take chances; to get the right feel in his paintings, it made sense that he would take risks too, to allow his art to become more impressionistic, less representational. Raised as he was to believe that somehow non-literal art was less honest, less "Christian," he could only push in that direction, not go the whole way, as his daughter had. The knife represented substantial artistic risk; that was good. It allowed him to express his creativity in a very direct, physical way, and in that there was happiness, and even a modicum of contentment.

17

THE EMPTY RED CANOE

WITH *WATERWALKER* FINALLY behind him, Bill painted, did occasional talks and played hard through the winter of 1987–88. His passion for hockey was almost eclipsed (but not quite) by a growing interest in telemark skiing, and if he couldn't be found on the rink at Meech Lake, all one had to do was listen to hear the hoots from higher up the slope as Bill would careen down through the trees on his steel-edged skis. He'd crash and laugh, and crash again in the deep snow. Anyone who came to the house, as always, was invited to join the outdoor activity of the day. And come April, as the creeks began to open, Bill and Paul and anyone else who happened by were out again playing in whitewater. Having found balance in the realization that painting needed to be combined with film making and books to get his message out, and having made time to paint and to play, the creative emphasis and tone of his life had changed. He was at peace with himself; his art was developing; he had many contributions yet to make. He finally seemed to have found the way to put his demons at rest.

On May 3, 1988, he sat down beside the carved model of Paddle to the Sea in the living room of the log house at Meech Lake to watch television with a large bowl of Joyce's homemade popcorn. He ate the lot, as he loved to do. Uncharacteristically, he couldn't keep it down. It was at that moment Joyce suspected that something was wrong.

Bill tried to laugh it off and carry on as usual. There was much else to think about. The canoe camping book, now called *Song of the Paddle*, was in final production stages and due out in the fall. Paul was getting ready to marry his fiancée, Judy Seaman. On May 7, Bill loaded up the rusty red Toyota, drove west and rode the spring freshet out of the southeast corner of Algonquin Park on the rollicking Opeongo River with friends, including the Seamans, Paul's in-laws-to-be. On May 24, Roy Bonisteel and a crew from the CBC program *Man Alive* turned up to film a profile of Bill and his life as a wilderness Christian. On June 4, he made his way back to Algonquin Park to meet Mike O'Connor, a friend and fan he'd met on Lake Superior, to do some kind of benefit for the Algonquin Wildlands League. O'Connor remembers wondering if something was wrong when Bill appeared to be having difficulty paddling the length of Canoe Lake.

Finally, Bill relented to Joyce's urging and went to see their family doctor about what he described as problems with digestion. X-rays were ordered and, when a shadow turned up on those pictures, more tests were scheduled.

On June 10, Bill had a flare-up of gout, which he'd had off and on for much of his life. This time, it was worse than ever before. His foot was so swollen he couldn't get his shoe on. Even Demerol would not relieve the pain. He wondered if he'd be able to walk for the wedding.

On June 16, he was admitted to the Ottawa Civic Hospital for the tests that were ordered the week before.

On Friday, June 17, with more tests scheduled, Mason signed himself out of the hospital for the wedding rehearsal. Nothing much was likely to happen with tests on Saturday and Sunday, so he decided to stay out for the weekend. Thankfully, the gout cleared. The digestive pain was still there and was now accompanied by nagging uncertainty that hovered over the whole family.

On Saturday, June 18, Paul and Judy married. Still on furlough from the Ottawa Civic, wearing his hospital identification band under the sleeve of his crisp white shirt, he barged on to the dance floor at the Carleton Place Canoe Club and broke up the reception with his impromptu canoe waltz.

On Sunday, June 19, Bill paddled the Petite Nation River with his nephews, Danny, Ian and Scott McKenzie—his sister's boys—and some other friends who had come to the wedding, but had to hurry back to the Civic to readmit himself in time to be prepped for a CAT scan and biopsy the following morning.

On Tuesday, June 21, Bill learned the X-ray shadow was a tumour in the duodenum that had spread to his liver. The cancer was in an advanced stage of growth and things did not look good. Joyce dropped Bill's sister, Liz, and her family at the Ottawa airport in the morning and stopped by the Civic, where she heard the news. There were no tears. With friends and family still at the house, held over from the wedding, and stunned by the news in ways she could see only long after the fact, Joyce left Bill and headed home to do what she has always done, look after her guests. It was a black day.

Still in hospital, Bill too did what he had always done. He covered adversity with activity, and, as was his practice during hospital stays, he put on his sneakers and donned shorts under his hospital gown, snuck out the front door of the hospital, stashed the gown, ran across Carling Avenue and set an easy jogging pace through the fields of the Experimental Farm. The June sun warmed his compact body, which was muscled, tanned and lean. He felt life in his legs and arms and looked down at the smooth brown skin of his torso rippling in rhythm to his step. It was unbelievable that this body, so alive and healthy on the outside, was so diseased on the inside. How could he run, faster, and faster, and faster, without losing his breath, and be dying? He lay down in the grass, and stared up into the blue, the warmth of the earth tickling his bare back. Tears would not come. He got up and ran again, faster, harder and harder, as if he could out-run the cancer. How could it be?

Finally exhausted, Bill walked back to the hospital, slipped on a gown, and settled back into his bed with pencil and sketchpad. He described what he had been thinking, how unbelievable it was that this seemingly healthy body could be harbouring such a sickening secret; he wrote and wrote, struggling to comprehend. It was a letter he would place in a drawer in the studio at Meech Lake that would be found only after the cancer had consumed its host.

On Friday, June 24, Joyce went to court in Ottawa on Bill's behalf to answer a charge of operating a dangerous vehicle. Some time earlier, Becky had been pulled over in the 1978 red Toyota rust-bucket, with its plywood bolted-through-the-roof canoe rack, and been issued the summons. The judge condemned the car. Joyce paid the fine and went looking for another vehicle. The finality of the news about Bill hit home like never before when she realized that, for the first time, the family car would have to be registered in her name.

On Monday, results of the biopsy were in. It was malignant. Paul and his new bride returned from their honeymoon, heard the news, delivered one rose to him in the hospital, and took him home. Finally, tears.

On Tuesday, Becky had an important art show. Becky and her dad had been working on a joint exhibition of their work they had done together in the studio since Bill had quit the NFB. Given the circumstances, they decided Bill's work would not be shown. When Becky's solo show opened at the Ottawa City Hall, everyone was there, including Bill, supporting Becky. There were smiles all around.

July 4 brought a first visit to the Cancer Clinic at the Civic. They learned the cancer had spread throughout Bill's body. There was no point in surgery. For what it was worth, he told them, the tumour was of a slow-growing variety. The doctors did not talk about how long Bill had to live. It was a wait-and-see scenario. "Can I go canoeing?" asked Bill. "As long as you feel up to it," the doctor replied.

They started to tell close friends the terrible news. Friend Wally Schaber recoiled but without hesitation said, "I'll go any place with anyone at any time for you." They decided to have one last run on the Nahanni.

The Nahanni trip had two groups: the first included Bill, Wally Schaber, Paul and his new spouse Judy, family friend and doctor Ken Gfeller and Bill's old friend and nemesis Barrie Nelson, who flew in from California to join them on this bittersweet last hurrah. As always, when Barrie and Bill met, like two cartoon characters, they spied each other, strode forward with right hands outstretched, then missed by a metre or so and passed each other.

"Mase!"

"Bar!"

These six started at the moose ponds at the foot of Mount Wilson and paddled the difficult upper section of the Nahanni where they were joined at Rabbitkettle Hotsprings by Becky, Joyce and Becky's friend and fellow artist Reid McLachlan, along with neighbour Barry Bryant and spouses Louise Schaber and Karen Gfeller. This second flight swelled the party to twelve, in six canoes.

With twelve people in six canoes and no real whitewater challenge to divert attention, the expedition took on the odd dynamic that might be expected, everyone trying to keep things as "normal" as possible, as they floated through the Nahanni Canyons. There was lots of joking and kibitzing, and at times it seemed like there was nothing to fear. People fished and hiked. At one point Bill and Joyce upset in one of the canyon rapids in the national park and managed to laugh the whole thing off. They recovered everything from the river except Bill's trademark floppy canvas hat, gone for good.

One day, the group decided to hike up out of the river valley to check out the view. Barrie Nelson walked with Bill, but Mason quickly stepped out ahead of his friend and disappeared. Assuming everyone was headed in generally the same direction, no one thought much more about it until, in late afternoon, when they were all back at the canoes, ready to paddle back across the river to their campsite, there was no sign of Bill. There was nothing they could do, so they all returned to camp. Finally, after people started to worry a little, there was a wolf howl from the opposite bank of the river. It was Bill, back from his solo time in the valley, wanting a lift back to camp. Ken Gfeller was there with all manner of analgesics and other paraphernalia to assist him if necessary. But, medically, the trip was without incident. Only on the way home, sitting with Joyce on the plane, did Bill finally ask for a painkiller.

Back in Ottawa, they returned to the Cancer Clinic for another scan. Bill was losing weight, and there was starting to be some distention of his abdomen. The doctors changed their minds. "It now looks like a fast-growing tumour." There was a 30 per cent chance that chemotherapy would slow down the growth rate of the tumour. Bill asked, "What's the point of going through all that pain for a 30 per cent chance of improvement? I want quality of life, and that's the way it's going to be." Joyce remembers leaving the clinic with that news and the doctor saying, as they walked out the door, "Have a nice weekend."

On September 8, Christopher Chapman and his wife, Glen, came to dinner, to say goodbye. This had been a sustaining friendship for both of them, and yet there is not enough time to speak of matters of the heart at a meal. They chatted and guffawed as always. Chapman returned home, unsatisfied by the encounter, and wrote to Bill:

> It was wonderful for Glen and me to be with you, Joyce and Becky—and to meet Judy.
>
> It meant so much to be able to talk with you and remember the past—and talk so freely about where you are now. You have talked so warmly about when we first met, what *The Seasons* has meant to you, *Quetico*—and our scattered relationship.
>
> If I have done anything for you then that means everything to me for I have watched you with so much admiration accomplishing what you believe in and using your talents to the full. You know you are unique and have touched millions—and that touch will never end.
>
> Your teamwork with Joyce and later with your children is an inspiration to all—and I know you know this.
>
> I feel your frustration over not being able to paint with the same energy as before. No one can help you with this— except to say that while you have not achieved completely what you have been searching for (and who has?) you have already discovered the magic and it does come through. We are so pleased to have a part of that magic hanging on our walls. . . .
>
> My prayer is to let go and let God speak to me. "God made us in his image and likeness—altogether perfect." But somewhere, somehow, humanly, we have strayed like lost sheep . . . but this does not change the fact that God's supreme love, God's supreme power is "closer than breathing, nearer than

hands and feet." It's a buoyant feeling. And in God's eyes we are still perfect.

We are all surrounded by the love of God—as well as family and friends. What an incredible thing that is.

Even though we know these wonderful things we need to be told again and again to help in the darker periods that this human mind puts us through.

During the days Bill played hockey with Wally Schaber and the Meech Lake cronies, in the morning and at night. He resurrected an idea to put together a book of the photos of his paintings and began writing and dictating text to describe the various images.[1] By September 22, Bill was in too much pain to play hockey. That day he and Joyce passed the big hurdle they'd been fearing and decided to begin morphine therapy to ease the pain. A week later, fulfilling plans that had been in the works with Keg Productions long before anyone knew Mason was ill, his old friend Ralph Ellis turned up with Ken Buck as cameraman to film a day-long interview that would be intercut with segments of Bill's films to make a one-hour television documentary entitled *Spirit of the Wilderness*. No one, least of all Joyce or his old friend Ken Buck behind the camera, knew how he mustered the energy to answer questions on camera that day.

By this time, word had spread throughout the environmental and canoeing community across North America and around the world, and letters were pouring into the house at Meech Lake. Bill had always found time to answer this kind of mail personally—he took great pride in the personal reply, even if it was only a scrawled word or two on the back of a postcard. But by now that was impossible. Driven by that same feeling of obligation to his fans, he worked with Joyce to produce a form letter that was reluctantly mailed to each and every correspondent. In it, he wrote:

I never thought I would see the day when I would resort to a form letter but there have been so many letters enquiring about my health and letters of concern and encouragement that it's impossible to keep up. I want to spend as much time as I can painting, writing, smelling the flowers and watching the clouds go by so I have decided to write all the details once and xerox it. This should in no way diminish my appreciation for your letter or phone call of concern.

In June, three weeks after the last game of the hockey season, I was diagnosed as having a malignant tumour in the duodenum. A week later they found the metastases in the liver. There is nothing they can do. Chemotherapy has little to offer and is such a long shot that I would much rather enjoy quality time rather than quantity. The thought has crossed my mind that maybe I should try an alternative life style such as smoking, drinking, carousing and junk food! But I couldn't get that one past Joyce.

Joyce, Becky, Paul and Judy have been absolutely amazing through all this. We have taken control over the situation and we are doing just fine. We live and cherish each day at a time as always. I am happiest when I am creating. One of the books I am writing is on creativity with an emphasis on painting and I am writing my memoirs to share all the wonderful experiences I have had and places I have been.

Actually our life has been so good I feel guilty when I see the misery that much of the world's population suffers. I have no sense of self-pity or why me? If anything I often wonder why not sooner. God has created us, placed us in a wonderful and beautiful world and set us free to create and utilize it and delight in it. We have the capacity to use it with compassion for all the creatures that share it with us but we have turned the air, water and land into a chemical soup. We are constantly in contact with carcinogenic substances so why should we complain when they do us in. I spend considerable time lamenting about what a mess I'll be leaving it in. However, I have never believed in harping on the negative. My obsession has been to share the wonder and infinite beauty of the world God has created and to help people develop an appreciation and concern for it. My optimism is rooted in my faith that God has not forsaken us. My relationship with God is in His son Jesus Christ and with a relationship like that there's really not a lot that can go wrong.

On October 1, a neighbour hosted a junk-food party for Mason. On the 11th, the *Man Alive* program was aired on television. Bill and Joyce watched. No popcorn this time. Joyce was dumbfounded by the difference, in such a short time, in Bill's physical condition. "He was so fit and robust in the film," she later remarked.

On October 18, Bill's canoe camping book *Song of the Paddle* was launched at the Château Laurier in Ottawa and speakers roasted Mason on a video camera. A friend from Toronto related the story of his son watching *Hockey Night in Canada* on television; during a break in the action the camera zoomed in on Pierre Trudeau sitting with a friend in the audience, at which point the son asked, "Who's that guy sitting beside Bill Mason?" Hundreds of other Mason fans in attendance were invited to speak to a video camera dressed up in one of Bill's other hats and a worn PFD, as if they were talking to the man himself. One man tearfully explained how Bill had had more effect on his two sons' upbringing than he himself, their father.

Bill spent the night at a campfire near the house, and watched the video bit by bit over the next couple of days. On October 20, he was still dictating for the painting book. Two days later, he was still outside in the sun, asking that his chair be moved as fall shadows crossed over him.

Everyone who spoke to Bill in these final days of his life was moved by his sense of peace and acceptance of what was to happen and how, even in the grip of his cancer, he could drink in the natural world around him at Meech Lake and rejoice in it. People would come dreading what they would find and invariably leave in tears, energized and strangely renewed by the clear-eyed way in which Bill faced the future without fear. In the end, there was no place on earth where he felt more at home than in the fresh air at Meech Lake, smelling the last vapours of summer being pulled from the cool forest floor by the radiance of the rising sun, feeling the warmth on his skin, listening to the cacophony of geese echo off the steep hillside, and watching the view

expand with the falling of the leaves. He was in the natural world. He
was surrounded by friends and family. He was home.

Canoeist George Grinnell was with a party of canoeists in the mid-
1950s who capsized in icy water on the Kazan River and nearly froze
to death.[2] Forty years later, he spoke about this experience at a wilderness symposium in Toronto, and provided insight into what it might
have been like for Bill Mason to face death. He recalled lying on the
shore of the river, knowing one of his party had already died:

> I remember passing out from the cold several times and hav-
> ing pleasant dreams. And the pleasant dreams would revive
> my will to live. And I had time to reflect in these sober mo-
> ments on what it meant to die. I thought, "Would I like not
> to have been on the trip but to have stayed in civilization and
> lived or to have been on the trip and died right then?" I had
> gotten to the point where I really wanted to die, but was so
> happy to have been on the tundra. . . . I can't explain why I
> was happy . . . [except to say] we had gotten into a relation-
> ship with the natural world and death was not the separation.
> The separation was . . . from civilization. I was happy to be
> separated from that. But what I would mourn was the sepa-
> ration from nature, from the relationship we had gotten into
> with the caribou, with the fish and the mushrooms, with the
> weather, with the beautiful lakes and rivers, with the sky. And
> this was the relationship it would have been death to be sepa-
> rated from, but it wasn't a separation to die . . .[3]

In a place he loved, perhaps more connected to the natural world
than he had ever been in his life, on the morning of October 29, 1988,
at fifty-nine years of age, Bill died.

In typical Meech Lake fashion, Steve MacDonald, a carpenter
neighbour, fashioned a casket from long boards of clear white ash another neighbour, Hugh Stewart, had saved for gunwales. The project
was done before Bill actually died, and, as Bill might have done, Steve
kept it in his living room. People remarked that his coffee table looked
just like a coffin. His wife sewed the liner.

Remembering the ongoing dispute on the Nahanni trip about the paddle Bill "stole" from Nelson's Boat Livery, Becky found and expressed her desire to have the NBL paddle placed on the top of the hand-rubbed wooden casket and together they went with Bill's body to an Ottawa crematorium. At the memorial service, it was St. Paul's Church pastor and old family friend Bill Duffy who likened Bill to Jeremiah and spoke of "fire in his bones."

> Then I said, I will not make mention of him, nor speak any more in his name. But his word was in mine heart as a burning fire shut up in my bones, and I was weary with forbearing, and I could not stay.[4]

The following July, at a solemn ceremony presided over by Joyce, a small group of family and friends travelled to Superior and Bill's ashes were scattered from canoes at the base of the cliffs at Old Woman Bay, amid echoes of wind, loons and the biblical sentiments on which Bill had based his life.

The flood of mail following Bill's death overwhelmed Joyce. Hundreds of letters came from people who'd never met Bill, from people he'd spoken to briefly at conferences; environmentalists, canoeists, conservationists, Christians, teachers, outdoor-equipment manufacturers, camp counsellors. Letters from Canada, the United States, England, Australia, Spain and Brazil. The letters spoke of a profound and intangible spiritual connection. One woman in Winnipeg said she felt a loss when her grandmother died but had not cried, and yet, having met Bill only once, she burst into tears when the news of his death was aired on CBC. They called him "leading light, our prophet, a guru, mentor, inspiration, natural ambassador, messenger, spiritual healer, part of the Canadian identity, and a connection between God and nature." One story told of a young boy asking his father in church what he would do if God walked in right now. His next question was, what would you do if Bill Mason walked in right now? The letters spoke of love, dedication, energy and authenticity, and illustrated the deep and abiding way in which he had touched the hearts and minds of people around the world, regardless of age, sex or point of view.

Awards and scholarships were established in his honour. His cameraman and friend Ken Buck, with colleagues at Rideau High School in Ottawa, commissioned a carving of a canoeist in Mason's memory that would serve as an annual award to an outdoor-education student who showed strong interest in enjoying and protecting the environment. The Carleton Board of Education built a new high school in Dunrobbin, just west of Ottawa, and established within the new school the Bill Mason Outdoor Education and Environmental Studies Centre. His close friend, hockey pal and whitewater canoeing partner Wally Schaber spearheaded an organization called the Friends of Bill Mason which worked on a number of projects, with friends and family in chapters in Toronto and Ottawa, to find a fitting and lasting tribute to Bill. Negotiations between the Ontario Ministry of Natural Resources and the Friends of Bill Mason to convert a Junior Ranger camp at Beaver Rock on the north shore of Lake Superior, just south of Lake Superior Provincial Park, into a centre to educate people about the beauty and fragility of the Superior wilderness was, ironically, quashed when Native people resident in the area rejected the fact that "another parcel of land with roots in the Native community has been set aside for use by a privileged group of non-residents."[5] The Friends also established the Waterwalker Film and Video Festival, which has been sustained on an biannual basis in the form of a formal adjudicated festival in Ottawa and, similar to the Banff Festival of Adventure Films, followed by a travelling best-of show that plays in dozens of cities across the country.

Bill's passion for nature was a beacon for environmentalism. His example was simple and genuine—somehow, even without the words to make the point in plain language, he conveyed to people the fact that his creative and spiritual fire was fuelled by love for the land. One outdoor educator in the United States remarked that he always shows the Path of the Paddle films to his students, even if they are mountain climbers or scuba divers—he could care less about the didactic canoeing lessons; what he wants his students to absorb is the film maker's ethic, the emotional feel and the forces of spirit of the man in the red canoe.

In spite of an abundance of other books, films and instructional materials about canoeing, Bill's work has risen to the top around the world, in Sweden, Germany, Britain, Scotland, South Africa, New Zealand, Japan,

Australia and elsewhere, in addition to, of course, just about every camp, river seminar, YMCA, club and backyard canoe gathering in Canada and the United States. Alan Oates, from Somerset, England, reports:

> In 1981 ten senior instructors met in a cold London dockland hut. They had with them a VCR and a couple of canoes. The weekend consisted of watching Path of the Paddle, talking about the strokes, then going out onto the diesel-polluted waters to try them out. From this weekend with Path of the Paddle techniques combined with the Canadian Recreational Canoeing Association's Standard Test of Achievement, the British Canoe Union Star tests for open canoes were written.
>
> The 1981 *British Canoe Union Handbook* reintroduced open canoeing to its thousands of members. The section on the Open Canoe by Geoff Good, Director of Coaching, listed as its main source, *Path of the Paddle: Solo Basic.*
>
> The 1989 *British Canoe Union Handbook* contains a slightly Anglicised article on whitewater by Bill Mason.[6]

In Britain, the decade from 1984 to 1994 had seen exponential growth in open canoeing, due, at least in part, to the teaching of Bill Mason.[7] And, across North America, his influence had helped to increase the popularity and the safety of all types of canoeing. The fact that just about every canoe company on the planet makes a "Prospector" model of some kind is no doubt linked to his conviction that this was the best all-round canoe in the world.[8] And although no one was quick to embrace the Baker tent Mason insisted was the best, that particular design of outdoor accommodation, with its open front, became a powerful symbol for the way in which Mason welcomed nature into his world. Mason somehow managed to infuse his life, and his spirit, into the very essence of wilderness recreation around the world.

Keg Productions' documentary *Spirit of the Wilderness* achieved great success in the television marketplace. It was translated into several languages and is played still on a regular basis in as many as fifty countries around the world—not, says Ralph Ellis, because people were all that interested in wolves or learning how to canoe, but because of the inexplicable way in which the man in the red canoe embodied something elemental about the Canadian wilderness experience. Ellis's film demonstrates the profound way in which Bill came to embody, in public consciousness, everyone who had come before. He was the best of the wilderness icons and pioneers. It didn't really matter what Bill said, what kind of boat he paddled, where he went; people responded to him at a much less tangible, deeper level. We responded to his authenticity, to his reverence for nature, and to his vital, youthful and energetic spirit of adventure.

In 1919, two years after the mysterious tragedy on Canoe Lake in Algonquin Park, Group of Seven founding member J.E.H. Macdonald painted *The Beaver Dam*, which features a prominent empty red canvas-covered canoe. The shaft of a wooden paddle stands akimbo across the centre thwart of the boat, as if waiting for its owner to return. This painting, and in particular the empty red canoe, was rendered as a tribute by Jock Macdonald to his friend and fellow artist, Tom Thomson, who had died so suddenly and so young. *The Beaver Dam* was recently designed into a featured exhibit in the Canadian art section of the Art Gallery of Ontario, and has been seen by thousands of new viewers, young and old, wilderness lovers all. Ironically, for nine out of ten people who view this painting, until they read the fine print in the exhibit, even those who remember images of Pierre Cadorai in Gabrielle Roy's *The Hidden Mountain*[9] or the opening sequences of Pierre Trudeau's television memoirs, the empty red canoe brings to mind one man only, the quintessential Canadian—Bill Mason.[10]

Bill Mason, the man, was human, with all the foibles and idiosyncrasies, triumphs and disasters, that such a condition can bring. That mortal soul, however, on which he built a myth, was as honest, loving, courageous, authentic, hard-working and well-intentioned as any two of the rest of us. And, as such, Bill Mason, the character in the films, the man in the red canoe, transcended art, film and the realm of the possible when it came to living a reverential life connected to nature. At the core of that integrated being was a love and a passion—a fire—for the sanctity of all life, for understanding, for compassion and for his

God, the God of all Creation. Bill Mason could have been a victim, and lived his life with all the misery and self-pity a perenially sick man could muster; instead, he got up in the morning, ran towards the dawn, lived each day as if was his last, and urged others to do the same. Of one champion, we could ask no more.

AFTERWORD

THE CANOEIST MAKES HIS WAY up the Dog River, heading back to Denison Falls. First, he paddled. Then he walked, pulling his boat with ropes that creased his hands. Now, at a sharp bend in the river, the current is even too strong for that. He stops on smooth grey rock and prepares to portage.

The river rises up-country, from springs and rivulets and the last pockets of melting snow. From here the water surges downstream, to the lake, and on to the sea. In time the clouds bring it back again, completing the great circle.

He dips a cup for a quick drink to nourish his bones. It's a toast to the source, and to coming again to the place of his great imaginings. He's almost there, but not quite.

Unloading first, he rolls the red Prospector out of the water and runs a hand over its bottom to check for damage, more out of habit than need. He throws a patched green pack onto his shoulders, a second on top, and the carry begins.

Picking his way in over driftwood and boulders, he works his way up the shore to a rock face blocking his way, where a frayed manilla rope hangs from an ancient white cedar. He ties both packs to the end of the line, scrambles himself to the crooked cedar, and hauls the packs up after. He pauses to admire the small falls where the river crosses the same precipice.

Standing there, beside the old tree, gripping the earth through wet moccasins, he loads himself again and carries on up the steep trail. The ragged breath he draws is compressed by the pack straps. Eventually, he feels the rumble ahead and forgets the burden.

The spindrift on his tongue is sweet. Head down, along the trail he goes, high above the river, hefting the load from left leg to right, smiling. First up, to skirt a sheer drop, then down, weight on his toes so not to slip, to a campsite near the base of the falls. Home.

Hands on his hips, he pulls his shoulders back and inhales. Then, kneeling, he drinks long sips from cupped, dirty hands. The last scoop he splashes over face and whiskers, rinsing salt from the corners of his eyes. He shivers, shrugs and heads back for the canoe.

With boat shouldered, he walks again to the small falls and props the prow as high as it will go beside the rope. Again, he climbs to the tree, carefully lifting the boat after him. In the footprints from last time, he flips the canoe over his head, and carries on up the narrow trail. As he steps again into the open, a breeze catches the boat, twisting his knees, quadrupling the strain.

Arriving at the packs, he sets down the canoe, strips and wades in. At the base of the falls, he stands before a pane of perfect green that churns, as it whitens, on his bare feet. He bends forward, sending cascades over his head. His skin blanches, muscles cooled and renewed by the pummelling.

In time, he pushes his whole body through the glass and sits inside on a mossy ledge. Behind the waterfall, the light is green and blue and impossibly clear. The hollow roar embraces him—so present, so predictable, so soothing—erasing any real sense of loneliness. Between the rock and the water, he sits immersed in a liminal world he finds only here.

Later, dry and warm in his tent with its open front, kipped up in his sleeping bag, feet slippery dry, the paddler finishes a sketch. Light from a single candle draws a crimson glimmer from the curve of a boat that has taken a country forward in time, delivering him to this restorative spot. Beyond that, the falls are suspended in motion and time, iridescent in the afterglow of evening.

ENDNOTES

2: CANOES AT GRAND BEACH

1   Canadian writer Barry Broadfoot was three years older than Bill Mason, but
    also lived in Riverview and spent his summers at Grand Beach. He writes
    about his growing up in *My Own Years* (Toronto: Doubleday, 1983).
2   Ibid., pp. 45–46.
3   The most striking of these is a large canvas called *The Beaver Dam*,
    which is on permanent display in the Art Gallery of Ontario in Toronto.
4   There are several excellent biographies of Grey Owl. Details here came
    from *Wilderness Man: The Strange Story of Grey Owl* by Lovat Dickson
    (Toronto: Macmillan of Canada, 1973).
5   *Men of the Last Frontier*, pp. 78–79.
6   *Path of the Paddle: An Illustrated Guide to the Art of Canoeing*
    (Toronto: Van Nostrand Reinhold Ltd., 1980), p. 5.

3: RED RIVER DAYS

1   *My Own Years*, p. 79.

4: FIRST NIGHT OUT

1   Curiously, this drawing has remarkable similarity to J.M.W. Turner's
    watercolour *Interior of Ely Cathedral*, painted in 1797, which hangs in
    the art gallery in Aberdeen, Scotland. This connection, when consid-
    ered in light of the other quasi-classical art instruction Bill received
    from Miss Carey, makes it plausible that Bill's love for Turner began at
    Kelvin when along with lessons on other masters he learned of the
    British Romantic painters as well.

2   IVCF *Venture* Newsletter, vol. 2. (April 1987), p. 2.
3   It's not clear why Bill's dad did not join the war effort overseas; he may have been a little too young for service in the First World War and marginally too old for active service in the Second World War.
4   IVCF *Venture* Newsletter, vol. 2. (April 1987), p. 1.

5: Growing Time

1   "Tom Thomson" by Harold Town in *The Canadian Encyclopedia* (Edmonton: Hurtig, 1985).

6: Weekends in Whiteshell

1   This note comes from an excellent account of Rutstrum's life that can be found in *Wilderness Visionaries* by Jim Dale Vickery (Merrickville, Indiana: ICS Books Inc., 1986), pp. 161–88.
2   Rutstrum's other books, including *North American Canoe Country, The Wilderness Cabin, The Wilderness Route Finder, Chips from a Wilderness Log,* and *Paradise Below Zero,* would become influential references for Bill but none more so than *Way of the Wilderness,* which Bill carried with him for many years in a tattered khaki canvas case purchased at Bill Rom's Canoe Country Outfitters in Ely, Minnesota.
3   *Wilderness Visionaries,* p. 172.
4   More than 10 per cent of the space in *Song of the Paddle* is dedicated to the tent Bill learned about from Calvin Rutstrum. This twenty-page eulogy includes eighteen photographs and ten diagrams!
5   *Way of the Wilderness,* pp. 65–66.
6   Ibid., p. 68.
7   *Wilderness Visionaries,* p. 167.
8   John Wadland's comments come from a paper entitled "Great Rivers, Small Boats: Landscape and Canadian Historical Culture" delivered at the 3rd International Camping Congress in Toronto, March 1994, and again at the annual conference of the Canadian Historical Association in June 1994. The "perfect machine" reference is from a CBC Radio program about the canoe by York University Dean of Fine Arts, Seth Feldman, broadcast in the *Ideas* series on May 23, 1995.
9   Some of this detail, including this quote, is drawn from Kenneth G. Roberts and Philip Shackleton, *The Canoe: A History of the Craft from Panama to the Arctic* (Toronto: Macmillan of Canada, 1983), p. 237.
10 See also "The Heritage of Peterborough Canoes" by John Marsh in *Nastawgan: The Canadian North by Canoe and Snowshoe,* edited by Bruce Hodgins and Margaret Hobbs (Toronto: Betelgeuse Books, 1985), pp. 211–22. There is also an interesting consideration of this

history in *The Canoe and Whitewater* by C.E.S. Franks (Toronto: University of Toronto Press, 1977), pp. 7–40.

11 In *Across the Sub-Arctic of Canada* (Toronto: Unwin, 1898), J.W. Tyrrell talks about three beautifully varnished Peterborough canoes, two of cedar, one of basswood.

12 Notes by Roger MacGregor accompanying a 1994 reprint of a 1950 Chestnut Canoe Company catalogue (Landsdowne, Ont.: Plumsweep Press), p. ii.

13 Ibid., p. iii.

14 *The Canoe*, p. 240.

15 Canoeist George Grinnell spoke about this notion at the 10th Annual Wilderness Canoeing Symposium in Toronto, January 1995, saying: "Canoeing in North America has taken the place today of the medieval pilgrimage in the sense that you put aside all your cares for a while and you focus on something else. Often what you're focusing on is to *not* focus . . . if you're beset by . . . various anxieties, simply to put those aside and to pile the canoe full of three months' worth of food to head into the wilderness. If it does nothing else for you it gives you a time to reflect." Grinnell's story is contained in a forthcoming book, *A Death on the Barrens.*

16 See "Purposeful Wanderers" and "Women of Determination," in *Nastawgan: The Canadian North.*

7: Heaven on Earth

1 Eric W. Morse, *Fur Trade Canoe Routes of Canada/Then and Now* (Toronto: University of Toronto Press, 1969), pp. 83–84.

2 From J.J. Bigsby, *The Shoe and the Canoe*, vol. II (London, 1850), p. 303.

8: Quetico

1 Sigurd F. Olson, *The Singing Wilderness* (New York: Alfred A. Knopf, 1945), p. 5.

2 Besides Olson's epic books that celebrate Shield country wilderness— *The Lonely Land, The Singing Wilderness* and *Runes of North* (to name just three)—Jim Dale Vickery's biographical account of Henry David Thoreau, John Muir, Robert Service, Bob Marshall, Calvin Rutstrum and Sigurd Olson (*Wilderness Visionaries*) sets this period in context. Mason was interviewed by Vickery for this book but did not make it in beyond an epigraph at the front of the book attributed to him: "It's very sad if our culture only sees wilderness as a place to play. What wilderness should be doing is speaking to our souls and teaching us about being quiet . . . and respecting the world we live in." One can hear echoes of many of Mason's preservationist predecessors in these words, especially Sigurd Olson.

9: Early Days at Meech Lake

1 "Lake Superior by Canoe" by Eric W. Morse in the *Ottawa Journal*, October 1960.
2 By now it seems that Bill is expert at starting and leaving jobs. His years of self-initiated summer lay-offs in Winnipeg gave him everything he needed to take a position with Crawley Films the year before he was married, leave the job to get married and film for a few months, return to fiddle for a few more months with the intention of returning to Crawley's when the Inter-Varsity funding ran out, and *still* be able to convince Budge Crawley, his on-again off-again employer, that it would be a good idea for him to come into the Crawley studios to work on his film at night, at no cost.

10: Paddle to the Sea

1 From "A Time-line of the National Film Board of Canada and the Canadian Film Industry from 1939 to 1989" contained in *The NFB Film Guide* published by the National Film Board in collaboration with the National Archives of Canada in 1991, editor-in-chief Donald W. Bidd.
2 In the relative absence of colleagues at the NFB making nature films, Bill's interest in this kind of tale may well have originated in the literary tradition of Canadian animal stories (i.e., Seton's *Wild Animals I Have Known* and Roberts's *The Last Barrier*), which Alec Lucas (*A Literary History of Canada*), among others, argues was in its heyday in the latter part of the nineteenth century and the early part of the twentieth century.
3 *Path of the Paddle*, pp. 148–51.

11: A Rising Star

1 One of the curious uses to which the film *Blake* was put during its early life in National Film Board distribution was for English-language training for military and government personnel in the Contact Canada Program in the 1960s and 1970s. People who took these courses remember watching the film while following along in a printed version of the script. Afterwards there was a *Blake* workbook, with all kinds of questions and exercises, to give students language practice. In other versions of this and related film-based language-training programs, Bill's earlier films *Paddle to the Sea* and *Rise and Fall of the Great Lakes* were also used.

12: Company of Wolves

1 Alec Lucas, *Farley Mowat* (Toronto: McClelland & Stewart, 1976), p. 22.
2 Letter from David A. Munro, director of the Canadian Wildlife Service, to Bill Brind, executive producer at the National Film Board, December 15, 1967.

3 These two books may have been *The Curse of the Viking Grave*, published later the same year, 1966, and *Canada North*, which was first published the following year, 1967, or perhaps an early version of Mowat's outport foibles in his little boat, *Happy Adventure*, published eventually in 1969.

4 National Film Board Contract CP9006.

5 NFB memo from Frank Spiller to Bill Brind, dated October 5, 1967.

6 Burt Heward, "Big, Bad, Wolf: Wright Family Filming in 'Secret.'" *Ottawa Citizen*, January 24, 1970, p. B1.

7 Patricia Thorvaldson, "The Canadian Filmmaker: Introducing Bill Mason." *Pot Pourri, National Film Board Newsletter*, September 1971, p. 7.

8 Notes taken at a meeting held to screen a cutting copy with draft narration of *Death of a Legend*, at NFB, 150 Kent Street, Ottawa, Thursday, June 17, 2:00 p.m. Present: Canadian Wildlife Service—Director and several staff members; Information Service—Messrs. D. Eagles and John Cameron; National Film Board—Miss E. Horne, Messrs. Barrie Howells, Bill Mason, T.V. Adams.

9 NFB memo from Barrie Howells to Bill Brind, dated June 25, 1970.

13: WATERSHED

1 "Some Private Thoughts" by William Mason. Undated, unpublished, mimeographed manuscript, probably written about 1978, pp. 55–56.

2 Typewritten juror comments sent to the NFB from the 20th Annual American Film Festival sponsored by the Educational Film Library Association, 43 West 61st Street, New York, NY 10023.

3 Bill Mason, "Whatever Happened to (That Film) Cry of the Wild?" Miscellaneous document 1184, National Film Board Records Centre, no date, pp. 3–4.

4 "50 Top-Grossing Films (week ending January 16)," *Variety*, January 23, 1974, compiled by Standard Data Corp., New York.

5 *Ottawa Citizen*, July 19, 1989.

6 Summary of *Cry of the Wild* Agreements and *Cry of the Wild* Distribution Report written by Gerry M. O'Halloran, Commercial Division, National Film Board, dated November 19, 1974.

7 Mason, "Whatever Happened to (That Film) Cry of the Wild?," p. 5.

8 Original article entitled "In the Footsteps of Walt Disney" by John Hofsess, *Maclean's*, April 1975. The letters to the editor were published in the subsequent issue.

9 "Headless Horsemen" by John Hofsess in *Cinema Canada*, April 1975. Mason's response appeared in the next issue.

10 Mason's letter, published in *Maclean's*, October 9, 1978, was a response to an article by Lawrence O'Toole entitled "The Days of Whine and Roses," in the October 2, 1978, issue.

11 "Some Private Thoughts" by William Mason, pp. 55–56.
12 Letter from Bill Brind, Audio Visual Branch, UNRVA Headquarters, Beirut, Lebanon, to Tom Shoebridge of Ottawa, dated Saturday, June 10, 1978.
13 From the narration of *Waterwalker.*
14 From handwritten notes prepared for a talk Bill gave at a Lake Superior Environmental Conference held in Michigan in April 1987.

14: MR. CANOEHEAD

1 Eric W. Morse, "Summer Travel in the Canadian Barrens." Reprint from the *Canadian Geographical Journal*, May 1967, published by the NWT Tourist Office, 400 Laurier Avenue West, Ottawa 4, Ontario, p. 2.
2 Letter from J.F. Kennedy to Marc Devlin, Director of Administration, NFB, dated November 12, 1974.
3 Founding Studio D was not universally supported by NFB administration. At one point, when the director of production suggested various ways for Studio D be absorbed by other units, because it was so small by comparison, Shannon realized that one way to get equal funding with the other studios within the Film Board was to take on an equal number of staff people. She was also concerned that if *all* the women at the NFB were organized in one studio they would have been isolated or even ghettoized. So, the solution she chose in consultation with the other women of Studio D was to invite selected men to join them. Until his retirement from the Board in 1984, Mason was one of six men, editors, writers and film makers, who eventually became part of Studio D. Had she had a choice, Shannon would have had no men, but, forced to compromise, she asked men she felt were simply decent people, people who would not play power games, people who would join in consensus-building, collaborative problem-solving and regular information-sharing.
4 The signature photograph of Bill silhouetted against the morning mist, taken by Paul, that became the cover image for the book *Song of the Paddle* was actually photographed under the cedars on the south shore of the Petawawa River opposite the cliffs on river right, just below the Natch Rapids. Some Petawawa River guides assert that this was the location at which Tom Thomson painted *Petawawa Gorges* when he was a fire ranger at Achray in 1916; however, it has been proven recently that the subject of this painting was in fact a canyon on the Barron River, 19 miles to the southeast, which at one time was called the South Branch of the Petawawa River.
5 Big Thompson Rapid was one of Bill's favourite locations for shooting and turned up regularly in his books and films. Using his novel soap/paint/ink combination for painting whitewater diagrams, he even rendered a drawing of Big Thompson that was used as a "test for running a complex rapid in low water" in *Path of the Paddle*, p. 113.

6 "Beyond Waterwalker" by Bill Mason. *Paddler*, Spring 1986, p. 12.

7 The shot the NFB chose to put on the cover of the instructional book-
   lets and on the posters advertising the Path of the Paddle series was one
   of these misty August morning shots, but, though it might have been, it
   was taken not on the Magnetawan River but a few miles north, at Blue
   Chute on the French River. The same moody shot is republished in *Path
   of the Paddle* on page 123. Although these rivers—and the Pickerel between them—flowed west into Georgian Bay, they were at exactly the
   same latitude and in identical Shield country to Bill's favourite rivers, like
   the Petawawa, Barron, Madawaska and Opeongo, flowing east out of
   the Algonquin highlands.

15: GOD ON WATER

1 Many environmental organizations, such as the Canadian Wildlife
   Federation, Sierra Club of Canada, and the Algonquin Wildlands
   League, took pride in inviting Bill to speak and making him an honorary
   member. It was about this time also that Bill joined the Board of
   Trustees for the Canadian Outward Bound Wilderness School at Black
   Sturgeon Lake, north of Lake Superior, ironically in almost the exact
   place where Paddle to the Sea had begun his epic voyage.

2 At times it appears that Bill was more fascinated by Plasticine and animation than the kids were. He had in mind a children's book featuring still
   photographs and the Dragon Castle story, and he even produced,
   around this same time, a manuscript for a how-to book, built around the
   story of making *Dragon Castle*, complete with tips on how to use pastry
   rollers, garlic presses and other sundry household items to make your
   own animated sculptures.

3 Letter from Terry Tempest Williams, Assistant Curator of Education,
   Utah Museum of Natural History, Salt Lake City, to the NFB, dated
   January 22, 1982.

4 Bill often complained about the fact that his books were not waterproof,
   and even tried to convince his publisher to produce *Song of the Paddle*
   on waterproof paper!

5 Letter from Rolf Kraiker, RR#1 Shanty Bay, Ontario, L0L 2L0, dated
   February 23, 1986.

6 Letter from Senior Editor Mary Alice Moore of Aqua-Field Publications,
   Inc., 728 Beaver Dam, Point Pleasant, New Jersey, dated November 16,
   1981.

7 The "guy" to whom Mason refers in this letter was either one Brian
   Creer or the legendary outdoorsman Jim Boulding, founder and co-
   owner with his wife, Myrna, of Strathcona Park Lodge and Outdoor
   Education Centre on Vancouver Island. Ironically, Boulding, a former
   teacher, much like Mason died young (at age fifty-four, in June 1986),

leaving behind a legion of former Strathcona students and staff members to carry on his tradition of outdoor pursuits as a way of building a deeply felt caring for the wilderness. The charismatic force of Jim Boulding's personality is illustrated by the fact that Bill didn't move easily from time-tested techniques he himself had developed on the trail. This encounter also illustrates the fact that Bill would listen to people and try what they had to say. He wasn't completely stuck on one way—his way—of canoeing. He was always of a mind that it was never too late to learn new tricks, and although the "guy" was closer to fifty years old than sixty when Bill encountered him, Jim Boulding was a western "canoe guru" for whom Bill developed a deep rapport and respect.

8 Letter from Mason to Mary Alice Moore at Aqua-Field Publications, undated, but likely written in late November or early December 1981.

9 Letter from Mason to Wendy Wolf, Pantheon Books, 201 East 50th Street, New York, New York, dated August 20, 1979.

10 *Path of the Paddle*, p. v.

11 A lawyer in Colombia tried many different schemes to get this project up and running and, in the absence of success in other attempts, had been put in touch with Sutherland. As it happened, the first World Congress of Aboriginal Peoples was taking place that winter in Peru and, through an even more serendipitous set of circumstances, Sutherland, a white from British Columbia, became a delegate at this auspicious conference for the Bella Coola Indian Nation. Bill found himself accompanying his friend and stand-in Bella Coola Indian as technical film expert on this most unlikely reconnaissance mission, from the jungles of the Amazon to the political thickets of international aboriginal politics.

12 National Film Board of Canada invoice of Motion Picture Equipment consigned to Bill Mason for shipment to Brasilia, Lima, Cusco and Bogotá from Montreal, Quebec, dated February 15, 1980.

13 From the undated show entitled "Wilderness Impressions: A Dialogue with the Arts" by William Mason, R.C.A.

14 "Perspectives on Wilderness and Creativity" by Bill Mason in *Park News*, summer issue 1982, p. 11.

15 Letter from Janine Edoin, NFB Personnel Branch, to the Superannuation Division of Supply and Services Canada, dated December 19, 1983.

16: IMPOSSIBLE FEATURE

1 Government of Canada memo from Bill Mason to Ian McLaren, dated February 2, 1978.

2 This reference is to a popular book of the day by Elizabeth Dobson Gray entitled *Green Paradise Lost* (Wellesley, Mass.: Roundtable Press, 1981) published first as *Why the Green Nigger?*

3 "A Motion and a Spirit: Bill Mason's Nature Films" by Gene Walz, published in *Border Crossings: Arts from Manitoba*, Spring 1989, p. 40.

4   "Creation, Creator in His Art" by Tim Bentley. *United Church Observer*, March 1983, pp. 55–58. Mason discovered the palette knife on paper technique as an animator, but it was not until this point much later in his life that he put the technique to use to express his feelings about the natural world in contrast to the animator's task of rendering someone else's idea from a story board or script.

17: THE EMPTY RED CANOE

1   This work became the basis of the manuscript for *Canoescapes* published by Boston Mills Press in fall 1995.

2   The first account of this trip was a two-part, posthumous publication of trip leader Art Moffatt's trip prospectus entitled "Man Against the Barrens," *Sports Illustrated*, March 9, 1959, pp. 68–76, and March 16, 1959, pp. 80–88. George Grinnell later wrote his account of the trip, entitled "Art Moffatt's Wilderness Way to Enlightenment" in *Canoe*, July 1988, pp. 18–56.

3   George Grinnell spoke at length about his trip with Art Moffatt at the 10th Annual Wilderness Canoeing Symposium in Toronto, January 27, 1995, remarks that were broadcast in more or less the same form in a CBC Radio *Ideas* program, "The Perfect Machine," May 23, 1995. This version of his remarks was taken from a tape of that program.

4   Jeremiah 20: 9.

5   "Is the MNR allocating park site to non-residents: A special report." *Aboriginal Voice*, Christmas 1989, p. 17.

6   Letter from Alan Oates, "Childrey," High Street, Dorlock, Somerset, U.K., dated March 13, 1995.

7   One, Two and Three Star awardholders in 1984 numbered 150, 54 and 31, respectively. In 1994, reports Alan Oates of the British Canoe Union, those numbers had risen to 1,771, 848, and 540, respectively.

8   The curious thing about this is that, in the heyday of canvas-covered canoes in the 1930s and 1940s, when Mason was learning to paddle, all the major Canadian canoe builders—Lakefield, Chestnut, Canadian, English—had similar shapes that carried the "Prospector" name. As with so many other things, Mason had not done exhaustive research on the subject; he had just happened to find a canoe that he liked, that worked, and decided to tell people about it. But, because people hung on his every word, contemporary canoe builders, of both composition and traditional construction, were quick to see the powerful marketing potential in playing up the "prospector" name for Mason aficionados.

9   There are chilling similarities between Gabrielle Roy's 1962 novel, *The Hidden Mountain*, and the life of Bill Mason. Protagonist Pierre Cadorai is an artist who travels alone by canoe and spends expanses of time on the Canadian Shield. Like Bill, Cadorai has a gift for sketching with a

pencil and yet hungers to work with paint to express his feelings. The artist is captivated by the light on a mountain that rises out of the vista before his tent. Try as he might, getting the essence of how he feels about that peak of nature eludes him. Ultimately, in Roy's novel, Pierre struggles to understand, finally having the great revelation that the mountain in his imagination has nothing at all to do with the mountain in Ungava, but he dies at his easel in Paris before he is ever able to paint that understanding or revisit the place where it all began. Strangely, a friend of Mason's guessed that Bill might find resonance in this story and passed along the book for him to read soon after he retired from the film board, not knowing how soon it would be before Mason, like Pierre Cadorai, would die at his easel at Meech Lake.

[10] Macdonald's 1931 painting *The Red Canoe* elicits similar sentiments and, although it is not as closely tied to the memory of Thomson, adds to the power vested in the red canoe as an icon of Canadiana.

FILMOGRAPHY/ BIBLIOGRAPHY

Wilderness Treasure (Manitoba Pioneer Camps) 20 minutes: researched, directed, filmed, edited, 1959–1962.

1) First Prize, Travel and Recreation Category, Canadian Film Awards, May 1963.
2) Chris Award, 11th Annual Columbus Film Festival, October 1963.

PADDLE TO THE SEA (National Film Board 106C 0166 061) 20 minutes: researched, directed, filmed, edited, 1962-1964.

1) First Prize, Stories for Children Category, American Film Festival, New York, 1967.
2) First Prize, Ex-aequo with Germany, Information Films Category, International Festival of 16mm and 8mm Films, Salerno, Italy, 1967.
3) Golden Plaque, Educational Films for Children, Second Children's Film Festival, Teheran, Iran, 1967.
4) Best Film, Creative Arts and Experimental Films, 9th International Film Festival, Yorkton, Saskatchewan, 1967.
5) Nominated for Best Short Film, Academy of Motion Picture Arts and Sciences, Hollywood, California, April 8, 1968.
6) Best Documentary Film (Silver Plaque), International Festival of Films for Children, La Plata, Argentina, October 13, 1968.

7) Award for Exceptional Merit, International Festival of Short Films, Philadelphia, Pennsylvania, November 13–18, 1971.

8) Certificate of Merit, International Film Review, Colombo, Sri Lanka, September 4–10, 1969.

9) Special Award, Montreal Society of Filmmakers, 1966.

10) For the Filmstrip: Silver Medal, Education—Language Arts Category, 30th Annual Awards Competition, International Film and Television Festival, USA, November 13, 1987.

RISE AND FALL OF THE GREAT LAKES (National Film Board 106C 0168 093) 17 minutes: researched, directed, filmed, edited, animation, 1965–1966.

1) Best Specialized Film, Society of Film and Television Arts, London, England, March 1971.

2) Certificate of Merit and Special Award for the Best Film of the Year, Canadian Amateur Film Association, Montreal, Quebec, May 1971.

3) Diploma of Merit, 1st International Film Festival on the Human Environment, Montreal, Quebec, June 1–10, 1973.

4) First Place, Documentary Category, 8th International Festival of Documentary and Experimental Films, Montevideo, Uruguay, July 2, 1971.

5) Winsted Rotary Club Award to Canada for the Best Movie, 2nd International Environmental Pollution Exhibition, Winsted, Connecticut, October 25, 1975.

6) Certificate of Merit, 1st International Film Festival, Tel Aviv, Israel, 1969.

7) Prize, Educational Category, 10th International Yorkton Film Festival, 1969.

8) Blue Ribbon, 12th American Film Festival, New York, 1970.

9) Silver Water Bucket Plaque, San Francisco Water Pollution Conference, 1970.

10) First Prize, Scientific Category, 6th International Scientific, Educational and Pedagogical Films, Teheran, Iran, 1969.

BLAKE (National Film Board 106C 0169 076) 20 minutes: researched, directed, edited, 1967.

1) Accepted, Society of Film and Television Arts, London, England, March 1971.

2) Etrog, Best Film under 30 minutes, Canadian Film Awards, Toronto, October 3, 1970.

3) Golden Sheaf Award, Best Direction, International Film Festival, Yorkton, Saskatchewan, October 18–23, 1971.

4) Golden Sheaf Award, Best Social Science Film, International Film Festival, Yorkton, Saskatchewan, October 18–23, 1971.

5) Grand Prix, Golden Boomerang, Melbourne Film Festival, Melbourne, Australia, June 4–19, 1971.

6) Nominated Best Live Action Short Film, Annual Academy of Motion Picture Arts and Sciences, Hollywood, California, April 1970.

DEATH OF A LEGEND (National Film Board 106C 0171 553) 52 minutes: researched, directed, filmed, edited, animation, 1968.

1) Award for Exceptional Merit, International Festival of Short Films, Philadelphia, Pennsylvania, November 11–18, 1971.
2) Diploma of Honour, 2nd International Days of Scientific and Didactic Films, Madrid, Spain, October 1972.
3) Etrog, Best Colour Cinematography, Canadian Film Awards, Toronto, October 1, 1971.
4) Gold Medal, 22nd International Festival for Tourist and Folklore Films, Brussels, Belgium, October 9–13, 1972.
5) Golden Rhododendron Award, 22nd International Festival of Exploration and Mountain Films, Trento, Italy, April 1974.
6) Golden Sheaf Award, Best Nature and Wildlife Film, International Film Festival, Yorkton, Saskatchewan, October 15–20, 1973.
7) Golden Sheaf Award, Best Cinematography, International Film Festival, Yorkton, Saskatchewan, October 15–20, 1973.
8) Red Ribbon Award, 14th American Film Festival, New York, May 9–13, 1972.
9) For *Au Pays des Loups* (French Translation): Coupe du Ministre des spectacles, 8e festival international de films pour enfants et adolescents, Salerno, Italy, July 1978.

WOLF PACK (National Film Board 106C 0174 501) 20 minutes: researched, directed, filmed, edited, 1971.

1) Best Film in the Professional Category, University of Montana, Missoula, Montana, April 1978.
2) Award given by *Learning* Magazine, Palo Alto, California, 1978.
3) Coupe du Ministre des spectacles, 8e festival international de films pour enfants et adolescents, Salerno, Italy, July, 1978.

IN SEARCH OF THE BOWHEAD WHALE (National Film Board 106C 0174 094) 52 minutes: researched, directed, filmed, edited, animation, commentary and narration, 1974.

1) Blue Ribbon Award, Environment, Nature and Wildlife Category, 17th American Film Festival, New York, June 2–17, 1975.
2) Chris Award, 24th International Film Festival, Columbus, Ohio, October 21, 1976.
3) First Award for Best Film in the Exploration Discovery Category, Black Orca Film Festival, Seattle, Washington, June 14–15, 1978.
4) Highest Merit in the Invited non-1977 films Category, University of Montana, Missoula, Montana, April 1978.

5) Silver Venus Medallion: Best Film in the TV Documentary Category, International Film Festival, US Virgin Islands, November 7–16, 1975.

6) Jules Verne Award for Best Exploration Film, First International Festival of Films on the Arctic, Dieppe, France, June 3–5, 1983.

CRY OF THE WILD (National Film Board 106C 0172 015) 90 minutes: researched, directed, filmed, acted, edited, graphics, commentary and narration, 1968–1971.

1) Diploma of Merit, 1st International Film Festival of the Human Environment, Montreal, 1973.

FACE OF THE EARTH (National Film Board 106C 175 109) 20 minutes: researched, directed, filmed, edited, 1975.

1) Blue Ribbon Award, Category 9: Elementary/Junior High Curriculum Films—Science, 19th Annual American Film Festival, New York, May 23–28, 1977.

2) Certificate of Recognition, Clarity and Correlation to Curriculum Area, Instructional Film Festival, Cleveland, Ohio, January, 1980.

PATH OF THE PADDLE—SOLO BASIC (National Film Board 106C 0177 008) 27 minutes: researched, directed, acted, edited, animation, commentary and narration, 1976.

PATH OF THE PADDLE—SOLO WHITEWATER (National Film Board 106C 0177 009) 27 minutes: researched, directed, acted, edited, animation, commentary and narration, 1976.

1) Best Script Film, First International Contest for White Water Films, Vénissieux, France, May 1983.

PATH OF THE PADDLE—DOUBLES BASIC (National Film Board 106C 0177 010) 27 minutes: researched, directed, acted, edited, animation, commentary and narration, 1976.

PATH OF THE PADDLE—DOUBLES WHITEWATER (National Film Board 106C 0177 011) 27 minutes: researched, directed, acted, edited, animation, commentary and narration, 1976.

1) Best Specialized Film, British Academy of Film and Television Arts, London, March 16, 1978.

2) Chris Bronze Plaque, Education Category, 26th International Film Festival, Columbus, Ohio, October 19, 1978.

3) Grand Prix of the Cultural Ministry of Nordrhein-Westfalen (cash award 5,000 DM), International Sport Film Festival, Oberhausen, West Germany, October 24–28, 1977.

4) Special Jury Award for Outstanding Achievement, Film as Communication Competition, 21st Annual International Film Festival, San Francisco, California, October 5–16, 1977.

5) For French Version: Prix. CIDALC Renée Barthélémy, 9e festival international CIDALC du film sportif, Rennes, France, May 1982.

6) Prix décerné au meilleur film a scénario (cash award 2,000 francs). Premier festival international du film de descente de rivière, Vénissieux, France, May 1983.

SONG OF THE PADDLE (National Film Board 106C 0178 111) 41 minutes: researched, directed, acted, edited, commentary and narration, 1976.

1) ANICA Award, 10th International Cinema Festival for Children and Young People, Salerno, Italy, July, 1980.

2) Award from the Tourist Bureau of the Veneto, 2nd International Adventure Film Festival, Cortina d'Ampezzo, Italy, July 20–25, 1980.

3) Chris Award, Travel Category, 28th Annual International Film Festival, Columbus, Ohio, October 23, 1980.

4) Etrog, Best Direction, Canadian Film Awards, Toronto, September 14–21, 1978.

5) Etrog, Best Cinematography in Documentary under 60 Minutes (Cinematographer, Ken Buck), Canadian Film Awards, Toronto, September 14–21, 1978.

6) Etrog, Best Sound Editing (Sound Editors, John Knight and Ken Page), Canadian Film Awards, Toronto, September 14–21, 1978.

7) Honourable Mention, 4th Annual Festival of Mountain Films, Banff, Alberta, November 1979.

8) Best Tourism Film, 29th International Festival for Tourist and Folklore Films, Brussels, Belgium, October 1979.

9) Red Ribbon Award, Nature and Wildlife Category, 21st Annual American Film Festival, New York, May 1979.

When the Wolves Sang (Greey de Pencier), 1980.

Dragon Castle (Bill Mason Productions) 13 minutes: produced, 15 International Awards to Paul and Becky Mason, 1980.

Path of the Paddle (Van Nostrand Reinhold), 1980. (Key Porter Books), 1984. Second edition published with text updated by Paul Mason (Key Porter Books), 1995.

COMING BACK ALIVE (National Film Board 1 0180 037), 1980.

PUKASKWA NATIONAL PARK (National Film Board 106C 0183 553) 16 minutes: directed, filmed, edited and commentary, 1981.

WHERE THE BUOYS ARE (National Film Board) 1981.

L'aviron Qui Nous Mene (French translation of *Path of the Paddle* published by Marcel Broquet in Quebec), 1981.

THE LAND THAT DEVOURS SHIPS (National Film Board 106C 0184 073) 58 minutes: directed, filmed, edited, animation and narration, 1984.
   1) Special Jury Award, 3rd International Festival of Films on Art and Archaeology, Brussels, Belgium, February 1986.

WATERWALKER (National Film Board and Imago) 87 minutes: researched, directed, acted, edited and narration, 1984.
   1) Nature and Environment Award, IVe festival international du film de descente de rivière, Valence, France, November 1989.

Die Kunst des Kanufahrens der Canadier (German translation of *Path of the Paddle* published by BusseSeewalk Herford in West Germany), 1987.

Song of the Paddle (Key Porter Books), 1988.

Canoescapes (Boston Mills Press [Stoddart]), 1995.

INDEX

(An "n" following a page number indicates an endnote.)

Art Gallery of Ontario, 271, 275n
Association of Canadian Clubs, 107
Audubon film series, 183
awards and scholarships, in Mason's honour, 269

Ct. Blue Herons

Eaton's Logging Camp 1940's

Pitcher Thistle

Trail

Sauna

Get jaw sounds

Falls

Viewseau

Cabin

Oiseau Bay

named after fisherman

Oiseau Pt.

Dampier Cove

Nicols Cove

nice Viewpoints

Campsite

one UK Isl

Caribou

Caribou

Campsite rainbow

Cabin (1950's)